Ferdinand Keller, John Edward Lee

The Lake Dwellings of Switzerland and other Parts of Europe

Vol. II

Ferdinand Keller, John Edward Lee

The Lake Dwellings of Switzerland and other Parts of Europe
Vol. II

ISBN/EAN: 9783337154288

Printed in Europe, USA, Canada, Australia, Japan

Cover: Foto ©ninafisch / pixelio.de

More available books at **www.hansebooks.com**

THE

LAKE DWELLINGS

OF

SWITZERLAND AND OTHER PARTS OF EUROPE

BY

DR FERDINAND KELLER

PRESIDENT OF THE ANTIQUARIAN ASSOCIATION OF ZÜRICH

SECOND EDITION, GREATLY ENLARGED

TRANSLATED AND ARRANGED

BY

JOHN EDWARD LEE, F.S.A. F.G.S.

AUTHOR OF 'ISCA SILURUM' ETC.

IN TWO VOLUMES

VOL. II.—PLATES, WITH EXPLANATIONS

LONDON
LONGMANS, GREEN, AND CO.
1878

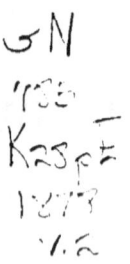

EXPLANATION OF THE PLATES.

FRONTISPIECE. VOL. II.

Piles of the lake dwelling of Möringen (bronze age), from a Photograph in the possession of J. Bürki, Esq., of Bern, p. 154.

PL. I. MEILEN.

Fig. 1. Ground plan, p. 12.—2. Section, p. 15.—3. Arrangements of the piles, p. 17.

PL. II. MEILEN.

Figs. 1, 5. Hammers of stag's horn, p. 30.—2. Stone celt set in stag's horn, p. 20.—3. Hafting of stag's horn with a chisel of nephrite at each end, p. 22.—4. Stone celt in hafting of stag's horn, p. 22.—6. Stone hammer partially perforated, p. 25.—7, 8. Corn-crushers, p. 27.—9. Hammer of stone like serpentine, p. 24.—10. Hammer of spotted serpentine, p. 26.—11. Cylindrical corn-crusher, p. 28.—12, 13. Stone celts, p. 19.

PL. III. MEILEN.

Fig. 1. Flint saw in handle of yew-wood, p. 26.—2, 3. Flint tongues or points, pp. 26, 27.—4. Stone awl, p. 27.—5. Whetstone, p. 27.—6. Perforated bear's tooth, p. 30.—7, 9, 24, 27. Earthenware vessels, p. 32.—8. Amber bead, p. 31.—10, 11. Implements of boar's teeth, p. 30.—12. Bronze armilla, pp. 15 and 31.—13. Spindle-whorl of earthenware, p. 33.—14. Oak club, p. 31.—15, 16, 19, 20, 21. Bone awls or piercers, p. 30.—17, 18. Bone needle and pin, p. 30.—22. Flint arrow-head, p. 27.—23. Grinding stone for making celts, p. 27.—25. Bone chisel, p. 29. 26. Bronze celt, pp. 15 and 31.

PL. IV. MOOSSEEDORF.

Fig. 1. Map of the district, pp. 35, 36. A, village of Münchenbuchsee; B, Hofwyl; C, Moosseedorf; D, Steinbruck; E, Eastern lake dwelling; F, Western lake dwelling; GG, Canal; HH, Commencement of the peat moor; KK, Shell marl (Weisser Grund, blancfond); LL, Peat; M, Schönsicht; N, 'Molasse' rock; O, Ancient outlet of the lakes; P, Great lake of Moosseedorf; Q, Smaller lake.—2. Ground plan of part of the Eastern settlement, p. 37. 3. Section of the Eastern settlement, p. 37.

VOL. II.   B

EXPLANATION OF THE PLATES.

PL. V. MOOSSEEDORF.
(N.B.—All the figures are half size except 14, 20, 22.)

Fig. 1. Celt hafting of fir-wood, p. 38.—2. Celt hafting of stag's horn, p. 38.—3. Harpoon of stag's horn, p. 38.—4. Bone lance-point, p. 38.—5. Flint saw in a handle of fir-wood, p. 38.—6, 7. Needles made of boar's tusks, p. 38.—8. Awl made of a bone of the roe, p. 38.—9. Bone knife, p. 38.—10. Bone chisel, p. 38.—11, 12. Wedge of fir-wood, p.38.—13. Bone awl, p. 38. —14. Fish-hook made of a boar's tusk, p. 38.—15. Boar's tooth ground to an edge and perforated, p. 38.—16. Needle (?) of boar's tusk, p. 38.—17, 19. Flint flakes for scaling fish (?) p. 38.—18. Arrow-head of rock crystal, p. 38.—20. Sharp celt of nephrite, p. 38.—21. Comb of yew-wood, p. 38.—22. View of the larger lake of Moosseedorf, taken standing on the site of the eastern lake dwelling, p. 37.

PL. VI. ROBENHAUSEN, &c.

Fig. 1. Plan of the lake of Pfäffikon, pp. 41,43.—2. Ground plan of part of the Aabach canal, p. 44.—3. Section of the relic-bed, p. 44.—4. Section of the Aabach canal, p. 43.—5. Bank at Himmerich, p. 62.

PL. VII. ROBENHAUSEN, &c.

View of the peat moor of Robenhausen, taken from Seegraben, p. 41. (The site of the lake dwelling is indicated by a bird flying.)

PL. VIII. ROBENHAUSEN.

Piles of the last settlement but one: round fir timber, p. 48.

PL. IX. ROBENHAUSEN.

Piles of the latest settlement: split oak-wood, p. 48.

PL. X. ROBENHAUSEN.

Figs. 1, 2, 3. Knives of yew-wood, p. 52.—4. Wooden ladle, p. 52.- 5 Wooden implement, p. 52. 6. Ring of bark, p. 52.—7. Club of ash-wood, with a stag's horn socket and stone celt, p. 52.—8, 8*a*, 8*b*. Boat ('Einbaum'), p. 53.—9. Flail, p. 53. 10. Bow of yew, p. 53.—11, 12. 'Arpion,' or fishing implement, p. 53. -13. Wooden ladle, p. 52.—14. Wooden club with a stone celt fixed in it, p. 52. 15. Implement of bark, p. 52. 16. Club with a celt fixed in it, p. 53. 17. Wooden ladle, p. 52.—18, 19. Implement of stag's horn, p. 57.

PL. XI. ROBENHAUSEN.

Figs. 1, 2. Clubs with celts, p. 54.—3. Yew club, p. 54.—4. Wooden club, p. 54. -5. Bark float, p. 52 -6, 7. Wooden suspension hooks, p. 54. 8. Earthenware spoon, p. 58. 9. Ladle of maple-wood, p. 52.—10. Tub of maple-wood, p. 55.

PL. XII. ROBENHAUSEN, &c.
(Fig. 1 is from Niederwyl; all the others are from Robenhausen.)

Fig. 1. Wooden implement, use unknown, p. 80. 2, 9. Agricultural implements of stag's horn, 57. 3. Wooden chisel, p. 55.—4, 5. Stone implement,

EXPLANATION OF THE PLATES.

p. 58.—6. Club of yew-wood, p. 54.—7. Ladle of maple-wood, p. 52.—8. Earthenware vessel, p. 58.—10. Wooden last, p. 55.—11. Knife or chisel of yew, p. 55.

Pl. XIII. Robenhausen.

Fig. 1. Rib bound with cord, p. 58.—2. Wooden implement, p. 55.—3. Yoke, p. 56.—4. Wooden club with celt, p. 56.—5. Wooden implement, p. 56.—6. Marble cone or hemisphere, p. 58.—7. Pile with a mortise in the head, pp. 56 and 80.—8, 9, 11. Earthenware vessels, p. 58.—10. Stag's horn implements, p. 58.—12. Clay cone, p. 58.—13. Flint arrow-head, p. 58.—14. Bone chisel, p. 58.

Pl. XIV. Robenhausen, &c.

Fig. 1. Bone awl, Wangen, p. 71.—2, 6. Balls of string, Robenhausen, p. 56.—3. Perforated wolf's grinder, Wangen, p. 71.—4, 5. Ornamentation on earthenware vessels, Robenhausen, p. 58.—7. Perforated stones, Wangen, p. 71.—8. Stag's horn implement, Wangen, p. 71.—9. Ornamentation on pottery, Wangen, p. 71.—10, 11. Flint arrow-head, Wangen, p. 71.—12. Perforated and sharpened boar's tusk, Moosseedorf, p. 38.—13. Dog's bone perforated, Wangen, p. 71.—14 to 20. Crucibles, Robenhausen, p. 59.—21. Bone awl with head of asphalt, Moosseedorf, p. 38.—22. Bone knife, Moosseedorf, p. 38.—23, 24. Bone fishing implements, Wangen, p. 71.—25. Bone implement, Moosseedorf, p. 38.

Pl. XV. Wangen.

Ornamentation on pottery, p. 70.

Pl. XVI. Niederwyl, &c.

(Fig. 2 is from Robenhausen; all the rest from Niederwyl.)

Fig. 1. Wooden platform, p. 78.—2. Section of beds, Rob. p. 46.—3. Section of platforms, Nied., p. 78.—4. Pile head with mortise, p. 80.—5. Wooden slab with mortise holes, p. 79.—6. Cone of baked clay perforated, p. 79.—7. Wooden mallet, p. 79.—8. View of the fascine work of part of the lake dwelling, p. 80.

Pl. XVII. Niederwyl.

View of the platform (from a photograph), p. 80.

Pl. XVIII. Wauwyl.

Fig. 1. Section, p. 84.—2. Section, p. 85.—3. Ground plan of part of the settlement, p. 83. The lower part of this plate contains a map of the district, p. 84.

Pl. XIX. Wauwyl.

On the left side of this plate are the ground plans of the five successive platforms, or layers of timbers, p. 82. *Figs.* 1, 2, 3. Position of piles and timbers, pp. 86 and 87.—4. Section of the timber platforms, p. 82.—5. Ground plan of a portion, p. 83. 6. End of pile, p. 85.

Pl. XX. Wauwyl.

The upper part is an ideal restoration of the settlement, but from late discoveries, the huts, *in all probability*, stood much nearer together, p. 87.

EXPLANATION OF THE PLATES.

Fig. 1. Stone for stirring melted asphalt, p. 88.—2. Celt hafted in stag's horn, p. 88.—3. Bowl of yew-wood, p. 88.—4, 12. Fragments of pottery, p. 88. —5. Ball of stone (corn-crusher?) p. 88.—6. Grinding stone for celts, p. 88. —7. Glass bead, p. 88.—8. Lump of asphalt, p. 89.—9. Knife of yew-wood, p. 89.—10. Awl of stag's horn, p. 89.—11. Bone saw, p. 89.—13. Bend of stag's horn, p. 89.—14, 15. Floats (?) p. 89.—16. Cutting implement of boar's tusk, p. 89.—17. Flint knife, p. 89.—18, 19, 20. Bone chisels, p. 89.—21 to 25. Bone awls or piercers, p. 89.—26. Barbed harpoon of stag's horn, p. 89.

Pl. XXI. Zug, Wangen, Robenhausen, and Nidau.

Zug. Fig. 1. Section, p. 130.—2. Plan, p. 131.—3. Stone celt, p. 133.— 4. Flint arrow-head, p. 133.—5. Stone half cut through for making celts, p. 130. *Wangen*, 6. Earthenware vessel, p. 70.—7, 8. Perforated balls of clay, p. 70.—9. Wooden club, p. 70.—10. Flint saw set in stag's horn, p. 70.— 11, 12. Earthenware spindle-whorls, p. 70.—13. Burnt straw (thatch?) p. 70. *Robenhausen*, 14. Crucible with portions of melted copper, p. 59. *Nidau*, 15. Earthenware figure of a lizard, p. 152.

Pl. XXII. Zug, Chevroux, Wauwyl, &c.

Fig. 1. Serrated bone arrow-head, Moosseedorf, p. 38.—2, 3. Earthenware vessels, Zug, p. 136.—4, 25. Implement of stag's horn, Moos., p. 39.—5. Fish-hook of boar's tusk, Moos., p. 39.—6. Fishing implement, Wangen, p. 71.— 7. Celt hafted in stag's horn, Wauwyl, p. 90.—8, 9, 10, 11. Stag's ribs, bifurcate one-third of the length, Wauwyl, p. 90.—12. Celt handle of wood, Wauwyl, p. 90.—13, 14. Implements of limestone, St. Andreas, Zug, p. 135.—15. Earthenware vessel, Lake of Sempach, p. 445.—16. Spoon of dark-coloured pottery, Cortaillod, p. 233.—17, 18. Ornaments of stag's horn, Wauwyl, p. 90.—19. Part of an earthenware vessel with three holes on each side of the handle filled with wooden plugs, Cortaillod, p. 233.—20 to 24. Singular bronze implement, use unknown, Chevroux, p. 461.—26. Bronze ornament, Cortaillod, p. 233.— 27, 28. Earthenware vessel with feet, Möringen, p. 155.—29. Bronze arrow-head, Estavayer, p. 265.—30. Bronze ornament, Cortaillod, p. 233.—31, 32. Earthenware vessel with the base perforated, Cortaillod, p 233.—33, 35. Bronze sickle, with a knob to secure the handle, Cortaillod, p. 233.—34. Handle of an earthenware vessel, Cortaillod, p. 233.

Pl. XXIII. Unter See, &c.

Fig. 1. Ground plan and sections, Allensbach, p. 93.—2. Flint scraper, Bodmann, p. 102.—3, 4. Fruit crusher (?) Allensbach, p. 95.—5. Portion of a stag's horn sharpened, Bodmann, p. 104.—6. Flint arrow-head, Allensbach, p. 98.

Pl. XXIV. Unter See, &c.

Figs. 1, 4. Net-weights (?), Allensbach, p. 96.—2, 3. Stone implements (fruit-crushers?), Allensbach, p. 96.—5. Earthenware vessel, Bodmann, p. 104. 6, 7. Stone celt, Allensbach, p. 95.—8, 9. Fruit-crusher (?), Allensbach, p. 95. 10, 11. Stone celt, Allensbach, p. 95.—12, 13. Battle-axe, Bodmann, p 103.—14. Stone hammer, Bodmann, p. 103.

Pl. XXV. Unter See, &c.

Figs. 1, 7. Half-perforated hammer, Allensbach, p. 96.—2, 3, 8. Stone hammer (?). Allensbach, p. 96. 4. Celt of diorite, Weiler Hegne, p. 98.—

5, 6. Broken stone hammer, Weiler Heyne, p. 99.—9, 10. Corn-crusher, Allensbach, p. 96.—11, 12. Stone celt, Allensbach, p. 97.—13, 14, 17. Unfinished hammer of serpentine, Bodmann, p. 103.—15, 16, 18. Unfinished stone hammer, Allensbach, p. 96.

Pl. XXVI. Ueberlinger See, &c.

Map of the district in the centre, p. 104.—Water-levels of Maurach, Nussdorf, Unter Uhldingen and Sipplingen, to the left, p. 109.—*a, b, c, d, e*. Flint arrow-heads, Nussdorf, p. 111.

Pl. XXVII. Ueberlinger See.

(All from Nussdorf.)

Figs. 1 to 7. Stone celts, p. 113 to 115.—8. Perforated stone, p. 116.—9. Small stone celt, p 114.—10. Flint saw, p. 112.—11. Celt with oval helve hole, p. 115.—12, 13, 14. Flint saws, p. 112.—15. Broken stone hammer, p. 116.—16. *a, b.* Stone celt in stag's horn hafting, p. 126.- 17. *a, b.* Stone celt, p. 115.—18. Chisel-shaped celt, p. 113.—19. Stone celt in stag's horn hafting, p. 114.—20. Flint saw, p 125.—21. Chisel-shaped celt, p. 113.—22. Stone celt, p. 115.—23. Celt with winglike edge, p. 115.—24, *a* and *b.* Part of celt with two helve-holes, p. 115.

Pl. XXVIII. Ueberlinger See.

Fig. 1. Stone hammer, Unter Uhldingen, p. 122.—2. Celt partially bored, Sipplingen, p. 125.—3. Lance-head of serpentine, Sipp., p. 125.—4. Stone celt, in process of manufacture, Sipp., p. 125.—5, 6. Stone celts, Nussdorf, pp. 113 and 114.—7. Perforated stone disc, Nuss., p. 116.—8. Comb of stag's horn, Nuss., p. 119.—9, 10. Flint saws in wooden handles, Nuss., p. 112.—11. Bone pin, Nuss., p. 118.—12, 13, 14. Bone chisels, Nuss., p. 118.—15. Perforated bear's tooth, Nuss., p. 119.—16, 17. Netting pins made of teeth, Nuss., p. 119.—18. Bone implement, Nuss., p. 118.—19. Perforated tooth of dog or wolf, Nuss., p. 119.—20, 21. Bone hammer-heads, Nuss., p. 119. —22. Hafting for celt of stag's horn, Sipp., p. 126.—23. Bone implement, Nuss., p. 118.—24. Wooden club for a celt, Nuss., p. 115.—25. Iron pruning knife, Unter Uhld., p. 124.—26. Iron lance-head, Unter Uhld., p. 124.—27. Iron arrow-head, Unter Uhld., p. 124.—28. Iron Roman key, Sipp., p. 126. —29. Steel for striking light (?), Unter Uhld., p. 124.—30. Bronze celt, Unter Uhld., p. 123.—31. Flint celt, Bodmann, p. 104.—32. Flint saw, sickle-shaped, Bodmann, p. 104.—33. Flint lance-head, Sipp., p. 125.

Pl. XXIX. Ueberlinger See.

(Fig. 19 is from Sipplingen ; all the rest are from Unter Uhldingen.)

Figs. 1, 2. Bronze armlets, p. 124.—3 to 18. Bronze pins, p. 124. - 19. Copper celt, p. 126.—20. Bronze celt, p. 123.—21, 22. Bronze fish-hooks, p. 124.—23. Bronze sickle, p. 124.—24. Bronze armlet, p. 124.—25. Bronze chisel, p. 124.—26. Bronze socketed celt, p. 124.

Pl. XXX. Ueberlinger See.

Fig. 1. Earthenware vase, Sipplingen, p. 126.—2. Ornamented cover, Unter Uhldingen, p. 123.—3. Earthenware implement, Sipp., p. 126.- 4. Ornamented pottery, Unter Uhld., p. 123.—5, 6. Earthenware vessels, Unter

EXPLANATION OF THE PLATES.

Uhld., p. 123.—7 Ornamented pottery. Unter Uhld., p. 123.—8, 9. Earthenware cups, Unter Uhld., p. 123—10. Earthenware vase, Sipp., p. 126.—11, 12. Earthenware jars with handles, Sipp., p. 126.—13. Earthenware pipkin, Sipp., p. 126.—14. Funnel-shaped earthenware vessel, Sipp., p. 126.

PL. XXXI. UEBERLINGER SEE.

Fig. 1. Ornamented cover, Unter Uhldingen, p. 123.—2, 3. Earthenware vessels, Unter Uhld., p. 123.—4. Pipkin, Sipplingen, p. 126.—5. Jar, with perforated base, Sipp., p. 126.—6. Crucible, Unter Uhld., p. 123.—7, 8. Earthenware vessels, Sipp., p. 126.

PL. XXXII. UEBERLINGER SEE.
(All Unter Uhldingen.)

Figs. 1 to 13. Bronze knives, p. 124.—14, 15, 16. Bronze lance-points, p. 123.

PL. XXXIII. NIDAU STEINBERG.
(All of bronze.)

Figs. 1, 2. Sickles, p. 143.—3 to 6. Knives, p. 144.—7, 8. Chisels, p. 145.— 9. Small anvil (?), p. 145.—10. Awl and knife all in one, p. 144.—11. Pin, p. 145.—12, 13. Lance-heads, p. 145.—14. Knob, p. 147.—15, 16. Rings, p. 146.

PL. XXXIV. NIDAU STEINBERG.
(All of bronze.)

Figs. 1 to 34. Pins, p. 145.—35, 36. Armlets, p. 146.—37. Hook, p. 147.

PL. XXXV. NIDAU STEINBERG.
(All of bronze, except Fig. 28.)

Figs. 1, 2. Armlets, p. 146.—3, 4. Lance-heads, p. 145.—5. Celt, p. 143.— 6. Broad chisel, p. 145.—7, 9. Ornaments, p. 147.—8. Knob, p. 147.—10, 11, 12. Arrow-heads, p. 145.—13 to 24. Cutting implements, p. 147.—25, 26, 27. Studs, p. 147.—28. Spiral of gold wire, p. 147.—29. Spiral of bronze, p. 147.— 30. Bronze implement, p. 147.

PL. XXXVI. NIDAU STEINBERG.
(All of bronze, except Fig. 42.)

Figs. 1, 2. Chisels and awls in one, p. 145.—3. Drill (?), p. 145.—4. Surgical instrument, p. 146.—5. Lingula, p. 146.—6 to 18. Needles, p. 145.—19 to 32. Fishhooks, p. 147.—33 to 41. Rings, p. 146.—42. Ribbed plate of gold, p. 147.

PL. XXXVII. NIDAU STEINBERG.

Figs. 1, 2, 3. Slingstones (?) drawn in section, p. 140.—4. Ornament (?) of earthenware, p. 152.—5. Bronze hammer, with an ear, p. 147.—6, 7. Cylinders of earthenware, p. 152.—8. Three bone arrow-heads, p. 152.—9. 'Crescent' of earthenware, p. 152.—10. Bowl of pot-stone, p. 142.—11. Implement of stag's horn, p. 152.—12. Implement of bear's tooth, p. 152.—13. Whistle of stag's horn, p. 152.—14. String of beads of glass and jet, p. 152.—15, 16. 'Crescents' of earthenware, p. 152. 17 to 24. Earthenware spindle-whorls, p. 151.—25. Perforated stone, p. 142.—26. Bead of serpentine, p. 142.—27, 27', 28. Coloured earthenware vessels, p. 150. 29. Perforated stone, p. 142.—30. Double cup of earthenware, p. 150.—31. Yoke of yew-wood, p. 153.—32. Bronze wire, p. 147.—33. Bronze implement like a snaffle-bit, p. 147.—34, 35. Bronze armlets, p. 146.

EXPLANATION OF THE PLATES.

Pl. XXXVIII. Nidau Steinberg, &c.

(Fig. 5 is from Meilen; all the rest from Nidau.)

Figs. 1 to 4, 7. Slingstones (?), p. 140.—5. Mealing-stone, Meilen, p. 142.—6, 8, 9, 10, 11, 12, 13. Earthenware vessels, p. 150.—14. Earthenware ring, p. 150.—15. Stone with an iron ring (net weight?), p. 140.—16. Conical weight, p. 152.—17. Earthenware spindle-whorl, p. 151.—18, 19, 20. Weights (?), p. 152.

Pl. XXXIX. Morges, Scheuss, &c.

Fig. 1. Bronze dagger, Chevroux, p. 461.—2. Net weight, Inkwyler See, p. 445.—3. Earthenware funnel-shaped vessel, À la Sauge, p. 462.—4. Bronze pin, Peter's Island, p. 454.—5. Serpentine hammer, Greng, p. 284.—6, 7, 8. Bronze mould for casting celts, Morges, p. 296 —9. Iron ornament, Scheuss, p. 456.—10. Neck of earthenware vessel, with tin ornament, Estavayer, p. 265.—11. Blunt serpentine hatchet, Estavayer, p. 265.—12. Cupped stone, Font, p. 460.

For comparison. Mainland.

Fig. 13. Cupped stone, Iolimont, p. 460.—14. Cupped stone, Bienne, p. 460. —15. Flint arrow-head fixed in the shaft, Geissbodenmoor, p. 130.

Pl. XL. Möringen, &c.

Fig. 1. Map of the lake of Bienne, p. 137.—2, 5. Iron sword, Möringen, p. 154.—3. Iron fork, Möringen, p. 154.—4. Boat ('Einbaum'), Möringen, p. 155.

Pl. XLI. Möringen.

Figs. 1, 2. Bronze knives, p. 155.—3. Bronze pin, p. 155.—4, 5. Bronze celt, p. 155.—6 Bone arrow-head, p. 155.—7. Ornamented bronze plate, p. 155.—8. Large wooden mallet, p. 155.—9. Weaver's shuttle of bone, p. 155.—10. Earthenware vessel with spout, p. 155.—11. Bronze awl set in wood, p. 155.—12, 14. Earthenware vessels, p. 155.—13. String of beads, p. 155.—15, 16. Earthenware vessel with the handle *inside*, p. 155.—17. Bronze ornament for suspension, p. 155.—18. Drinking cup, p. 155.

Pl. XLII. Möringen, &c.

Fig. 1. Harpoon of stag's horn, Lattringen, p. 450.—2. Handle of stag's horn, Lüscherz, p. 197.—3. Hafting of stag's horn in wood, Lüscherz, p. 197.—4. Flint saw in stag's horn handle, St. Aubin, p. 459.—5. Bone dagger in stag's horn handle, Lattringen, p. 450.—6, 7. Bronze needle in a case made of the bone of a stork, Greng, p. 290.—8. Bone pointer or dagger in stag's horn handle, St. Aubin, p. 459.—9. Ornament for suspension, St. Aubin, p. 459.—10. Stag's horn hammer, Sutz, p. 448.—11. Hafting of stag's horn, St. Aubin, p. 459.—12. Pointer of stag's horn, Möringen, p. 180.—13. Spatula of stag's horn, Lüscherz, p. 200.—14. Spoon cut out of yew-wood, Gerlafingen, p. 452.—15. Three-toothed stag's horn comb (?), Lüscherz, p. 197.—16 and 17. Small boxes of stag's horn, Concise, p. 272.—18. Bone awl in a handle of stag's horn, Lattringen, p. 450.

Pl. XLIII. Möringen, &c.

Fig. 1. Horse's bit, of stag's horn, Möringen, p. 174.—2. Necklace ornament, of stag's horn, Lüscherz, p. 197.—3. Necklace ornament, of stag's horn, Lüscherz, p. 197.—4. Necklace ornament, of stag's horn, Lüscherz, p. 197. 5. Ornament of stag's horn, Lüscherz, p. 198.—6. Ornament of bone, Möringen, p. 179.—

EXPLANATION OF THE PLATES.

7. Double pointer of stag's horn, Sutz, p. 449.—8. Handle of stag's horn, Möringen, p. 179.—9. Arrow-head of stag's horn, Auvernier, p. 684.—10. Horse's bit, of stag's horn, Möring-n, p. 174.—11. Ornament for suspension, stag's horn, Lüscherz, p. 197. — 12. Arrow-head of stag's horn, St. Aubin, p. 459.— 13. Ornamented disc of stag's horn, Auvernier (the figure to the left shows the section), p. 244.—14. Double-hooked implement of stag's horn, St. Aubin, p. 459.—15 and 15a. Spoon made of stag's horn, Sutz, p. 448.

PL. XLIV. ST. AUBIN, &c.

Fig. 1. Celt hafted in stag's horn, St. Aubin, p. 459.—2. Necklace, ornament of stag's horn, Auvernier, p. 243.—3. Bone hook, St. Aubin, p. 459.—4. Hook of stag's horn, Lake of Bienne, p. 156.—5. Celt hafted in stag's horn, St. Aubin, p. 459.—6. Ornament of stag's horn, Estavayer, p. 262.—7. Bone ornament, St. Aubin, p. 459.—8. Scraper of bone, St. Aubin, p. 459.—9. Arrow-head of stag's horn, St. Aubin, p. 459.—10. Bone implement, St. Aubin, p. 459. —11. Bone chisel, St. Aubin, p. 459. -12. Stag's horn hafting, Lüscherz, p. 200. 13. Stone chisel hafted in a bone handle, St. Aubin, p. 459.—14. Ornament for suspension, stag's horn, St. Aubin, p. 459.—15. Glass bead, St. Aubin, p. 459. 16. Amber bead, St. Aubin, p. 459.—17. Bead of stag's horn, St. Aubin, p. 459.—18, 19, 20. Perforated small bones, St. Aubin, p. 459.—21. Bone pointer, Lake of Bienne, p. 156.—22. Bone pointer, St. Aubin, p. 459.—23. Amber bead, Möringen, p. 459.

PL. XLV. ST. AUBIN, &c.

Fig. 1. Stag's horn handle, St. Aubin, p. 459.—2. Worked horn of the elk, Lake of Bienne, p. 156.—3. Horse's bit, of stag's horn, Estavayer, p. 262.— 4. Stag's horn implement, hollowed out, St. Aubin, p. 459.—5. Bone lance-head, St. Aubin, p. 459.—6. Lance-head of stag's horn, St. Aubin, p. 459.—7. Goblet of stag's horn, St. Aubin, p. 459.—8, 9. Horse's bit, of stag's horn, Möringen, p. 174.—10. Small hammer of stag's horn, Sutz, p. 449.—11. Bear's tooth perforated, St. Aubin, p. 459.—12. Ornament for suspension made of boar's tusk, Möringen, p. 186.—13, 14. Wolves' teeth, St. Aubin, p. 459.—15. Ornament for suspension, stag's horn, St Aubin, p. 459.

PL. XLVI. ESTAVAYER, &c.

Fig. 1. Bronze sword, Estavayer, p. 684.—2. Bronze sword, Cortaillod, p. 234.—3. Bronze sword, Möringen, p. 158.—4. Point of a large bronze hook, Möringen, p. 165.—5. Bronze sword with a handle, Auvernier, p. 239. 6. Bronze arrow-head, Möringen, p. 161.—7. Bronze 'ferrule,' Möringen, p. 180. —8. Bronze lance-head, Auvernier, p. 240.—9. Bronze lance-head, Gerlafingen, p. 452.

PL. XLVII. MÖRINGEN, &c.

Fig. 1. Bronze sword, Conciso, p. 684.—2. Bronze sword, Palafitte Forel, p. 684. 3. Bronze sword, Zihl. Nidau, p. 147.—4. End of a bronze sword used as a lance, Möringen, p. 161 -5. Bronze lance-head, Möringen, p. 180. 6 Bronze arrow-head, Estavayer, p. 262. 7. Dagger of bronze, Gerlafingen, p. 452. 8. Fragment of an implement, use unknown, Estavayer, p. 262. 9. Bronze arrow-head, Möringen, p. 161. 10. Bronze end of a sword-sheath, Möringen, p. 159. 11. Bronze arrow-head, socketed, Möringen, p. 161.

PL. XLVIII. AUVERNIER.

Fig. 1. Handle of bronze sword, Auvernier, p. 239.—2. Handle of bronze sword, Auvernier, p. 258.

EXPLANATION OF THE PLATES. 9

Pl. XLIX. Möringen, &c.

Fig. 1. Handle of bronze sword inlaid with iron, Möringen, p. 159. - 2. Bronze sword-handle, the blade of iron, Möringen, p. 159.—3. Bronze swordhandle, Cortaillod, p. 234.

Pl. L. Auvernier, &c.

Fig. 1. Bronze knife (*a, b* section), Auvernier, p. 240.—2. Knife and handle of bronze, Möringen, p. 163.—3. Bronze knife with a stag's horn handle, Möringen, p. 163.—4. Bronze ornament for suspension, Corcelettes, p. 281.— 5. Knife and handle of bronze, Auvernier, p. 241.—6. Knife and handle of bronze, Auvernier, p. 240.

Pl. LI. Auvernier, &c.

Fig. 1. Ornamented bronze knife, Colombier, p. 457.—2. Ornamented bronze knife, Auvernier, p. 246.—3. Knife and handle of bronze, Möringen, p. 163.— 4. Knife with a stag's horn handle, Möringen, p 164.—5. Knife and handle of bronze, Möringen, p. 164.—6. Socketed bronze knife, Colombier, p. 457.

Pl. LII. Möringen.

Fig. 1. Bronze cutting implement, Möringen, p. 164.—2. Bronze cutting implement, Möringen, p. 164.—3. Bronze cutting implement with stag's horn handle, Möringen, p. 164.—4. Bronze cutting implement, Möringen, p. 164.— 5. Bronze cutting implement, Möringen, p. 164.—6. Bronze cutting implement, Möringen, p. 164.

Pl. LIII. Auvernier, &c.

Fig. 1. Bronze cutting implement, Möringen, p. 164.—2. Bronze cutting implement, Auvernier, p. 684.—3. Bronze cutting implement, Auvernier, p. 684. —4. Bronze cutting implement, Auvernier, p. 684.—5. Bronze cutting implement, Möringen, p. 164.— 6. Bronze cutting implement, Corcelettes, p. 281.

Pl. LIV. Möringen.

Figs. 1 and 1 *a*, 1 *b*, 1 *c*. Wooden handle of a bronze sickle, Möringen, p 162.

Pl. LV. Auvernier, &c.

Fig. 1. Bronze ornamented gouge, Auvernier, p. 241.—2. Bronze chisel, Möringen, p. 180.—3. Bronze gouge, Auvernier, p. 241.—4. Bronze socketed chisel, Auvernier, p. 241.—5. Bronze hammer, Auvernier, p. 241.—6. Bronze hammer, Auvernier, p. 246.—7. Bronze anvil, Auvernier, p. 241.—8. Bronze hammer, Möringen, p. 165.—9. Bronze hammer, Auvernier, p. 241.—10. Bronze saw, Möringen, p. 165.

Pl. LVI. Möringen, &c.

Fig. 1. Bronze fibula, Möringen, p. 170.—2. Bronze fibula, Möringen, p. 170. —3. Ornament for suspension, bronze, Island of St. Peter, p. 454.—4. Small bronze chain, Island of St. Peter, p. 454.—5. Girdle buckle (?) Möringen, p. 169. —6. Bronze ornament for suspension, Möringen, p. 172.—7. Bronze ornament for suspension, Möringen, p. 172.

PL. LVII. AUVERNIER, &c.

Fig. 1. Part of a bronze girdle buckle, Möringen, p. 169.—2. Bronze ornament, Auvernier, p. 243.—3. Bronze ornament, Auvernier, p. 243.—4. Bronze implement, use unknown, Auvernier, p. 243.—5. Amber bead, Möringen, p. 173. —6. Bronze ornament for suspension, Möringen, p. 172.—7. Bronze ornament, Auvernier, p. 246.—8. Bronze ornament, Auvernier, p. 243.—9. Gold ornament, Möringen, p. 173.—10. Bronze ornament, Auvernier, p. 243.—11. Bronze ornament, Corcelettes, p. 281.—12. Bronze ornament, Corcelettes, p. 281.—13. Bronze ornament, Corcelettes, p. 281.

PL. LVIII. AUVERNIER, MÖRINGEN, &c.

Fig. 1. Bronze ear-pendant, Auvernier, p. 243.—2. Ornament for suspension, Möringen, p. 172.—3. Fibula of bronze, Nidau, p. 147.—4. Bronze spiral, Möringen, p. 180.—5. Bronze repoussée plate, Möringen, p. 180.—6. Bronze ornament for suspension, Auvernier, p. 684.—7, 8. Ferrules (?) for a bronze knife handle, Auvernier, p. 240.—9. Bronze fibula, Sutz, p. 449.—10. Bronze spatula, Möringen, p. 161.—11. Bronze pins in a case, Möringen, p. 170.—12. Bronze awl in a wooden handle, Möringen, p. 165.—13. Bronze spoon, Lüscherz, p. 200. —14. Bronze repoussée plate, Auvernier, p. 246.—15. Bronze vessel, Möringen, p. 180.—16. Bronze hammer, Möringen, p. 165.—17. Bronze implement, use unknown, Möringen, p. 180.—18. Gold finger-ring, Möringen, p. 180.— 19. Small gold rosette, St. Aubin, p. 459.—20, 21. Gold ornaments, St. Aubin, p. 459.

PL. LIX. AUVERNIER, MÖRINGEN, &c.

Fig. 1. Bronze finger-ring, Auvernier, p. 243.—2. Bronze stud, Cortaillod, p. 234.—3. Bronze ear-ring, Möringen, p. 180.—4. Bronze finger-ring, Möringen, p. 180.—5. Bronze crescent ornament, Cortaillod, p. 234.—6, 7. Bronze fibulæ, Möringen, pp. 170 and 180.—8, 9. Copper chisels, Gerlafingen, p. 452.—10. Bronze ornamented sickle, Möringen, p. 162.—11. Bronze twisted bar, Möringen, p. 180.—12. Bronze celt without an ear, Auvernier, p. 162.—13. Bronze ornamented socketed celt, Auvernier, p. 240.—14. Bronze chisel with circular rings, Möringen, p. 180.—15. Bronze pliers, Möringen, p. 684.—16. Bronze ear pendant, Möringen, p. 172.—17. Bronze ornament, Auvernier, p. 246.—18. Round bell of bronze, Möringen, p. 180.

PL. LX. MÖRINGEN, &c.

Fig. 1. Bronze implement, use unknown (dagger ?), Möringen, p. 161.— 2. Bronze hair-pin with double shank, Gerlafingen, p. 452.—3. Bronze hair-pin, Auvernier, p. 246.—4. Bronze fibula, Möringen, p. 170.

PL. LXI. AUVERNIER, &c.

Fig. 1. Bronze hair-pin with the head flattened, Bevaix, p. 457.—2. Bronze hair-pin with a hollow head, Nidau, p. 147.—3. Bronze hair-pin with gold plates set in the head, Auvernier, p. 242.—4. Bronze hair-pin, the head ornamented with silver, Estavayer, p. 262.—5. Bronze hair-pin ornamented, Möringen, p. 170. 6. Bronze hair-pin ornamented, Auvernier, p. 246.

PL. LXII. MÖRINGEN AND AUVERNIER.

Fig. 1. Bronze armilla, Möringen, p. 180.—2. Bronze armilla, Möringen, p. 180.—3. Bronze armilla, Auvernier, p. 242.—4. Bronze armilla, Auvernier, p. 242.

Pl. LXIII. Auvernier, &c.

Fig. 1. Bronze armilla, Auvernier, p. 246.—2. Bronze armilla, Auvernier, p. 242.—3. Bronze torque, Auvernier, p. 242.—4. Bronze armilla, Möringen, p. 180.—5. Bronze armilla, Möringen, p. 180.

Pl. LXIV. Estavayer, &c.

Fig. 1. Bronze armilla, Estavayer, p. 262.—2. Bronze armilla, Möringen, p. 171.—3. Bronze armilla, Auvernier, p. 243.—4. Bronze armilla, Auvernier, p. 242.—5. Bronze armilla, Möringen, p. 171.

Pl. LXV.[1] Möringen, Auvernier, &c.

Fig. 1. Bronze armilla, Möringen, p. 171.—2. Bronze armilla, Auvernier, p. 684.—3. Bronze armilla, Auvernier, p. 243.—4. Bronze armilla, Auvernier, p. 243.—5. Bronze armilla, Auvernier, p. 243.—6. Bronze armilla, Auvernier, p. 242.

Pl. LXVI. Auvernier, &c.

Fig. 1. Bronze armilla, ornamented both inside and out, Auvernier, p. 243. —2. Bronze armilla, inlaid with iron bands, Möringen, p. 172.—3, 4. Bronze armilla, or ear-rings, Möringen, p. 180.—5. Bronze armilla, Möringen, p. 180.— 6. Bronze armilla, Auvernier, p. 246.

Pl. LXVII. Möringen, &c.

Fig. 1. Bronze armilla, Bevaix, p. 457.—2. Bronze armilla, Auvernier, p. 243. —3, 4. Bronze ornamented armilla, Auvernier, p. 243.—5. Bronze armilla for a child, Auvernier, p. 243.—6. Bronze armilla, Möringen, p. 180.

Pl. LXVIII. Morges.

Fig. 1. Hollow bronze ring, p. 309.—2. Smaller solid ring, p. 310.—3. Great bronze hook, p. 310.

Pl. LXIX. Morges, Auvernier.

Fig. 1. Bronze armilla, Morges, p. 310.—2, 2 *a*, 2 *b*. Hollow bronze ring, Auvernier, p. 246.—3. Curved knife for under cutting (?) Morges, p. 310.

Pl. LXX. Möringen, &c.

Fig. 1. Horse's bit, bronze, Möringen, p. 173.—2. Horse's bit, of iron, Möringen, p. 174.—3. Horse's bit, of bronze, Auvernier, p. 244.—4. Horse's bit, of bronze, Auvernier, p. 244.—5. Horse's bit, of bronze, Möringen, p. 174.

Pl. LXXI. Möringen, Auvernier, &c.

Fig. 1. Umbo of a shield, bronze, or part of harness, Auvernier, p. 244.— 2. Bronze implement, use unknown, Möringen, p. 173.—3. Hollow cylinder of bronze, Auvernier, p. 241.—4. Bronze implement, use unknown, La Broie, p. 465.—5. Bronze implement, use unknown, Estavayer, p. 262.

[1] In this plate, and in one or two others, there appears in some few cases (probably an error of the printer) to be a slight discrepancy as to localities between the short list of objects given in the Swiss report and the letterpress description; in these instances the letterpress or full description has been followed, as being more likely to be correct.—[Tr.]

PL. LXXII. AUVERNIER AND MÖRINGEN.

Figs. 1, 2. Ornamental discs in cast bronze, Auvernier, p. 244.—3, 4, 5. Ornamental discs of repoussé bronze, Möringen, pp. 175 and 180.

PL. LXXIII. MÖRINGEN, AUVERNIER, &c.

Fig. 1, 2. Ornamental discs of repoussé bronze, Möringen, pp. 174 and 175.—3. Discs of cast bronze, Auvernier, p. 244.—4. Bronze ornament, Möringen, p. 180. —5. Bronze ornament, Auvernier, p. 246.—6. Bronze ornament, Möringen, p. 180. —7. Bronze rings on a ring of tin, Estavayer, p. 262.—8. Ornamental bronze disc, Möringen, p. 174.—9. Bronze ornament, Auvernier, p. 246.—10. Hollow bronze ring, Auvernier, p. 239.—11. Bronze ornamental disc, Möringen, p. 180.

PL. LXXIV. MÖRINGEN.

Fig. 1. Mould for a socketed knife, p. 167.—2. Mould for a knife with a tang, p. 167.—3. Mould for a lance-head, p. 168.—4 *a* and *b*. Mould for a hammer, p. 167.—5. Mould for pins, p. 168.—6. Fragment of a pipe, p. 168.

PL. LXXV. MÖRINGEN AND AUVERNIER.

Fig. 1 *a* and *b*. Mould for a chisel, Möringen, p. 166.—2. Fragment of a mould for a bracelet, Auvernier, p. 244.—3. Clay crucible, Möringen, p. 168.— 4. Bored stone implement, Auvernier, p. 246.—5. Mould for a sickle, Möringen, p. 167.—6. Fragment of a mould for a celt, Möringen, p. 167.

PL. LXXVI. MÖRINGEN AND AUVERNIER.

Fig. 1. Large earthenware painted plate, Möringen, p. 176.—2, 5. Ornamented vessels, Auvernier, p. 246.

PL. LXXVII. AUVERNIER, &c.

Figs. 1, 2, 3, 4, 5. Earthenware vessels of the stone age, Lüscherz, pp. 194 and 200.—6, 7. Fragments of rings, Auvernier, p. 246.—8. Vessel of the bronze age, Lüscherz, p. 200.—9, 9 *a*. Vessel with a spout at the side, Estavayer, p. 262.— 10. Fragment of pottery, ornamented with circles, Auvernier, p. 246. —11. Stone mould for making pottery, Auvernier, p. 245.—12. Perforated stone, use unknown, Auvernier, p. 246.—13. Fragment of cullender of earthenware, Auvernier, p. 246.

PL. LXXVIII. AUVERNIER, &c.

Fig. 1. Figure of a mole, child's toy, Auvernier, p. 245.—2. Figure of a bird, child's toy, Auvernier, p. 246.—3, 4. Child's toys, earthenware cups, Möringen, p. 175.—5. Earthenware vessel, Auvernier, p. 245.—6. Earthenware cup, Auvernier, p. 246.—7. Earthenware vessel, with a division (for salt, &c.), Möringen, p. 175.

PL. LXXIX. AUVERNIER, &c.

Figs. 1, 2. Child's toy, earthenware, Möringen, p. 176.—3. Child's toy (?) of earthenware, Möringen, p. 180 —4. Child's cup, Auvernier, p. 246.—5. Earthenware vessel, with a division for salt, &c., Möringen, p. 175.—6. Earthenware vessel, with two connecting tubes, Auvernier, p. 245.

Pl. LXXX.

Figs. 1 to 4, 6, 8 to 11. Crescents of earthenware, from various lake dwellings, p. 502.—Figs. 5 and 7 are from the mainland station of Ebersberg, p. 558, &c.

Pl. LXXXI.

Figs. 1 to 12. Crescents of earthenware from various lake dwellings, p. 502.

Pl. LXXXII.

Fig. 1. Plan, and fig. 2. View of the tomb at Auvernier, p. 249.

Pl. LXXXIII. Auvernier, &c.

Figs. 1 and 8. Flint saws in wooden handles, St. Aubin, p. 459.—2. Ornamented wooden staff, Möringen, p. 179.—3. Wooden implement, Auvernier, p. 242.—4 and 6. Wooden implement, Lüscherz, p. 198.—5. Netting needle (?), Möringen, p 179.—7. Pebble enclosed in a covering of bark, Lüscherz, p. 196. —9. Child's toy, wooden boat, Gerlafingen, p. 452.

Pl. LXXXIV. Tomb at Auvernier.

Fig. 1. Stone celt, p. 251.—2 to 5. Perforated teeth, p. 251.—6. Bone disc, p. 251.—7. Copper bead, p. 251.—8. Amber bead, p. 252.—9 and 10. Bronze armillæ, p. 252.—11. Bronze pin, p. 251.—12. Small bronze ring, p. 251.—13. Bronze knob or pendant, p. 252.

Pl. LXXXV. Möringen and Auvernier.

Figs. 1 to 12. Spindle-whorls from Möringen and Auvernier, pp. 169 and 245.

Pl. LXXXVI. Vingelz.

Figs. 1 to 6. Oak canoe, p. 224.

Pl. LXXXVII. Cudrefin, &c.

Figs. 1 and 2. Canoe of poplar wood, Vingelz, p. 224.—3, 4, 5. Small oak canoe, Cudrefin, p. 282.—6. Rod of wood wound round with thread, Lüscherz, p. 198.—7. Basketwork, Sutz, p. 449.

Pl. LXXXVIII. La Tène, Morges, Geneva, &c.

Fig. 1. Iron javelin-head, La Tène or Marin, p. 415.—2. Bronze knife, Thonon, p. 467.—3. Netting-hook of bronze, Morges, p. 310.—4, 5, and 6. Bronze pins, Geneva, p. 466.—7. Bronze hairpin, with a double head, Geneva, p. 466.—8. Flat tin ring, Geneva, p. 466.—9 and 10. Handles of bronze swords, Lake of Luissel, p. 467.—11. Bronze knife, Thonon, p. 467.—12. Mould for making rings, Geneva, p. 466.—13, 14, 15. Earthenware vessels, Geneva (?) p. 466.—16. Earthenware vessel, Nyon, p. 466.—17. Earthenware vessel, Geneva, p. 466.

Pl. LXXXIX. Geneva, Möringen, &c.

Fig. 1. Flint arrow-heads fixed to the shaft with asphalt, St. Aubin, p. 459. —2. Bronze celt, hafted with wood, Möringen, p. 180.—3. Bronze comb, Geneva, p. 466.—4 and 5. Crescents, Geneva, p. 466.—6. Bronze ring, Möringen, p. 180.

—7, 8. Socketed bronze celt, Morges, p. 310.—9. Bronze knife, Geneva, p. 466. —10. Fragment of ornamented pottery, Möringen, p. 180.—11. Bronze armilla, Geneva, p. 466.—12. Earthenware vessel, Geneva, p. 466.

Pl. XC. Sutz, Lattringen, &c.

Fig. 1. Stone hammer, Sutz, p. 447.—2. Iron lance-heads, Sutz, p. 447.— 3. Bronze dagger, Lattringen, p. 450.—4. Bronze sword, Sutz, p. 447.—5. Gold ornament, Little Island, p. 455.—6. Cup of wood with handle, Möringen, p. 155. —7. Bronze sword, between Sutz and Lattringen, p. 447.—8. Bronze crescent implement, Möringen, p. 155.—9. Bronze knife, Möringen, p. 155.—10 and 11, Oak lances, Sutz, p. 447.—12. Bronze hook, Scheuss, p. 456.—13. Bronze hook, Lattringen, p. 450.—14. Bronze hook, Sutz, p. 447.—15. Bronze pin, Scheuss, p. 456.—16. Crescent of earthenware, Möringen, p. 155.

Pl. XCI. Cortaillod, &c.

Figs. 1 to 4. Fragments of earthenware vessels ornamented with tin, Estavayer, p. 265.—5. Earthenware vessel, also ornamented with tin, Cortaillod, p. 230.

Pl. XCII. Cortaillod.
(All bronze.)

Fig. 1. 'Neck' of a casting, p. 232.—2, 3. Armillæ, p. 232.—4, 5. Chariot wheel, p. 231.—6, 7, 8. Crescent implements, p. 232.—9. Arrow-head, p. 232.

Pl. XCIII. Cortaillod.
(All bronze, except figs. 11, 12, 14 to 16.)

Figs. 1, 2, 3. Ornaments for suspension, p. 232.—4. Armilla, p. 232.— 5. Ring, p. 232.—6, 7.—Portions of armilla (?) p. 232.—8. Crescent cutting implement, p. 232.—9. Section of Pl. XCII. fig. 3. p. 232.—10. Armilla, p. 232.— 11, 12. Ear-ring of gold, p. 233.—13. Bronze hook, p. 232.—14. String of beads of bluish-white glass, p. 233.—15. Bronze ear-ring, the drop earthenware, p. 232. —16. Bone (netting) implement, p. 233.

Pl. XCIV. Auvernier, &c.

Fig. 1. Bronze lance-head, Auvernier, p. 236.—2. Bronze ring, Auvernier, p. 236.—3. Bronze implement, Corcelettes, p. 280.—4. Bronze knife, Conciso, p. 280.—5. Bronze knife, Corcelettes, p. 280.—6. Bronze knife, Bevaix, p. 457. 7. Iron lance-head, near Zihlbrücke, p. 462.—8 to 12, 14 to 20. Bronze pins, Corcelettes, pp. 280 and 281.—13 and 21. Bronze pins, Cortaillod, p. 232.— 22. Hairpin of stag's horn, Conciso, p. 281.—23. Flint arrow-head, Auvernier, p. 236.—24. Bronze armilla, Corcelettes, p. 281.—25. Bronze armilla, Cortaillod, p. 232.—26. Earthenware drinking cup (in section), Auvernier, p. 236.—27. Bronze fish-hook, Auvernier, p. 236. 28. Bronze implement, Cortaillod, p. 233. —29. Horn-shaped earthenware vessel, Auvernier, p. 236. 30 to 34. Earthenware vessels, Auvernier, p. 237. 35. Mortar (?) of stone, Auvernier, p. 237. 36. Small bronze chisel, Auvernier, p. 237.

Pl. XCV. Estavayer.

Fig. 1. Bronze chisel, p. 259. 2. Bronze spiral, p. 260. 3 to 14. Bronze pins, pp. 257, 258, and 259. 15. Section of part of the cover, Pl. XCVI. fig. 1, p. 261. 16, 17, 21, 23. Bronze armillæ, p. 260. 18. Bronze ring, p. 260. 19, 20. Bronze button (?) p. 260. 22. Bronze spiral, p. 260. 24. Bronze fish-hook, p. 260.—25. Flint arrow-head, p. 255.—26. Bronze arrow-head, p. 257.—27. Hammer of stag's horn, p. 255.—28. Bronze celt, p. 259.—29. Stone hammer, p. 256.—30. Celt of serpentine, p. 261.—31. Bronze sickle, p. 260.

Pl. XCVI. Estavayer, &c.
(All from Estavayer, except figs. 5 and 6.)

Fig. 1. Earthenware cover, ornamented with tin, p. 260.- 2, 3. Bronze knives, p. 258.—4. Bronze dagger-blade, p. 260.—5. Hatchet of stag's horn, La Crasaz, p. 263.—6. Flint tongue, La Crasaz, p. 262.—7 to 15. Bronze knives, p. 258.

Pl. XCVII. Estavayer and Lake of Morat.

Fig. 1. Bar of tin, Estavayer, p. 264.- 2. Bronze arrow-head, Est., p. 264. 3. Bronze saw, Est., p. 264.—4. Bronze ferrule, Est., p. 264.—5. Bronze armlet, Est., p. 265.—6. Bronze ornament, Est., p. 265.—7, 8. Disc of elk's horn, Est., p. 265.—9, 10. Bronze nail with socket, Est., p. 265.—11. Bronze boss, Est., p. 265.—12, 13. 'Slingstones,' Est., p. 265.—14. Tinned vessel (section) Lake of Morat (Guévaux), p. 464.—15. Earthenware vessel, Lake of Morat, p. 464.

Pl. XCVIII. and XCIX. Montellier.

The whole of the specimens drawn on these two plates consist of earthenware vessels and spindle-whorls, from Montellier, on the Lake of Morat, described pp. 291, 292, and 293.

Pl. C. Montellier.

Figs. 1, 2, 3. Fragments of a mould for casting rings (figs. 2 and 3 are the front and back of the same piece), p. 294.—4. Trellis-shaped implement of black earthenware, p. 293.—5. Fragment of pottery, ornamented with tin, p. 294.—6. Flint arrow-head, p. 294.—7. Bronze arrow-head, p. 294.—8 a, b, c. Fragment of a ring of tin, p. 294.—9. Small armlet of tin, p. 294.—10. Sewing needle of horn, p. 294.—11. Bronze ornament for suspension, p. 294.—12, 13. Bronze knobs, p. 294.—14. Bronze ornamented disc, p. 294.—15, 16. Bronze screws, p. 294.—17. Thin bronze plate, p. 294.—18. Fragment of bronze buckle, p. 294.—19. Bronze ring, p. 294.—20, 21, 22. Bronze fish-hooks, p. 294.—23. Bronze ornament in the shape of a crescent moon, p. 294.—24. Amber bead, p. 294.

Pl. CI. Montellier.

Fig. 1. Earthenware dish, perforated, p. 294.—2. Bronze knife, p. 294.

Pl. CII. Concise, &c.[1]

Fig. 1. Plan of the lake of Neuchâtel, in the neighbourhood of Yverdon, p. 266.—2. Section of the ground at Les Uttins, p. 266.—3. Plan of Concise harbour, p. 267.—4, 5, 6, 7, 8. Stag's horn haftings for celts, p. 268. 9, 10. Stone celt, p. 269.—11. Flint saw, p. 269.—12. Hatchet hammer of stag's horn,

---

[1] The objects drawn on this and the two following plates are described in M. Rochat's account of the lake dwellings in the neighbourhood of Yverdon, and apparently refer to the specimens in the interesting museum there. From his notice, which is given nearly in full in the present volume, it seems as if the whole of the objects drawn are from Concise, though this is not definitively stated; if, however, any of them are not from Concise, they must be from Corcelettes, and, as the two places are at no great distance apart, this small amount of uncertainty is of less importance.—[Tr.]

p. 269.—13. Hammer of stag's horn, p. 269.—14, 15, 16. Hatchet hammer of stag's horn, p. 269.—17. Bronze sword, p. 274.—18. Spiral bronze wire, p. 273. —19. Necklace bead (?) p. 273.—20. Bead of stag's horn, p. 273.

Pl. CIII. Concise, &c.

Figs. 1. 2. Hatchet hammers of stone, p. 270.—3. Perforated pebble, p. 270. —4, 5. Perforated pebbles (spindle-whorls ?) p. 271.—6. Spindle-whorl, p. 271. —7, 8, 9. Flint arrow-heads, p. 275.—10. Bone piercer, p. 271.—11. Piercer made of a boar's tooth, p. 271.—12 to 17. Bone arrow heads, p. 275.—18. Bone lance. p. 275.—19. Bone bead (?) p. 273.—20, 21. Hairpins (?) of stag's horn, p. 272.—22, 23, 24. Bone hairpins, p. 272.—25. Plate of enamel of tusk, p. 273. —26, 27. Harpoons of stag's horn, p. 275.—28, 29. Implements of boars' tusk, p. 277.—30, 31, 32, 34. Bone pottery tools, p. 278.—33. Bone point, p. 278.— 35. Bone needle, p. 272.—36. Fragment of jet bracelet, p. 273.—37. Amulet (?) of bear's tooth, p. 273.—38. Bone chisel, p. 277.—39. Oval plate of enamel, p. 273.—40. Bone gouge, p. 278.—41. Bone pottery tool, p. 278.

Pl. CIV. Concise, &c.

Fig. 1. Part of clay ring, p. 276.—2, 3, 5 to 9, 11, 12. Earthenware vessels, p. 276.—4. Earthenware ladle, p. 276.—10. Goblet of stag's horn, p. 276.—13, 14. Drinking vessels of stag's horn, p. 276.—15. Boar's tusk, partially perforated, p. 273.—16. Lozenge-shaped flint, p. 275.—17, 18. Bone potter's tools, p. 277 and 278.—19. Bronze button, p. 273.—20. Bronze knife, p. 279.—21. Implement made of a rib, 277.

Pl. CV.

Plan of the lake dwellings in the lakes of Neuchâtel, Bienne, and Morat.

Pl. CVI. Lake of Bourget.

Fig. 1. Earthenware vessel with Greek pattern, p. 332.—2. Perforated earthenware vessel, p. 332.—3. Earthenware vessel with spout, p. 332.—4. Earthenware vessel with rope ornament, p. 332.—5. Fragment of pottery, p. 332.— 6. Earthenware spindle-whorl, p. 332. 7. Earthenware ring, p. 332.—8, 9. Earthenware beads, p. 332.

Pl. CVII. Lake of Bourget.
(All bronze.)

Figs. 1 to 7. Socketed knives, p. 339.—8. Knife with a tang, p. 339.— 9. Bronze knife, p. 339.

Pl. CVIII. Lake of Bourget.
(All bronze.)

Figs. 1 and 4. Celts with loops, p. 339. 2, 3. Socketed celts with loops, p. 340. 5. Socketed and looped hammer (?) p. 340. —6. Socketed chisel, p. 684. 7. Socketed and looped chisel, p. 340.

Pl. CIX. Lake of Bourget.
(Pottery.)

Fig. 1. Pottery ornamented with alternate squares, p. 337.—2 Pottery with a fern leaf ornament, p. 337. 3, 4, 5, 6, 7, 8. Ornamented pottery, p. 337.

EXPLANATION OF THE PLATES. 17

PL. CX. MERCURAGO.

Figs. 1 and 2. Bronze pin, p. 348.—3. Bronze pin, p. 349.—4. Bronze lance-head, p. 348. 5, 6. Flint tongue, p. 349.—7 to 11. Flint arrow-heads, p. 349.—12, 13, 22. Fragments of pottery, p. 349.—14, 16, 17. Earthenware vessels p. 349.—15. Earthenware disc, p. 348.—18. Section of the ground with piles, p. 349.—19, 20. Wooden wheels, pp. 350 and 351.—21. Ground plan, p. 349.—23. Boat, p. 348.

PL. CXI. TERRAMARA.

Figs. 1 to 6. Paalstabs and lance-heads of bronze, p. 386.—7. Cylinder-shaped implement of earthenware, p. 386.—8. 'Slingstone' of porphyry, p. 384. —9. Mould for casting combs, p. 386.

PL. CXII. TERRAMARA.

Figs. 1 and 2. Piles in section, p. 381.—4, 5. Ground plans, p. 381.—6. Hearthstone (?) p. 382.—7 to 10. Earthenware vessels, p. 383.

PL. CXIII. TERRAMARA.

Figs. 1, 2. Earthenware vessels, p. 383.—3 to 10. Variously shaped handles to earthenware vessels, p. 383.—11, 13, 14. Fragments of pottery ornamented, p. 384.—12. Fragment of pottery inlaid with bronze, p. 384.

PL. CXIV. TERRAMARA.

Figs. 1, 2. Bronze pins, p. 385.—3 to 6. Bronze implements (5 and 6 are set in wooden handles), p. 385.—7, 8, 9. Implements of bone and horn, p. 385. —10. Bronze chisel, p. 385.—11, 12, 13. Bone implements, p. 385.—14, 18. Fragments of crescent implements, pp. 385 and 504.—15. Bone implement, p. 385.—16, 17. Bronze sickles, p. 385.—19. Bronze arrow-head, p. 386.—20, 24, 25, 28 to 30. Bone arrow-heads, p. 385.—21, 22, 23. Bronze pins, p. 385. —26, 27. Bone implements, p. 385.

PL. CXV. TERRAMARA.

Figs. 1 to 5. Bronze dagger-blades, p. 386.—6, 15. Bone combs, p. 385.—7. Bronze comb, p. 385.—8, 9, 10. Mould for casting, p. 386.—11. Bone implement, p. 385.—12. Bronze lance-head, p. 386.—13, 14. Horn implement, p. 385.

PL. CXVI. TERRAMARA.

Figs. 1 to 10. Wooden implements, Castione, p. 384.—11. Basket bottom, p. 384.—12 to 16, 18. Earthenware spindle-whorls, p. 386.—17. Spindle-whorl of stag's horn, p. 386.—19. Disc of earthenware, p. 386.

PL. CXVII.

N.B.—The specimens drawn on this plate are from the mainland; they are *for comparison* with those of the lake settlements.

Fig. 1. Earthenware vessel, San Martino, p. 353.—2. Bronze sword, Lago di Viverone, p. 353.—3. Serpentine knife, Cumarola, p. 303.—4, 7, 8, 9. Flint arrow-heads, Cumarola, p. 303.—5, 6. Tools of serpentine, Cumarola, p. 303.—10. Earthenware implement, Cumarola, p. 303.—11, 12. Bronze arrow-heads, Cumarola, p. 303.—13. Bronze celt, Cumarola, p. 303.—14. Bronze implement,

VOL. II.   C

Cumarola, p. 393.—15 to 20. Vessels and fragments of earthenware, Sesto Calende, p. 393.—21 to 25. Stone celts and tools, Imola, p. 393.

Pl. CXVIII. Peschiera.
(All bronze.)

Figs. 1, 3, 4. Daggers, p. 365.—2, 5 to 9. Spear-heads, p. 365.—10 to 14, 16 to 22. Pins, p. 365.—15 and 23. Needles, p. 365.

Pl. CXIX. Peschiera.

Figs. 1, 2, 3. Small bronze harpoons, p. 365.—4, 11 to 14. Bronze pins, p. 365.—5. Bronze armilla, p. 365.—6, 9. Bronze spiral, p. 365.—7, 8. Bronze fibulæ, p. 365.—10. Bronze knife, p. 365.—15, 16, 17. Copper tools, p. 365.—18. Bronze tube engraved with spiral, p. 365.—19. Bronze celt or chisel, p. 365. —20. Granite disc (slingstone?), p. 365.—21. Plan of Peschiera, p. 365.

Pl. CXX.

N.B.—This plate represents specimens drawn *for comparison* with those of the lake dwellings Figs. 1 to 28 are all drawings of *copper* implements from the mainland in Hungary, p. 369.

Pl. CXXI. Marin.
(All Iron.)

Figs. 1 to 9, 13. Fibulæ, p. 423.—10 to 12. Clasps of buckles, p. 423.

Pl. CXXII.

Figs. 1 to 5. Clasps of iron buckles, p. 423.—6. Ringed iron staple, p. 420.— 7, 8, 9, 10, 11. Iron rings for buckles (?) p. 423.—12, 13, 15 to 21. Iron studs, knobs, or nails, p. 423.—14. Part of iron buckle (?), p. 423.—22. Part of iron buckle, p. 423.—23. Mat of flax or bast, p. 409.

Pl. CXXIII. Marin.

Figs. 1 to 5. Iron swords and sheaths, p. 410.—6, 7. Iron sickles, p. 423.— 8. Steel for striking light (?), p. 421.—9, 10. Iron knives, p. 421.—11 to 16. Iron spear-heads, p. 415. -17. Small iron dagger (?), p. 421.—18. Three-pronged iron fork, p. 420.—19, 20. Iron hedging bills, p. 421.—21. Iron gouge, p. 421.—22, 23, 24. Iron celts and hatchet, p. 420.—25. Stone and iron anchor, p. 422.—26. Iron shears, p. 421.—27. Iron currycomb, p. 421.—28. Iron fibula, p. 423.

Pl. CXXIV. Marin.

(The late Col. Schwab's Museum.) N.B. The error of inserting &c. after Marin at the foot of this plate in the first edition has inadvertently been perpetuated in the present edition; *all* the specimens drawn on this plate are from Marin. Fig. 16, ½; 1 to 3, ¼; 5, 13, 15, 18, 19, 21 to 27, ½; 14, 17, ⅓; 28, ⅔; and the rest full size.

Figs. 1, 2 Iron spear-heads, p. 415 and 417.—3. Iron knife, p. 421.—4. Bone die, p. 409. 5. Iron bit, p. 409.—6. Part of blue glass armlet, p. 408.—. 7, 8, 9. Glass beads, pp. 408 and 409.—10. Bone ornament, p. 409.—11. Incised tooth, p. 109.—12. Glass ball (head of pin?), p. 409.—13. Iron Roman key, p. 409. 14. Iron taper drill, p. 421. 15. Iron linch-pin, p. 422.—16, 19. Iron hook, p. 421.- 17. Iron pliers, p. 423. 18. Iron hatchet or gouge, p. 421.—20. Stone ball for a game (?), p. 407.—21. Earthenware ring polished black, p. 408. 22, 23. Parts of iron sheaths, p. 410.—24, 25. Iron fibulæ, p. 422.— 26. Iron fibulæ with bronze knobs, p. 422.—27. Scraping iron, p. 421. -28. Bronze needle, p. 408.

EXPLANATION OF THE PLATES.

Pl. CXXV. CXXVI. CXXVII. CXXVIII.

All are drawings of iron swords and sheaths from Marin; nearly the whole of them are in the collection made by the late Col. Schwab. Fig. 6, Pl. CXXVIII. is in the possession of Professor Desor. The 'marks' on this plate, figs. 11 to 14, are drawn of the full size; all the other figures on these four plates are half-size, with the exception of the swords drawn Pl. CXXVI., which it was of course impossible to get into an octavo plate, and of which only the two extremities have been represented (half-size), p. 410.

Pl. CXXIX. Marin.
(Iron.)

Spear-heads, Figs. 3, 4, in the collection of Professor Desor. Figs. 1, 2, 5, in the late Col. Schwab's collection. Fig. 1 weighs about 8¼ ounces troy, and Fig. 2 nearly 10 ounces troy, p. 415.

Pl. CXXX. Marin.
(Iron.)

Figs. 1 to 4, and 7 to 9. Spear-heads, p. 415.—5, 6. Sickles, p. 423.

Pl. CXXXI. Marin.
(Iron.)

Figs. 1 to 7. Spear-heads, p. 415 (Fig. 1 weighs 14 ounces troy).—8. Shield plate or strap, p. 419.

Pl. CXXXII. Marin.

Fig. 1. Bronze hatchet, p. 408.—2, 3. Bronze pliers, p. 408.—4, 5, 6. Iron handles (?), p. 420.—7. Iron staple, p. 420.—8. Iron ring and staple, p. 420.—9. Bronze fibula, p. 408.—10, 11, 12. Iron plate (shield plate), p. 420.—13, 14. Iron shield plate or strap, p. 419.—15, 16. Lance-shaft ferrules, p. 419.—17 Bronze ring, p. 408.—18. Blue glass ring, p. 408.—19. Bronze spiral with glass bead, p. 408.—20. Bronze ring, p. 408.—21. Iron wire, p. 420.—22, 23. Bone implement, p. 409.—24. Iron ring, p. 420.—25. Iron hook, p. 420.—27. Bronze ring, p. 408.—28, 29. Iron rings, p. 420.

(N.B. Fig. 26. Bronze ring from Montellier has been drawn on this plate in error, p. 291.)

Pl. CXXXIII. Marin.

Fig. 1. Iron ladle, p. 420.—2, 3. Glass bead, p. 408.—4, 5, 6 and 9. Bronze plates, p. 408.—7. Bronze ring, p. 408.—8. Bronze cauldron with iron rings for handles, p. 407.—10, 11. Bronze ring with shank, p. 408.—12 to 15. Iron horn-like implements, p. 420.—16, 17. Gaulish gold coin (Philipp's money), p. 423.—18, 20 to 24. Gaulish coins ('Potin'), p. 424.—19. Silver coin of Massilia, p. 424.—25 Bronze pin, p. 408.

Pl. CXXXIV. Robenhausen and Wangen.

Various specimens of platted 'bast' and flax, pp. 507 and 508.

Pl. CXXXV. Robenhausen and Wangen.

Platted 'bast' and flax, and thread, string, and rope of flax, see pp. 409 and 507.

Pl. CXXXVI. Robenhausen and Wangen.

Platted and woven flax, see pp. 509 and 510.

c 2

PL. CXXXVII. ROBENHAUSEN.

Fig. 1. Pocket sewed on to coarse cloth, p. 512.—2. Net, p. 510.

PL. CXXXVIII. WANGEN AND CORTAILLOD.

Fig. 1. Flax plat (top of a cap?), Wangen, p. 70.—2. Strap or bag of a sling made of flax, Cortaillod, p. 233.

PL. CXXXIX. IRGENHAUSEN, &c.

Fig. 1. Fragment of pottery with peculiar ornament, Wangen, p. 71.—2, 2*a*. Embroidered cloth, Irgenhausen, p. 63.—3. Agricultural tool of stag's horn, Robenhausen, p. 58.—4. Bronze celt, Unter Uhldingen, p. 123.

PL. CXL. CORTAILLOD, &c.

Figs. 1, 2. Earthenware vessel ornamented with tin, Cortaillod, p. 231.—3, 4, 5. Round bronze plates, Möringen, p. 155.—6. Mat of flax or bast, Robenhausen, p. 57.—7. Stone beads, Bodmann, p. 105.

PL. CXLI. AND CXLII.

Plants and seeds of the lake dwellings : see the full description of the figures in the abridgment of Professor Heer's Treatise, p. 532.

PL. CXLIII. EBERSBERG. (Mainland for Comparison.)

Fig. 1. Slingstone (?) of porphyry, p. 141.—2, 3. Clay spindle-whorls, p. 565.—4. Bronze ring, p. 568.—5, 6. Stone celts, p. 566.—7. Part of crescent of red sandstone, p. 566.—8, 9. Earthenware vessels, p. 563.—10. 'Restoration' of the forms of pottery, p. 563.—11. Bone lance-head, p. 567.—12. Bronze knife, p. 568.—13, 14, 18, 19. Bronze pins, p. 568.—15, 16, 17. Bronze chisels, p. 568.

PL. CXLIV. EBERSBERG. (For Comparison.)

Figs. 1 to 15. Ornamentation on pottery, all drawn half-size, p. 563.—16. Impression of wattlework on the clay coverings of the huts, p. 565.

PL. CXLV. EBERSBERG. (For Comparison.)

Fig. 1. Earthenware vessel perforated, p. 563.—2. Glass bead, p. 567.—3. Cup and ring, p. 565.—4. Earthenware vessel, p. 563.—5. 'Crescent' terra cotta, p. 566. 6. Bone lance-head, p. 567.—7 to 9, 14 to 16. Bronze pins, p. 568.—10. Bronze knife, p. 568.—11. Earthenware loom-weight, p. 565.—12, 20, 21. Earthenware spindle-whorls, p. 565.—13 and 23. Bronze spirals, p. 568.—17. 'Crescent' of sandstone, p. 566.—18. Bronze finger-ring, p. 568.—19. Bronze ear-ring, p. 568.— 22. Stone corn-crusher, p. 566.—24. Celt of nephrite, p. 566. 25. Bronze arrow-head, p. 568.

PL. CXLVI. UETLIBERG AND WINDISCH. (Mainland for Comparison.)
(N.B.—Figs. 1 to 10 from Uetliberg. Figs. 11 to 14 from Windisch.)

Fig. 1. Red pottery coarsely ornamented, p. 570.—2. Black pottery, p. 570. 3. Bronze chisel, p. 570.—4. Stone celt, p. 570. 5. Bone piercer, p. 570. 6. Bronze pin, p. 570. 7. Four bronze ornaments, p. 570.—8. Small bronze wheel,

p. 570.—9. Handle of a 'crescent' cutting implement (?) p. 570.—10. Bronze ornament, p. 570.—11. Flint tongue or knife, p. 571.—12. Flint scraper, p. 571. —13. Stone celt, p. 571.—14, 15. Corn-crushers of stone, p. 571.—16. Perforated bear's tooth (amulet?), p. 571.

PL. CXLVII.   IRISH CRANNOGES.

Fig. 1. Section of crannoge in Ardakillin Lough, p. 648.—2. Ground plan of a crannoge in Drumaleague Loch, p. 648.—3. Section of another crannoge in the same lake, p. 648.—4, 5, 6. Bone cloak-pins, Ballinderry, p. 650. 7. Head of bronze pin, Ardakillin, p. 651.—8. Ringed bronze pin, Dunshaughlin, p. 651. — 9. Sandstone mould for casting celts, Lough Scur, p. 651.— 10. Iron spear-head, Lagore, p. 651.—11, 12. Double-edged iron sword, Lagore, p. 651. —13. Scimitar-shaped iron blade, Lagore, p. 651.—14. Iron knife, Lagore, p. 651.

PL. CXLVIII.   WELSH CRANNOGE, LLANGORSE LAKE.

Fig. 1. Plan of the crannoge, p. 661.—2. Island as seen from the lake near Brecon, p. 660.—3. Section between the island and the shore, p. 661.—4. Section on the east of the island, p. 662.—5, 6. Piles or slabs, p. 661.

PL. CXLIX.   RODENHAUSEN.

Wooden door (?) p. 56.

PL. CL.   MÖRINGEN, &c.

Figs. 1, 2, 3. Bone pins, Gerlafingen (Oefeli), p. 453.—4. Earthenware cup mended with asphalt, Niederwyl, p. 80.—5. Wooden shutter with bolt, Schaffis, p. 218.— 6. Bone skate, Moosseedorf, p. 39.—7. Implement made of boar's tusk, perforated, Gerlafingen, p 453.—8. Chisel of nephrite (?) Gerlafingen, p. 453.— 9. Needleholder of earthenware, Möringen, p. 170.

PL. CLI.   LAKE OF BOURGET.

Fig. 1. Earthenware vessel standing on four feet, p. 336.—2, 3, 4. Small earthenware vessels, p. 336.—5. Jar with peculiar ornamentation, p. 336.— 6. Neck of small vessel with spout, p. 336.—7. Vessel with a band running round it, p. 336.—8. Ornamented vessel, p. 336.—9, 10, 11, 14. Pottery ornamented with circles, p. 336.—12, 13, 15, 16. Ornamented pottery, p. 336.

PL. CLII.   LAKE OF BOURGET.

Figs. 1, 2, 3. Lamps (?) p. 337.—4, 5, 6, 7, 8. Pottery with various incised ornamentations, p. 337.

PL. CLIII.   LAKE OF BOURGET.

Fig. 1. Stone weight (and section), p. 335.— 2. 'Slingstone' (?) p. 335.— 3, 4. Polishing stones perforated (touchstone?) p. 336.—5. Spindle-whorl, p. 336. —6. Lozenge-shaped stone, p. 336.—7, 8. Flint arrow-heads, p. 336.

PL. CLIV.   LAKE OF BOURGET.
(All bronze.)

Fig. 1. Clasp or buckle, p. 340.—2 and 6. Cutting implements, p. 340.— 3. Socketed knife, p. 340.—4, 5. Ornamented knives, p. 340.

Pl. CLV. Lake of Bourget.
(All bronze.)

Figs. 1, 2, 3, 4. Armillæ, p. 340.— 5. Ornamented disc, p. 340.—6. End of clasp (?) p. 341.—7. Implement, use unknown, p. 341.—8. Ring with projecting radii, p. 341.— 9. Ring with three other rings cast on it, p. 341.—10. Short and strong chain, p. 341.

Pl. CLVI. Lake of Bourget.
(All bronze.)

Fig. 1. Part of a sickle, p. 341.—2, 5. Lance-heads, p. 341.—3. Dagger or lance, p. 341.—4. Knife, p. 341.—6. Arrow-head of thin bronze turned over, p. 341.—7, 8, 9. Arrow-heads, p. 341.—10. Arrow-head with a tang or stalk, p. 341.—11. Portion of ornamented plate, p. 341.

Pl. CLVII. Lake of Bourget.
(All bronze.)

Figs. 1 to 6. Pins, p. 341.—7, 8, 10, 11. Needles, p. 341. 9, 14, 16. Pointers or chisels, p. 341.—12, 13, 15, 18, 19. Hooks, p. 341.—17. Cutting implement ornamented, p. 341.

Pl. CLVIII. Lake of Bourget.

Fig. 1. Rude figure of an animal or lizard in earthenware, p. 337.—2, 3. Rude figures of animals (?) in earthenware, p. 337.—4. Ornamented pottery, p. 338. - 5. Wooden implement (distaff?), p. 684.—6. Double bronze armilla joined with a ring, p. 340.—7. Bronze knife, very thin and short, p. 340.

Pl. CLIX. Lake of Bourget.

Fig. 1. Bronze vase found in its mould, p. 342.—2, 4. Bronze celts, p. 342.—3. Earthenware vessel (the upper figure is the side view, the lower figure the base), p. 338.—5. Arrow-head of bronze of a peculiar form, p. 342.

Pl. CLX. Lake of Bourget.

Plan of the lake on a scale of $\frac{1}{10000}$.

Pl. CLXI. Lake of Bourget.

Fig. 1. Hollow bronze ball, use unknown, p. 342.—2. 'Crescent' (?) of a much longer form than is usual, p. 338.—3. Clay (said to be part of the hut covering) with the 'croix gammée' impressed on it, p. 339.—4. Seal or stamp for making this impression, p. 339.—5. Seal or stamp for making concentric impressions, p. 339. 6. Bone harpoon, p. 342.—7. Bronze tube ornamented with rings, &c., p. 342.—8, 9. Bronze pins with large heads, p. 342.

Pl. CLXII. Bodio, Lago di Varese.

Figs. 1 to 10. Flint arrow-heads, p. 359.—11. Bronze lance-head, p. 360.—12. Bronze lance-head, p. 360.—13. Spindle-whorl (?) p. 358.—14, 15, 16, 17. Bronze hooks, p. 360.—18. Bronze pin, p. 360.—19. Perforated stone, p. 360.—20. Net weight (?) p. 360. 21. Quartzite ring, p. 360.—22, 23. Bone pointers, p. 358.

Pl. CLXIII. Bodio, Lago di Varese.

Figs. 1, 2 and 6. Ornamented pottery, p. 359.— 3, 4, 5. Spindle-whorls, p. 358.

PL. CLXIV. LAGO DI VARESE.

Fig. 1. Two-handled cup, Monate, p. 404.—2, 3. Ornamented pottery, p. 358.
—4. Cone ornamented at the base (spindle-whorl?) p. 358.—5. Bone pointer
(Isola Camilla), p. 358.—6, 8. Flint lance-heads, p. 360. 7. Flint scraper, p.
360.—9, 12, 13. Flint knives, p. 360.—10, 11. Bone pointers, p. 358.

PL. CLXV.
Plan of the lakes of Varese and Monate.

PL. CLXVI.
Plan of the lakes of Pusiano and Garda.

PL. CLXVII. LAIBACH MOOR.
Figs. 1, 2, 3, 4, 5, 6, 8, 9, 11, 12. Ornamented pottery, p. 614.—7. Earthenware cylinder, use unknown, p. 614.—10. Spindle-whorl (?) p. 614.

PL. CLXVIII. LAIBACH MOOR.
Figs. 1, 2, 3 and 5. Hammer-axes of stag's horn. p. 609.—4. Bone pointer
or dagger, p. 609.—6, 7. Bone pointers, p. 609.—8. Ornament of stag's horn,
p. 611.—9, 10. Bone pins, p. 610.—11. Bone needle, p. 610.—12. Perforated bone
pointer, p. 609.—13 and 17. Clothes hooks, p. 611.—14. Perforated arrow-head
or ornament, p. 610.—15. Needle of stag's horn, p. 610.—16. Borer or ornament
of stag's horn, p. 610.—18. Bronze pin, p. 612.—19. Cylindrical bone (used for
netting?), p. 610.—20. Bone (spear- or arrow-head?) perforated, p. 610.

PL. CLXIX. LAKE OF FIMON.
Sections of the 'relic bed' of the stone and bronze ages, p. 368.

PL. CLXX. LAKE OF FIMON.
Figs. 1, 2. Flint arrow-heads, p. 369.—5, 6, 8. Flint lance-heads, p. 369.—
3, 4. Flint knives, p. 369.—7. Stone corn-crusher (or slingstone), p. 369.

PL. CLXXI. LAKE OF FIMON.
Figs. 1, 2, 3. Pottery ornamented with diagonal lines and circular bands,
p. 371.

PL. CLXXII. LAKE OF FIMON.
Figs. 1, 2, 3, 4. Earthenware vessels of various forms, p. 372.—5, 6. Handles
of earthenware vessels, p. 374.

PL. CLXXIII. LAKE OF FIMON.
Figs. 1, 2, 3, 4. Ornamented pottery, pp. 374 and 375.

PL. CLXXIV. LAKE OF FIMON.
Figs. 1, 2, 3. Ornamented pottery, p. 374.

PL. CLXXV. LAKE OF FIMON.
Figs. 1 and 2. Ornamented pottery, pp. 376 and 377.

Pl. CLXXVI. Lake of Fimon.

Figs. 1, 2, 3. Bronze celt, p. 376.—4. Clay ring, p. 377.

Pl. CLXXVII.

Map of the district near the lake of Fimon, p. 367.

Pl. CLXXVIII. Lake of Starnberg (Rosen-Insel).

Fig. 1. Ornamented bronze plate, p. 593.—2, 3. Earthenware counters, p. 594.—4. Glass bead, p. 595.—5. Clay bead, p. 594.—6, 7. Clay net-weights, p. 594.—8. Clay bead, p. 594.—9. Part of a bronze armilla, p. 594.—10, 11. Iron javelin-heads, p. 595.—12. Iron knife, the blade and handle in one, p. 595. 13. Bronze ornamented knife, the blade and handle in one, p. 594.—14. Bronze dagger, p. 594.

Pl. CLXXIX. Lake of Starnberg (Rosen-Insel).

Figs. 1, 3, 4, 6, 9, 10, 11, 12. Bronze pins, p. 594.—*Fig.* 7. Bronze pin with the upper end pressed flat, p. 594 (note).—*Figs.* 2 and 5. Bronze needles, p. 594.—8. Bronze pointer or awl, p. 594.

Pl. CLXXX. Lake of Starnberg (Rosen-Insel).

Figs. 1 to 23 give a selection from the ornamentation on the pottery, p. 595.

Pl. CLXXXI. Lake of Starnberg (Rosen-Insel).

Figs. 1, 2, 3. Bronze pins, p. 594.—4, 5. Ornamented knives, p. 594.— 6. Bronze socketed arrow-head, p. 594.—7. Bronze fish-hook, p. 594.— 8. Anchor-shaped bronze implement, use unknown, p. 594.

Pl. CLXXXII. Lake of Starnberg (Rosen-Insel).

Figs. 1 to 3. Flint arrow-heads, p. 593.—4. Celt of nephrite, p. 593.— 5. Stone celt in stag's horn hafting, p. 593.—6. Stone celt, p. 593.— 7, 8. Polishing stones, p. 593.—9, 10. Ornaments of wild boar's teeth, p. 593. —11, 12, 13, 17, and 33. Bone arrow-heads, p. 593.—14, 15, 16, 23, and 41. Horn hammers, p. 593.—18, 20, 24, 26, 30, 31, 32, 34, 35, 37, 38, and 42. Tools of bone and teeth, p. 593.—19, 21, 39, and 43. Bone or horn haftings or handles, p. 593.—22, 25, and 28. Shuttles (?) p. 593.—27. Horn knife, p. 593. —29. Bone awl or pointer, p. 593.—36. Bone skate, p. 593.—40, and 44. Ornament of boar's tusks, p. 593.

Pl. CLXXXIII. Lake of Starnberg (Rosen-Insel).

The upper part is a plan of the platform, p. 591, and the lower part is a plan of part of the lake in which Rosen-Insel lies, p. 590.

Pl. CLXXXIV. Mond See.

Figs. 1 to 13. Forms of earthenware vessels without any ornamentation, p. 602.

Pl. CLXXXV. Mond See.
(Pottery.)

Figs. 1 to 7. Various patterns of ornamentation on the pottery found here; the incised lines are filled with white or chalky matter, pp. 603 and 604.

Pl. CLXXXVI. Mond See.
(Pottery.)

Figs. 1 to 7. Various patterns on pottery, made in a similar way to those drawn on the last plate, pp. 603 and 604.

Pl. CLXXXVII. Mond See.

Figs. 1, 2, 3. Rude figures of animals made of baked clay, p. 604.

Pl. CLXXXVIII. Mond See.

Fig. 1. Half-moon-shaped flint knife, p. 598.—2, 3. Flint knives with a kind of handle (?) p. 599.—4, 5. Flint lance-heads, p. 599.—6. Stone hammer partially bored, p. 600.—7. Forked bone pointer, p. 600.—8. Flint arrow-head, p. 599.—9, 10. Bored and polished stone hammers, p. 599.—11. Stone celt with the cutting edge diagonal, p. 600.

Pl. CLXXXIX. Mond See.

Figs. 1 and 2. Ornamented earthenware vessels, p. 604.—3. Crucible of baked clay for melting metal; it has a kind of socket for a handle, p. 597.

Pl. CXC. Atter See.

Fig. 1. Large earthenware vessel, Puschacher, p. 624.—2, 3, 4, 5, and 7. Pottery ornamented in various ways, Weyeregg, p. 624.—6. Perforated stone of serpentine, Puschacher, p. 624.—8. Flint arrow-head, Seewalchen, p. 621.—9, 12. Small specimens of iron implements (?), Seewalchen, p. 621.—10. Bronze awl, Seewalchen, p. 621.—11. Bronze pin, Seewalchen, p. 621.—13. Flint lance-head, Seewalchen, p. 623.

Pl. CXCI. Atter See.

Figs. 1, 2, 3, 4, 5. Flint arrow-heads, Seewalchen, p. 621.—6. Stone perforated and worked, Seewalchen, p. 621.—7, 8, 9. Stone celts, Seewalchen, p. 621.—10, 11. Bone pointer, Weyeregg, p. 623.—12, 13. Forked bone pointers, Weyeregg, p. 623.—14, 15. Tines of horn with circular incisions, Weyeregg, p. 623.—16. Perforated bear's tooth, Weyeregg, p. 624.—17, 18, 19, 20, and 21. Pottery with various ornamentation, Seewalchen, p. 622.

Pl. CXCII. Lake of Paladru.

Fig. 1. Iron knife-blade, p. 637.—2. Iron lance-head, p. 637.—3. Iron key, p. 637.—4 and 9. Iron horse-shoes, p. 637.—5 and 7. Bone counter, p. 637.—6. Iron spur, p. 637.—8. Iron axe, p. 637.—10. Iron curry comb, p. 637.

Pl. CXCIII. Lake of Paladru.

Fig. 1. Wooden spoon, p. 637.—2. Wooden comb, p. 638.—3, 4, 5, 6. Ornamented pottery, p. 637.—7. Earthenware jug of a peculiar form, p. 638.

PL. CXCIV. LAKE OF PALADRU.

Ground plan of the piles and lake dwelling at Grands Roseaux in this lake, p. 636.

PL. CXCV. LAKE OF PALADRU.

Plan of this lake, p. 631.

PL. CXCVI. MOOR OF SCHUSSENRIED.

District of the Feder See, p. 589.

PL. CXCVII. SCHUSSENRIED.

View of the lake dwelling, p. 580.

PL. CXCVIII. SCHUSSENRIED.

Fig. 1. Pipkin with a handle, p. 582.—2, 3, 5, 6, 8, and 9. Ornamented pottery, p. 582.—7. Jar with four knobs round the bulge, p. 582.

PL. CXCIX. SCHUSSENRIED.

Figs. 1 and 11. Hammer of stag's horn, p. 585.—2. Dagger of stag's horn, p. 585.—3, 4. Stone chisels hafted in stag's horn, p. 585.—5, 6, and 9. Flint arrow-heads, p. 583.—7. Flint implement with asphalt adhering to it, p. 583.—8. Flint scraper, p. 583.—10 and 12. Stone hatchets, p. 584.—13. Flint knife, p. 583.

PL. CC. SCHUSSENRIED, &c.

Figs. 1, 2, 3. Ornamented pottery, p. 582.—4. Pipkin with short handle, p. 582.—5. Earthenware vessel with four perforated knobs, p. 582; the whole of the above are from Schussenried.—6. Bronze ring inlaid with iron, Möringen, p. 172.

PL. CCI. CONSTANCE.

Fig. 1. Broken perforated serpentine hammer, p. 574.—2. 'Core' from boring, p. 574.—3. Half of a perforated serpentine hammer, p. 574.—4. Half of a partially perforated serpentine hammer, p. 574.—5. Half of a perforated hammer of serpentine, p. 574.—6. Celt of diorite, p. 574.—7, 8. Celts of serpentine, p. 574. —9. Small serpentine celt, p. 574.—10, 11, 12, 13, 14. Flint implements, p. 574.

PL. CCII. CONSTANCE.

(All drawn half-size, and the material grey earthenware.)

Figs. 1 and 2. Spindle-whorls, p. 574.—3. Jar with two handles, p. 574.— 4 and 5. Ornamented pottery, p. 575.—6. Cup with a handle, p. 575.—7. Pot or pipkin without a handle, p. 575.

PL. CCIII. CONSTANCE.

Fig. 1. Ornamented earthenware plate, p. 575.—2. Neck of vessel with circular lines perforated in a diagonal direction, p. 575.—3, 4. Ornamented pottery, p. 575. 5, 6. Ornaments of bronze, p. 575.—7. Bronze pin, p. 575.—8. 'Drop ornament' of a cup, p. 575.—9. Fragment of light green glass, p. 575.—10. Fragment of bluish-green glass, p. 575.

Pl. CCIV. Terramara of Seniga.
(The upper part is a plan of the district.)

Figs. 1 and 2. Flint arrow-heads, p. 396.—3, 4, 5. Flint knives, p. 396.—6. Earthenware vessel with knobs outside, p. 396.—7. Handle of earthenware vessel, p. 396.—8, 9. Coarsely ornamented pottery, p. 396.

Pl. CCV. Lake Mohrya.

View of the lake dwellings in Lake Mohrya (Central Africa), copied (with permission) from Captain Cameron's 'Across Africa,' p. 500.

Pl. CCVI.

General map of the lake-dwelling district.

N.B.—The terramara settlements are not included. It would also be manifestly impossible in so extended a map as this to have every settlement laid down, but all the more important ones will be found in it coloured red.

THE END.

LONDON : PRINTED BY
SPOTTISWOODE AND CO., NEW-STREET SQUARE
AND PARLIAMENT STREET

Pl. I.

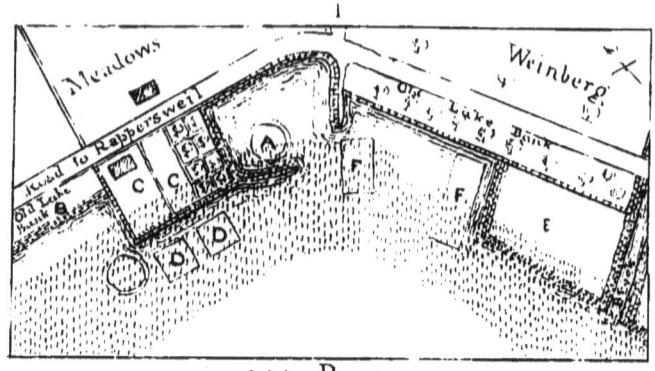

GROUND PLAN

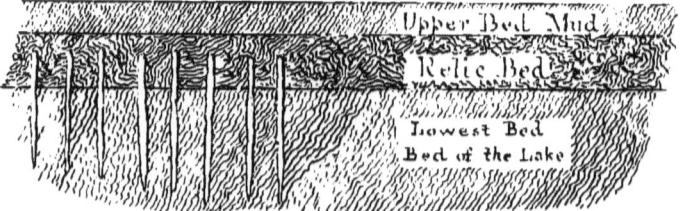

SECTION

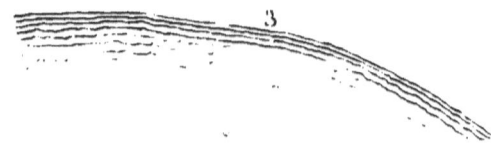

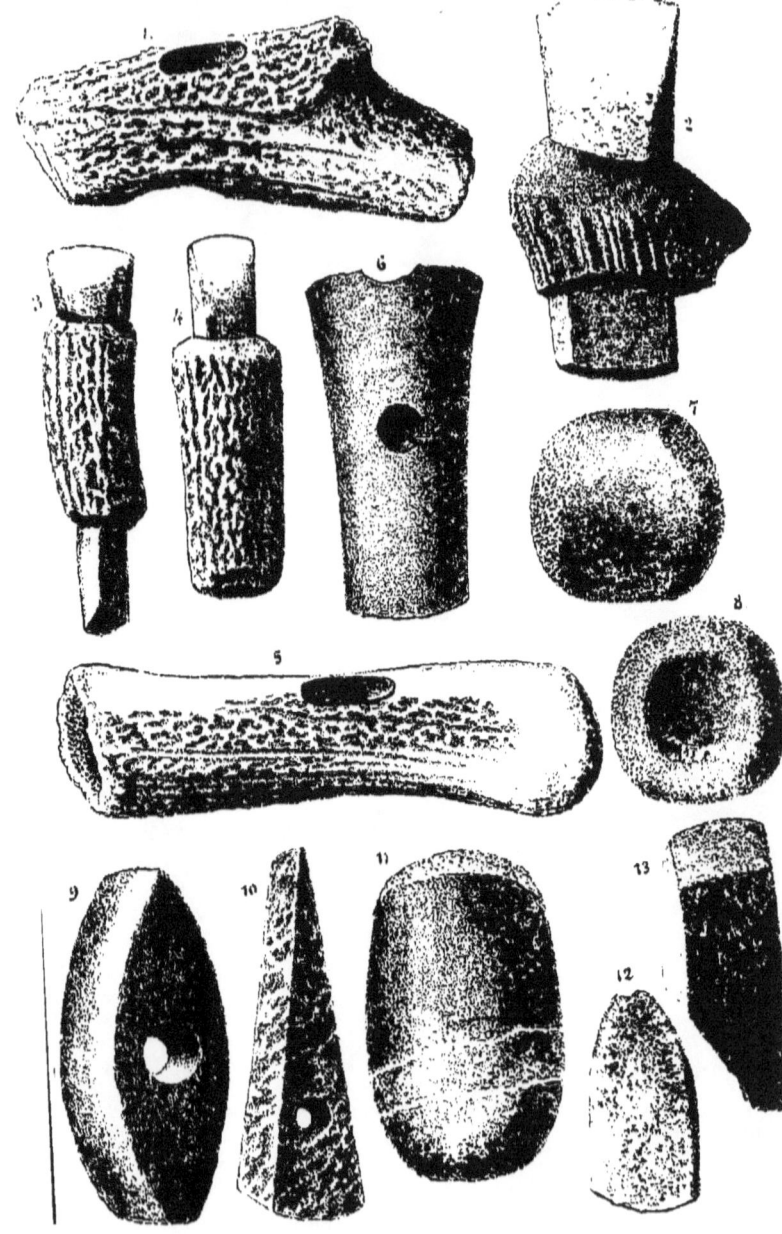

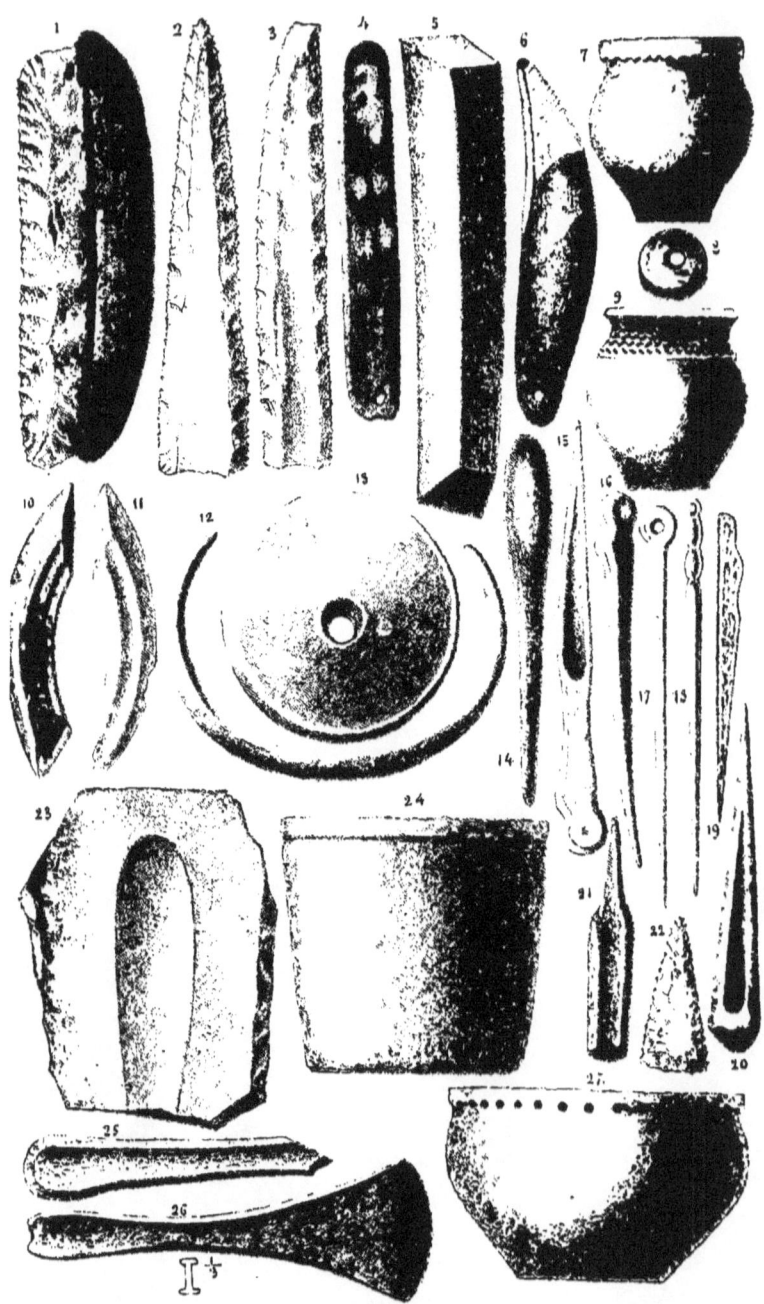

MEILEN.

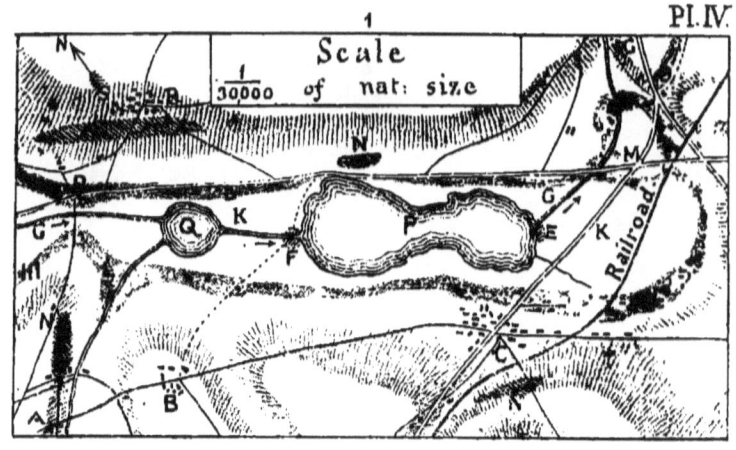

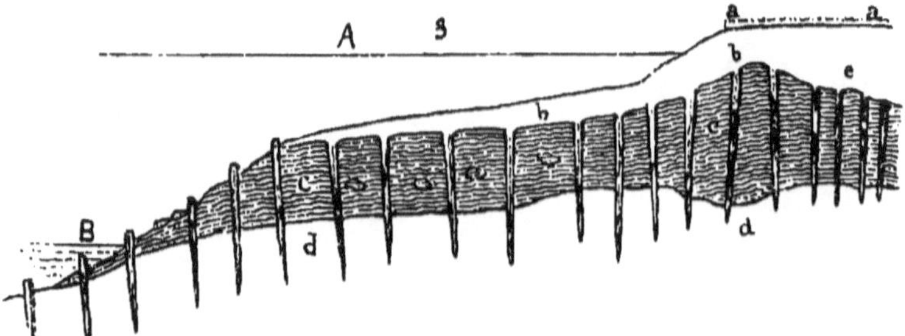

MOOSSEEDORF

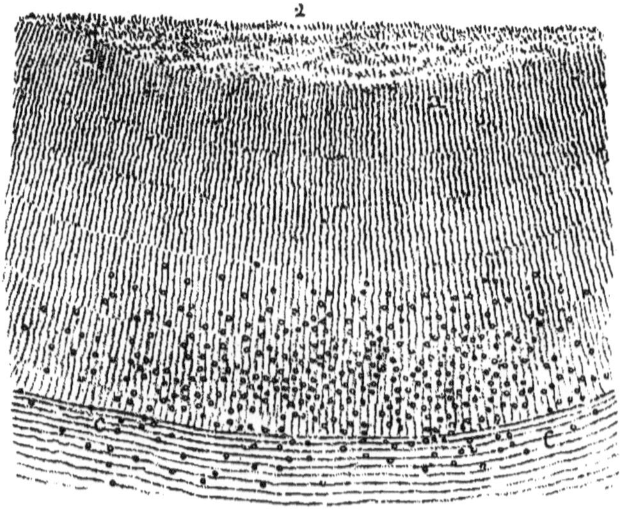

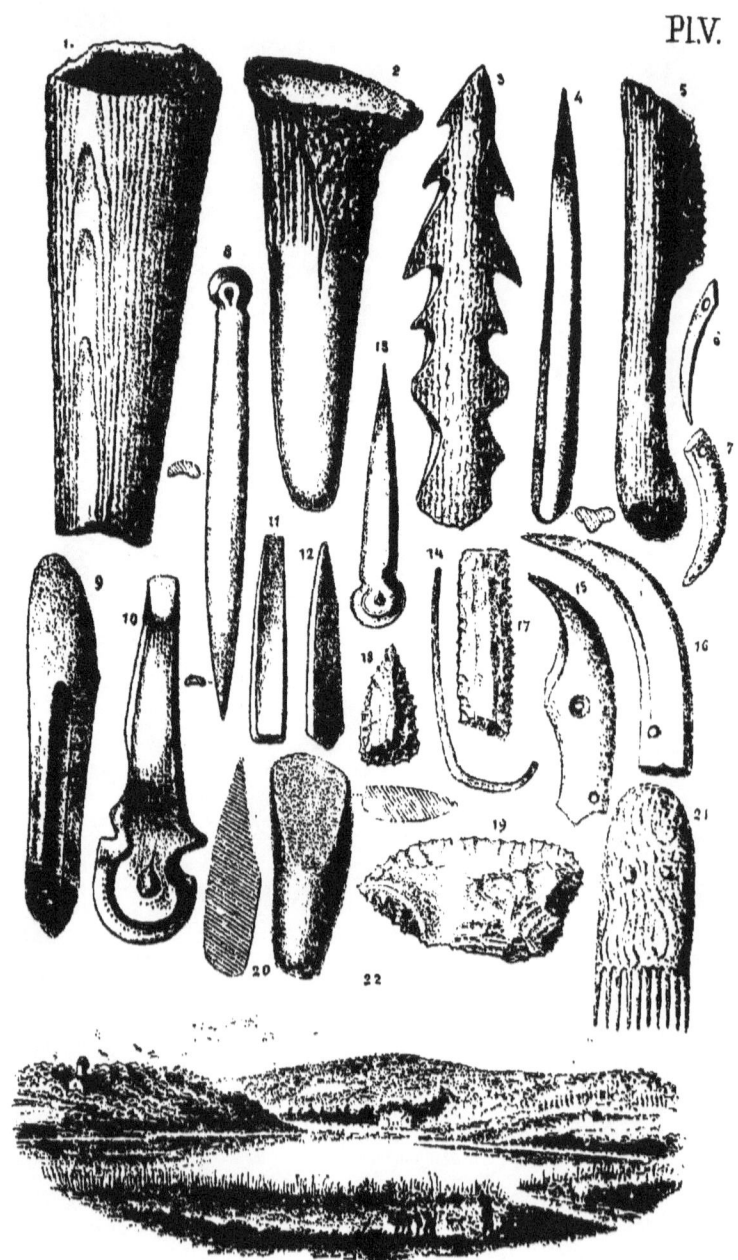

Pl. V.

MOOSSEEDORF.

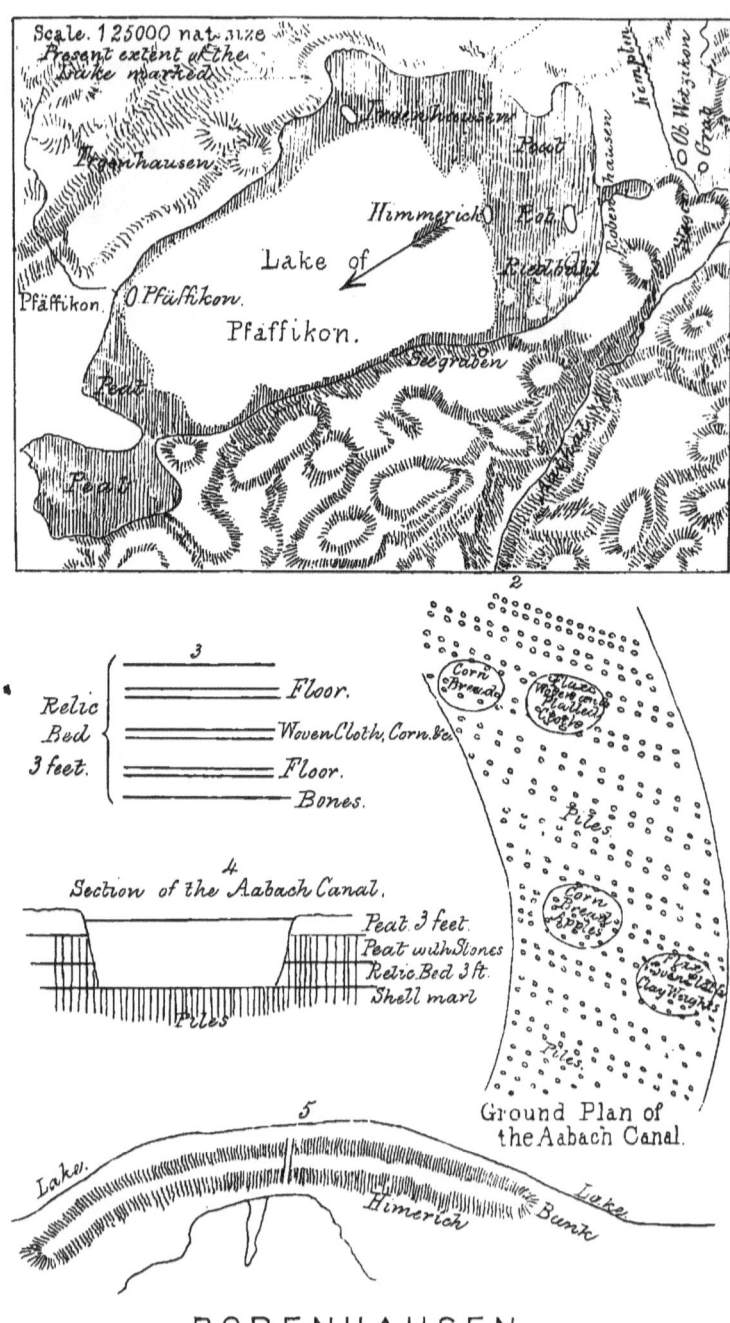

ROBENHAUSEN

Peat Moor of ROBENHAUSEN *with part of the* LAKE PFÄFFIKON *as seen from* SEEGRABEN.

ROBENHAUSEN.
as seen 20 June 1865.
Piles of the last settlement but one – Round Fir Timber.

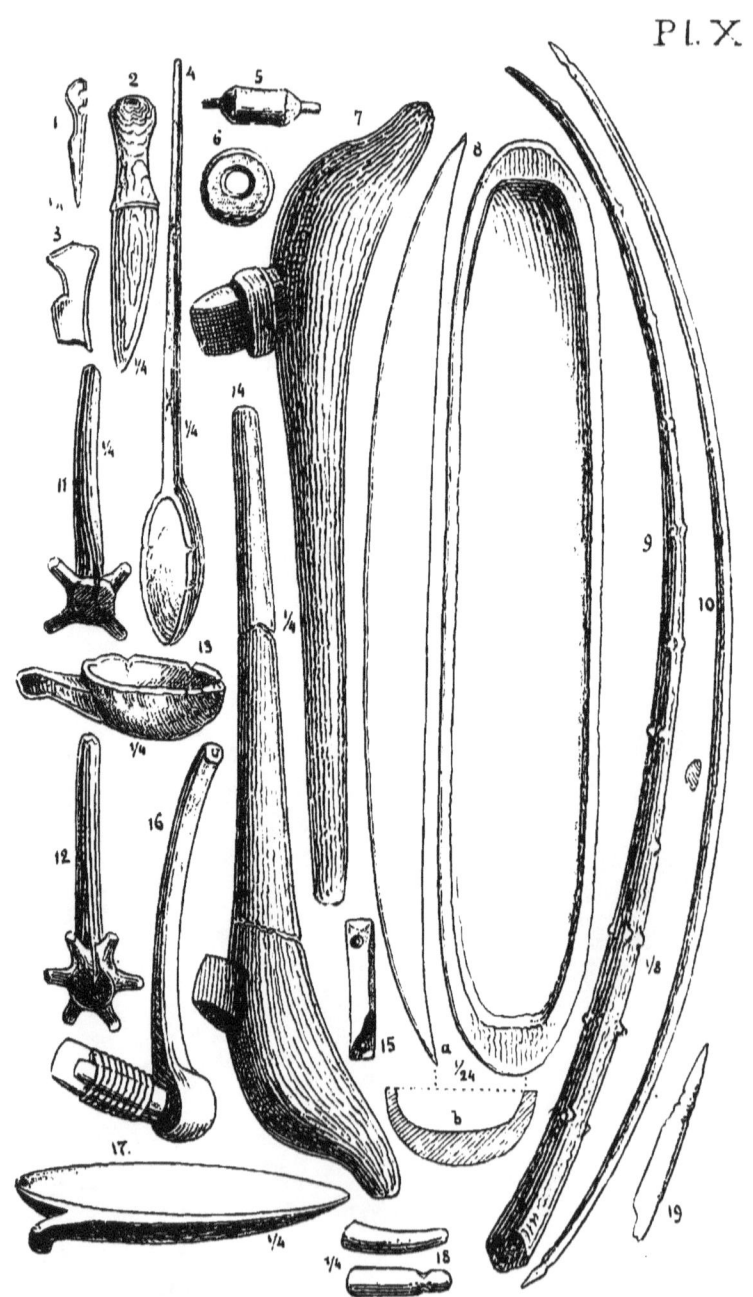

ROBENHAUSEN Wood &c.

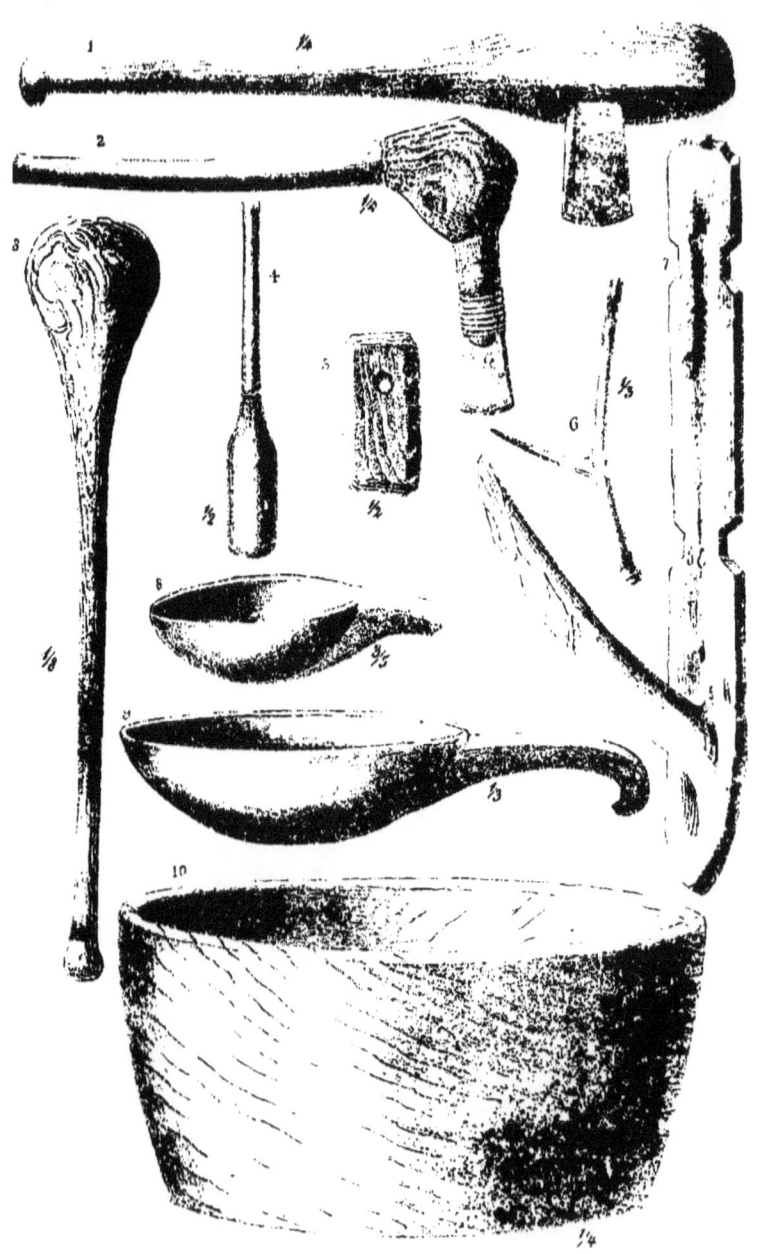

ROBENHAUSEN.

Pl. XII.

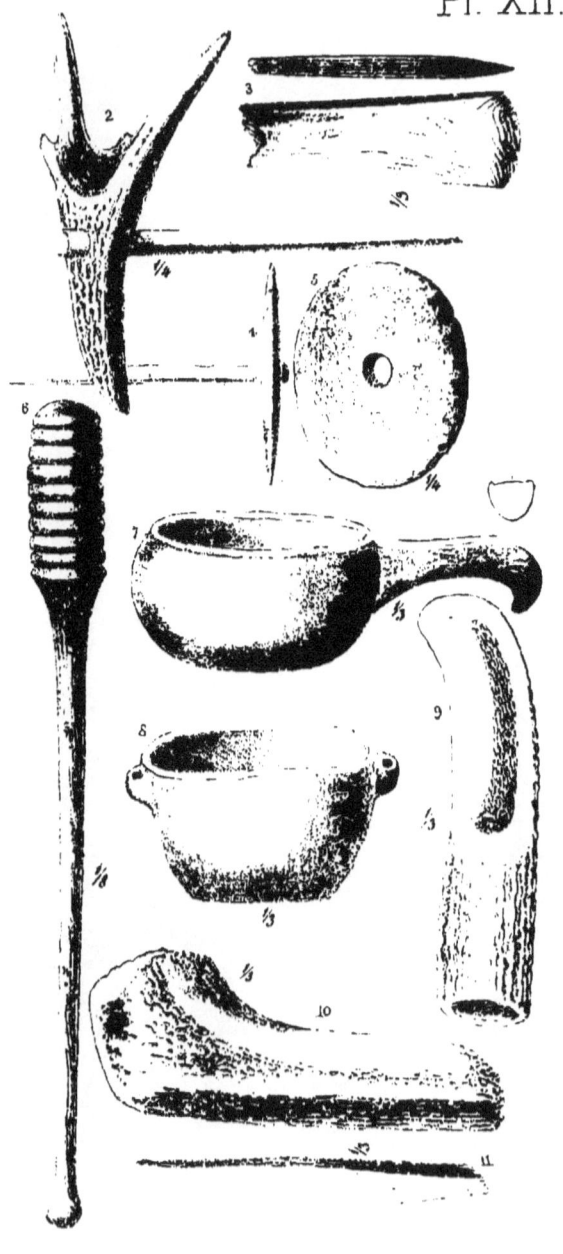

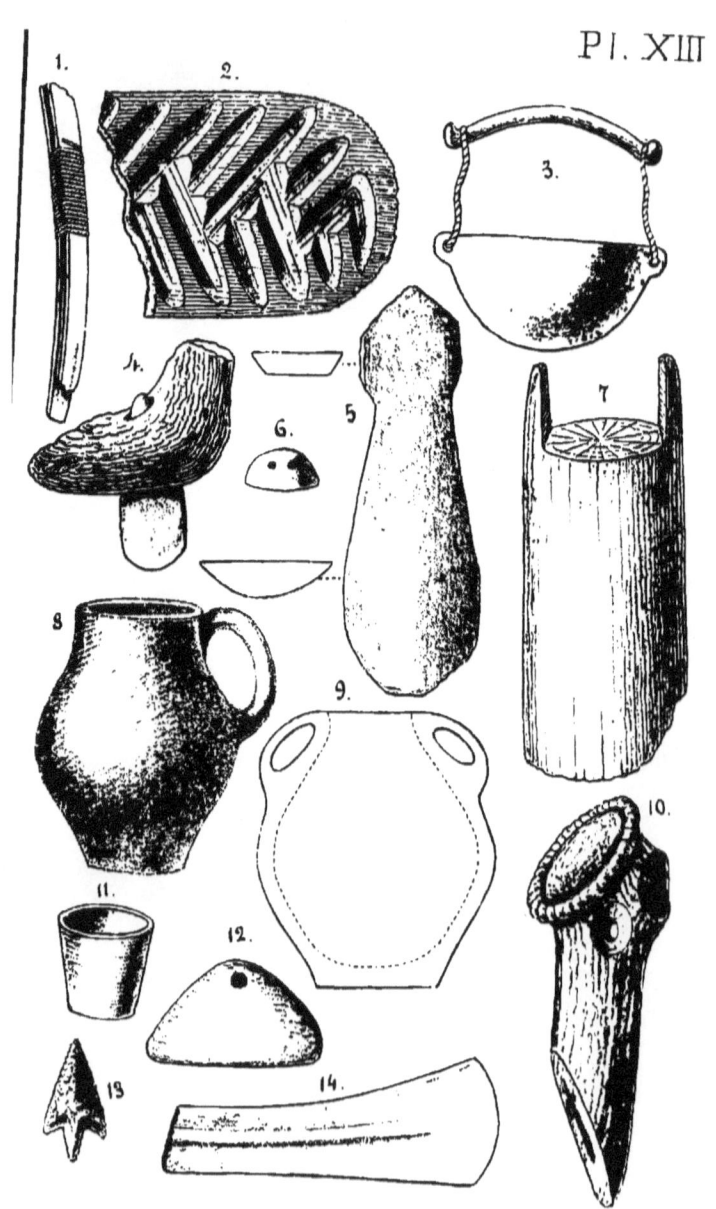

Pl. XIII

ROBENHAUSEN

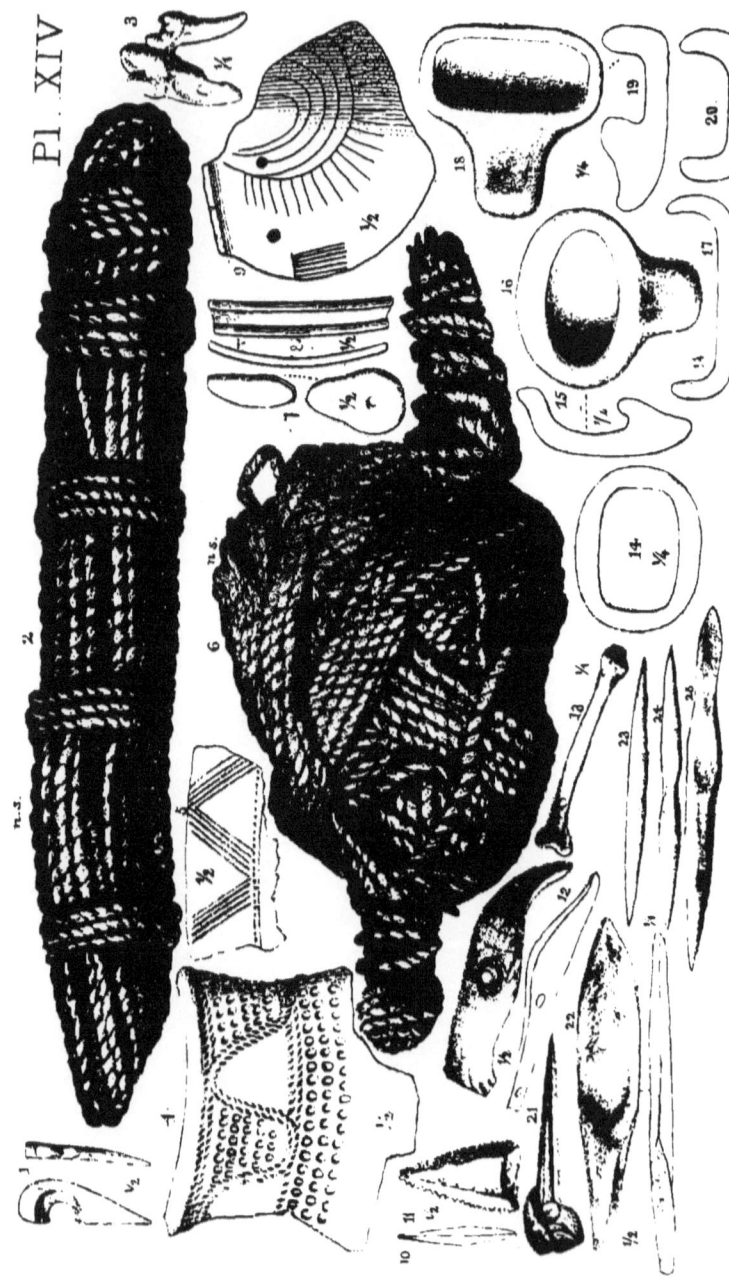

Pl. XIV

ROBENHAUSEN WANGEN & MOOSSEEDORF.

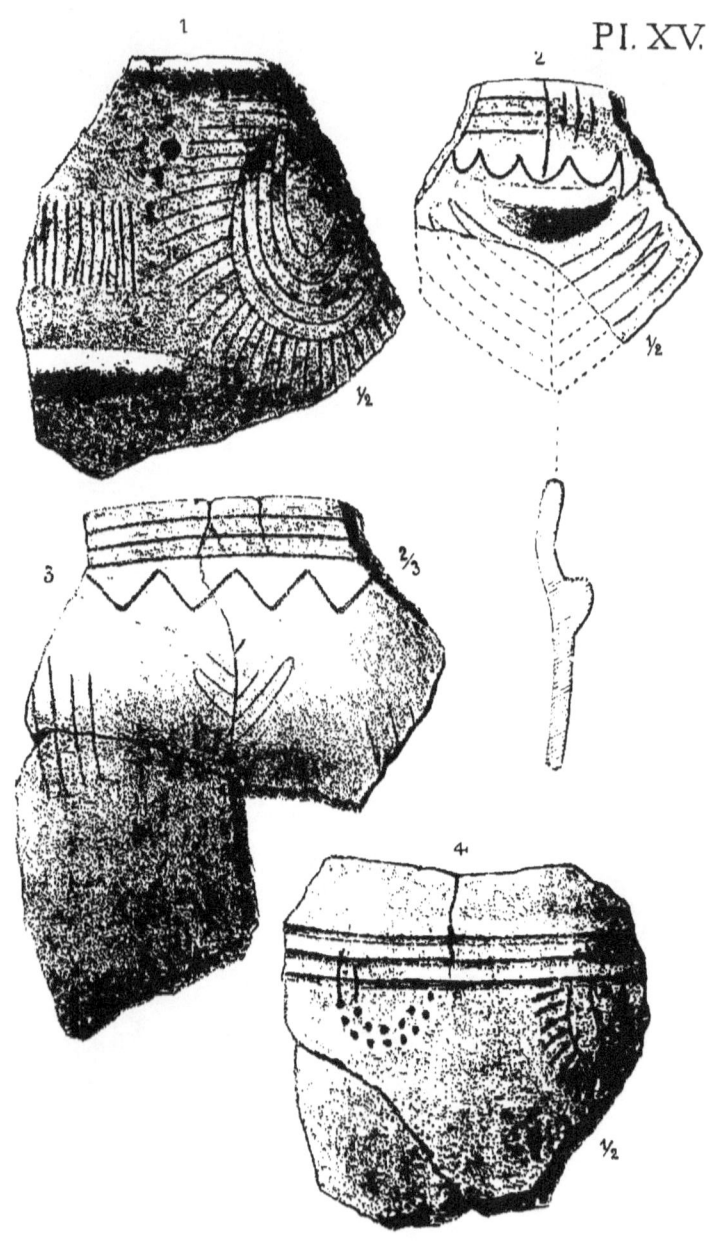

WANGEN

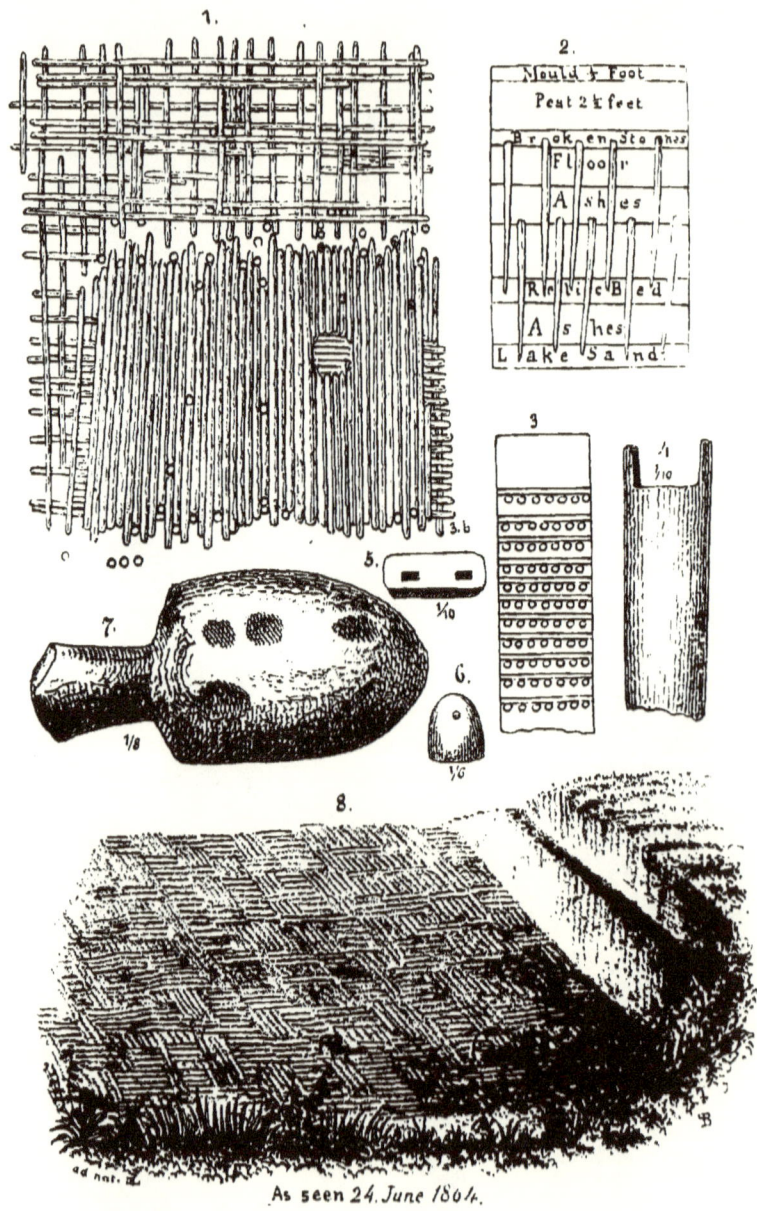

As seen 24. June 1864.

NIEDERWYL &c.

Pl. XVII.

Niederwyl.

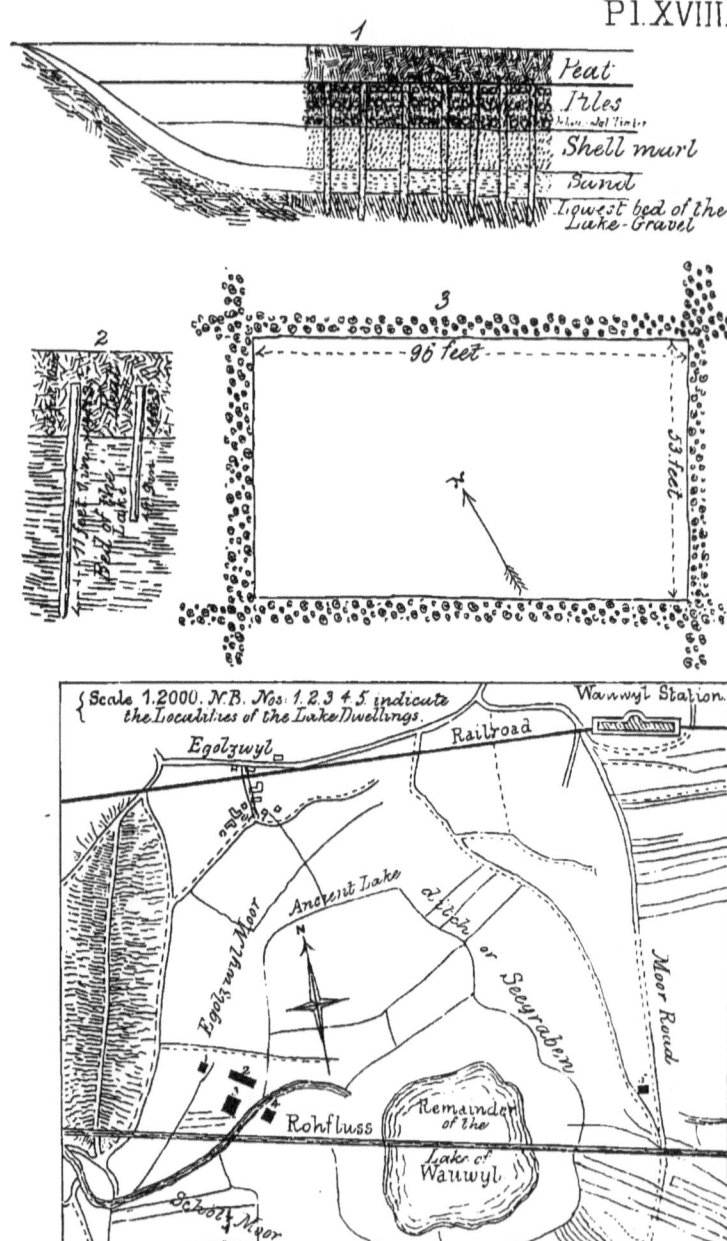

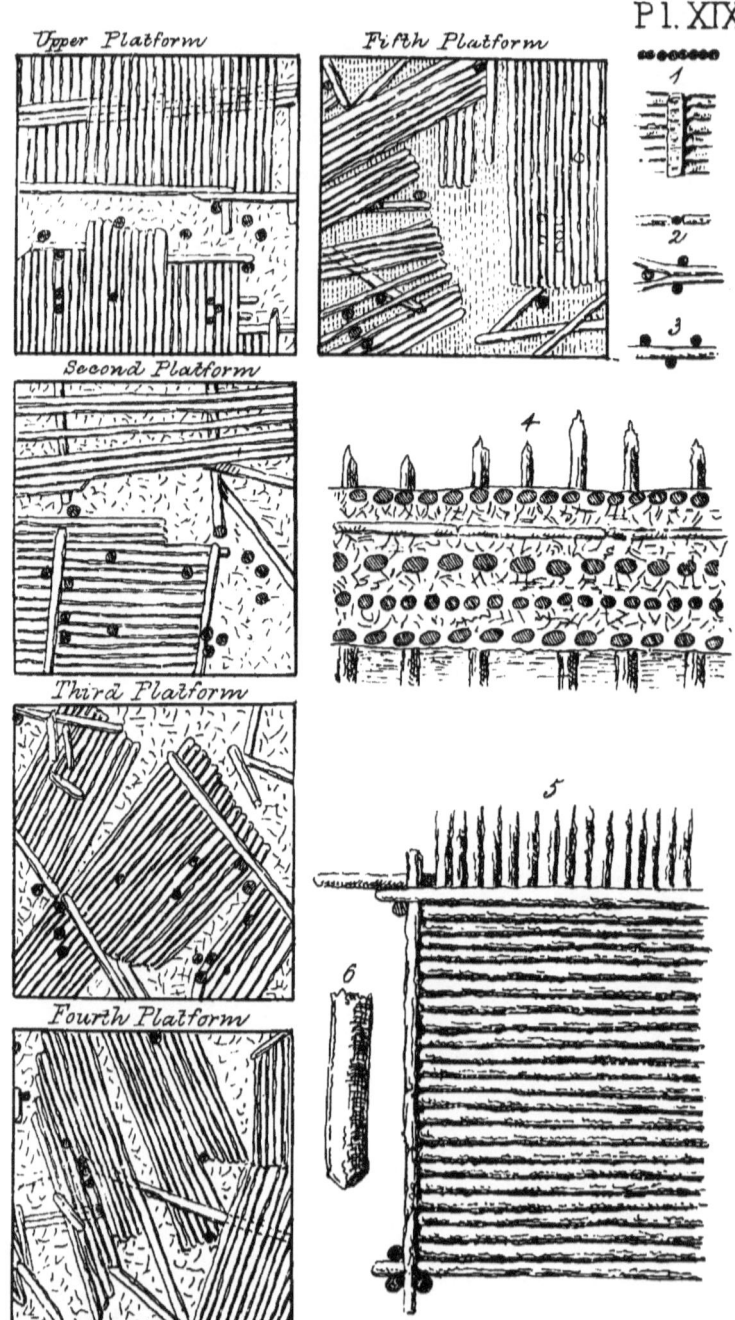

WAUWYL.

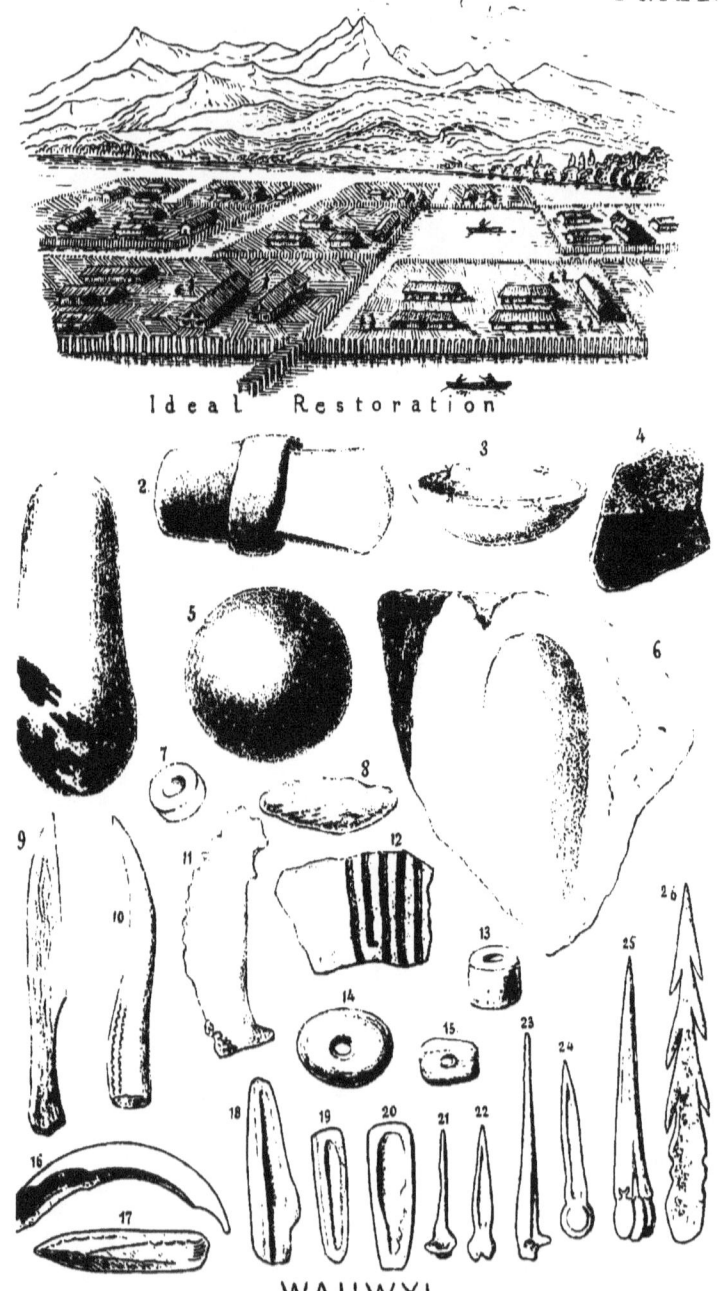

Ideal Restoration

WAUWYL.
Fig. 7. Nat. Size Remainder. ⅓

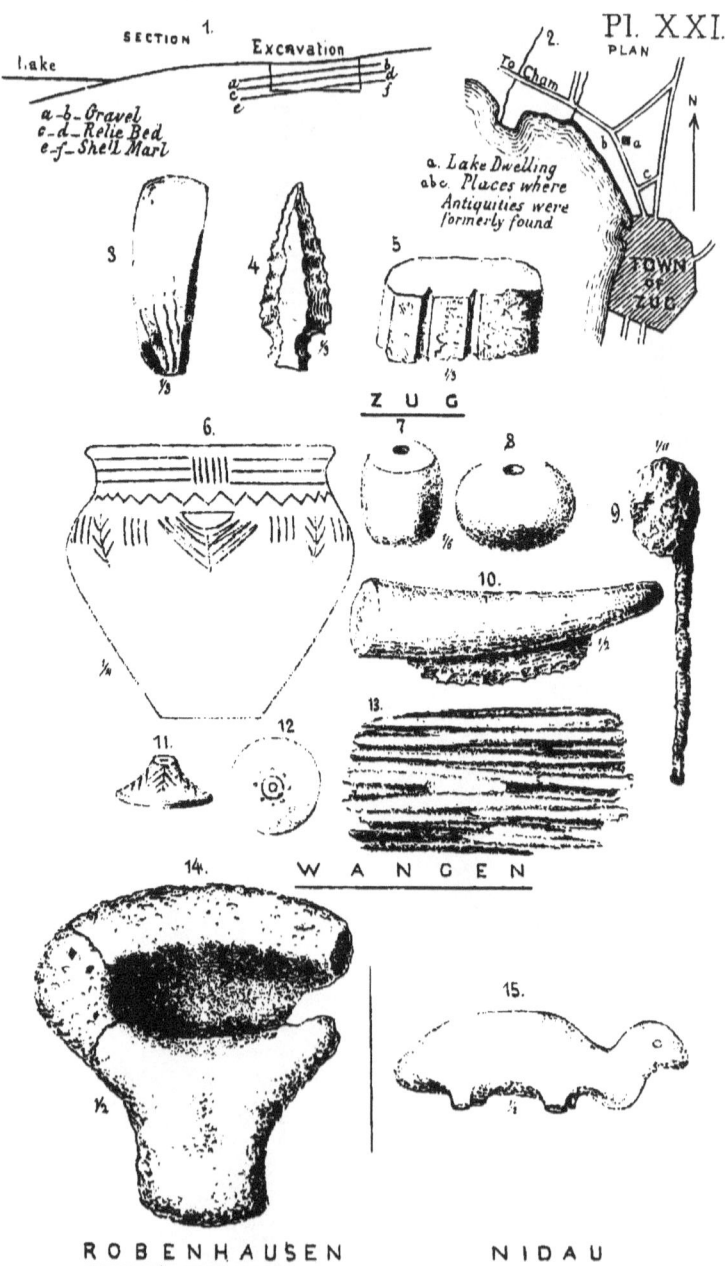

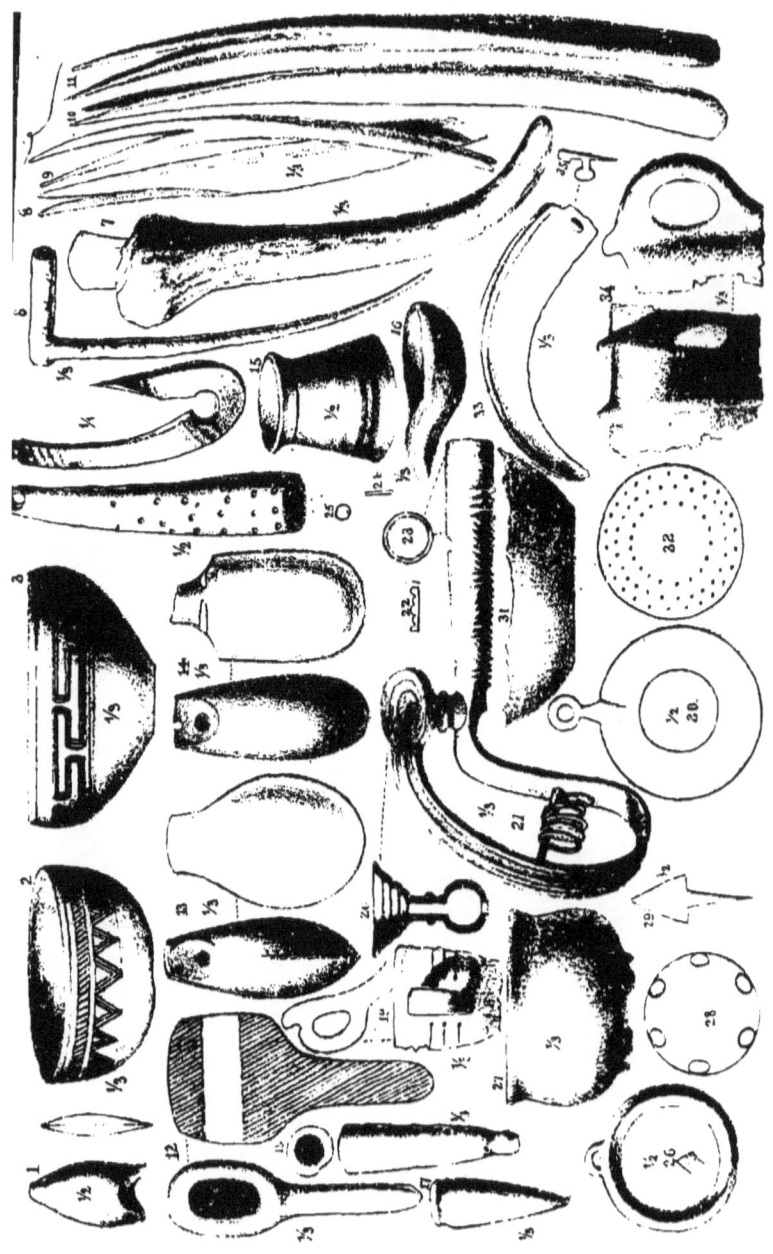

ZUG CHEVROUX WAUWYL &c.

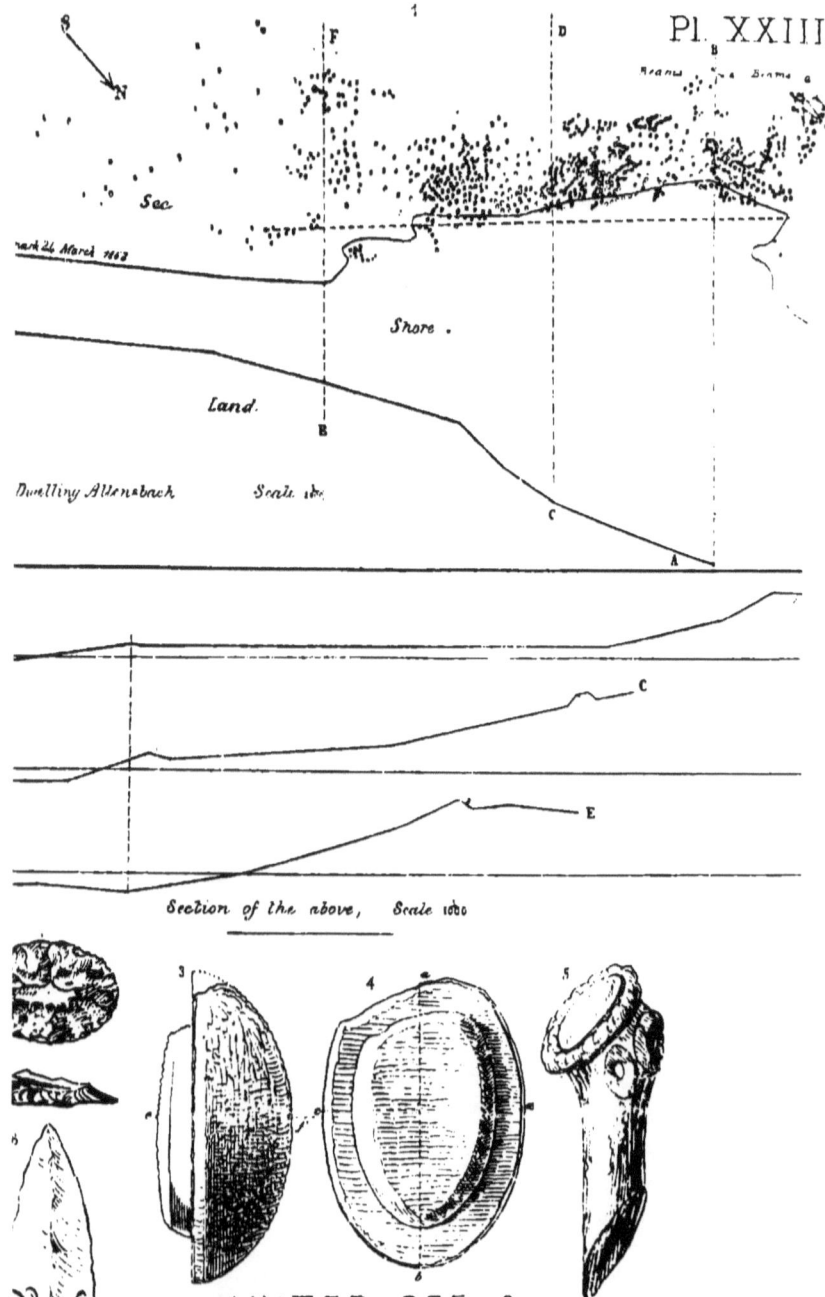

Pl. XXIV.

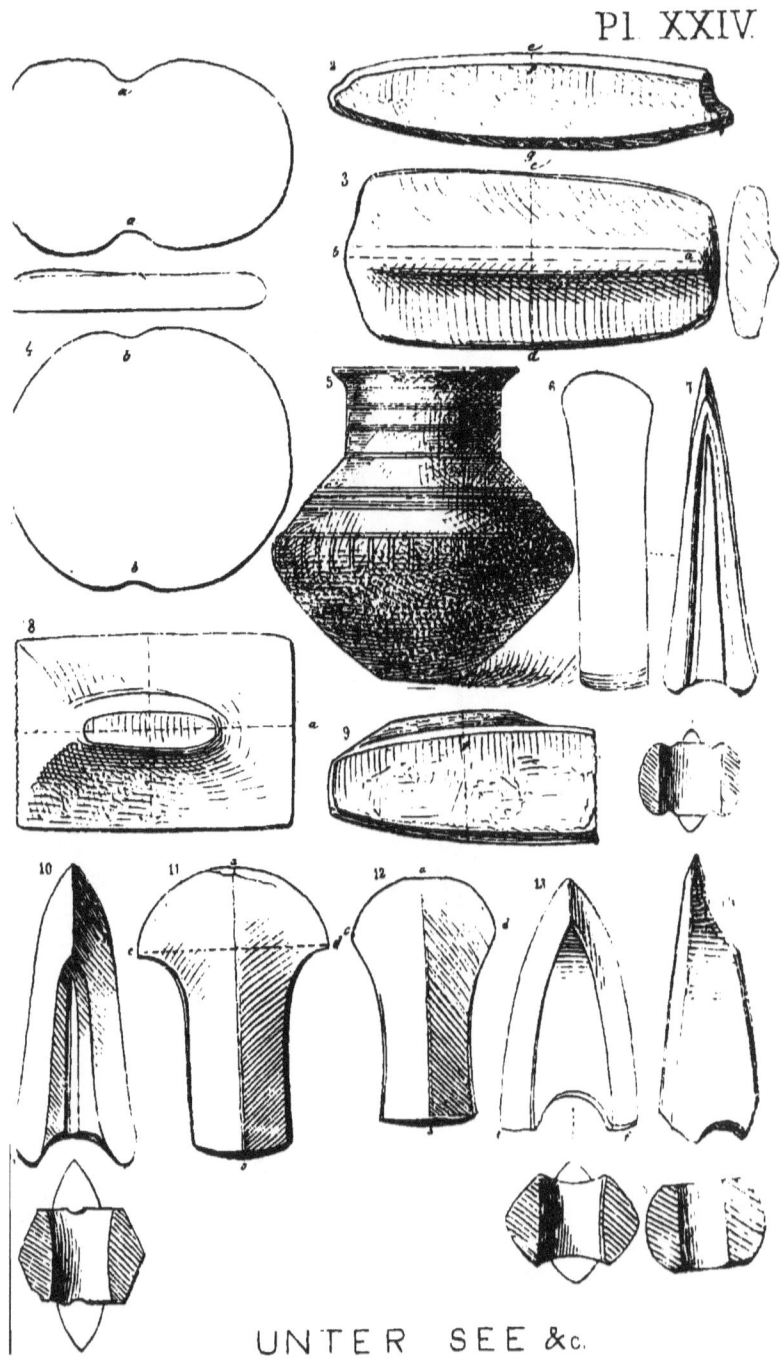

UNTER SEE &c.

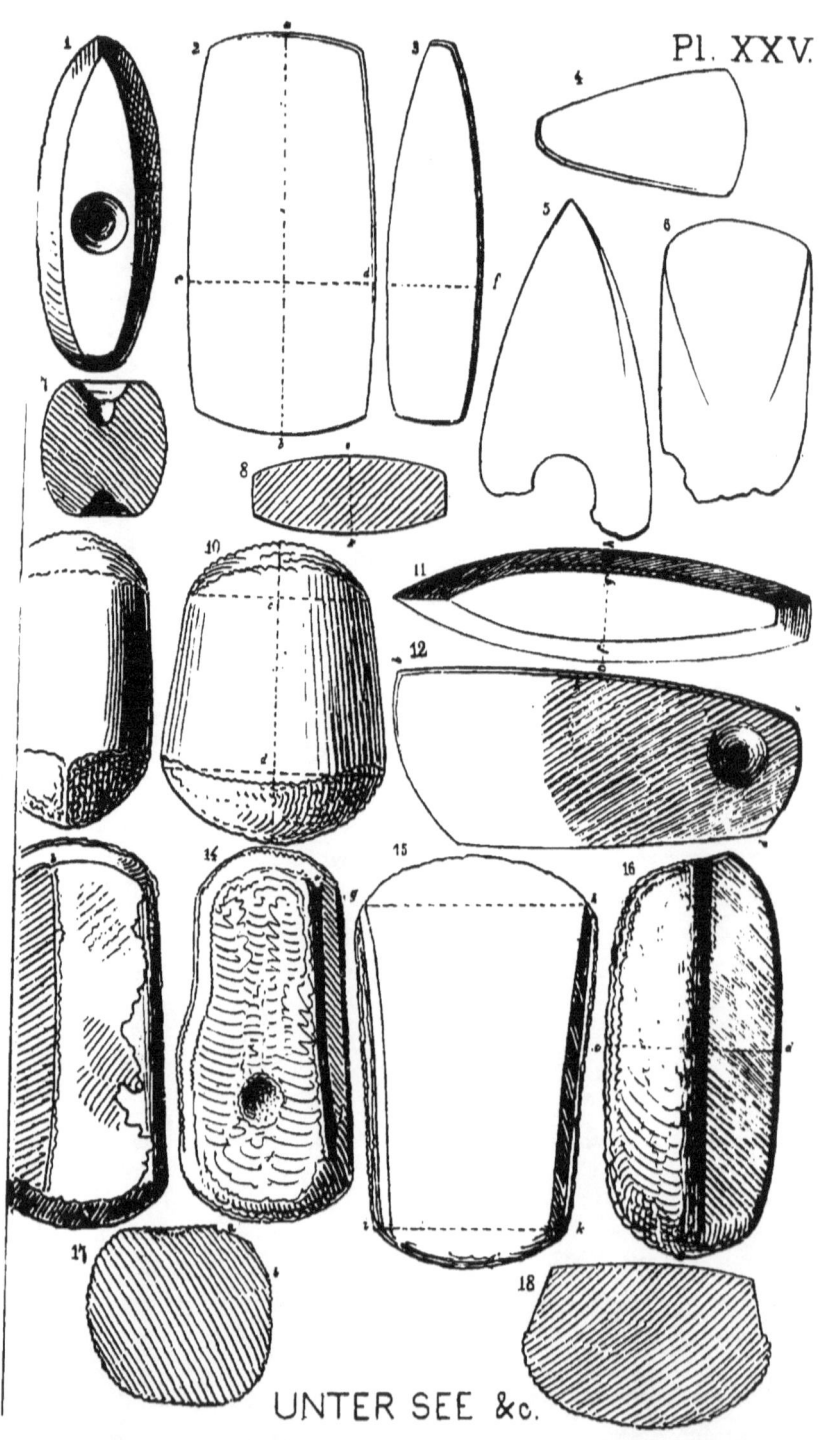

Pl. XXV.

UNTER SEE &c.

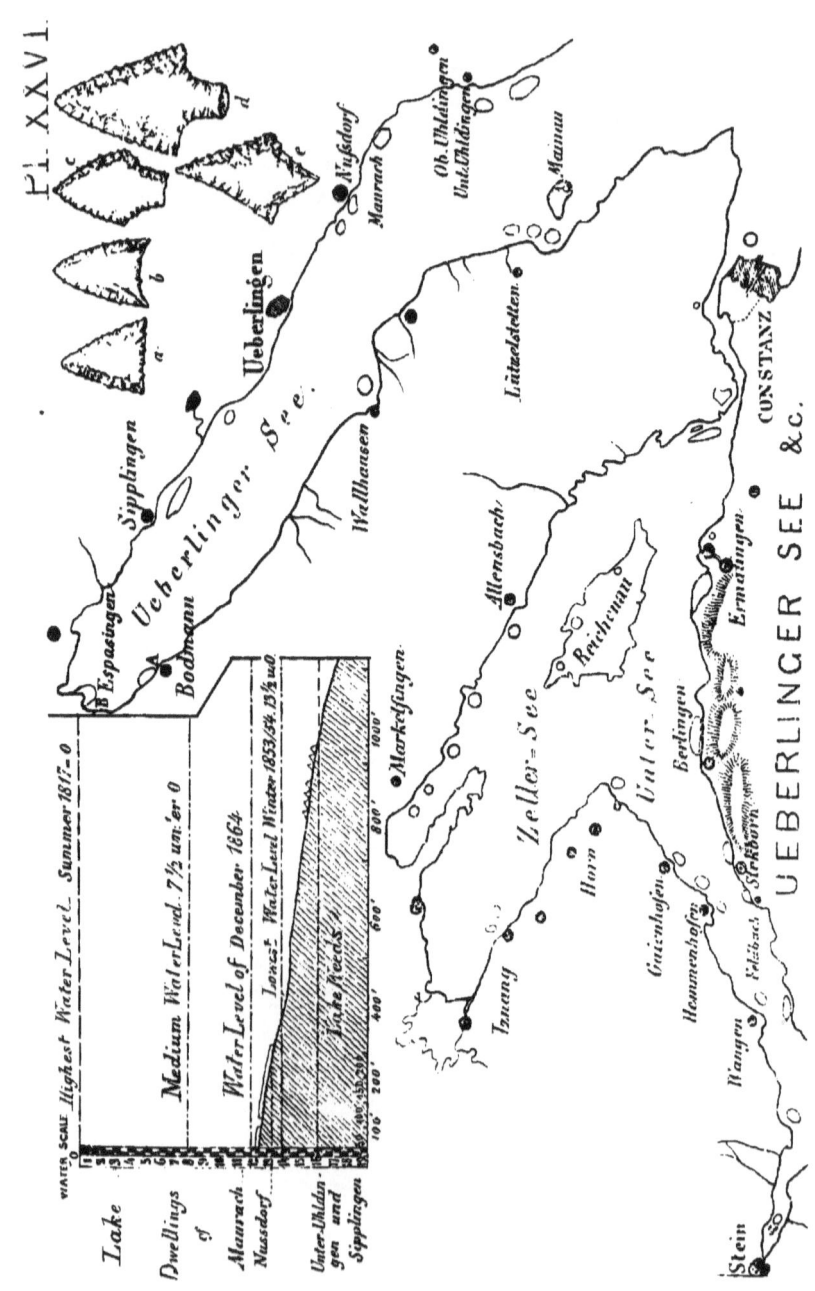

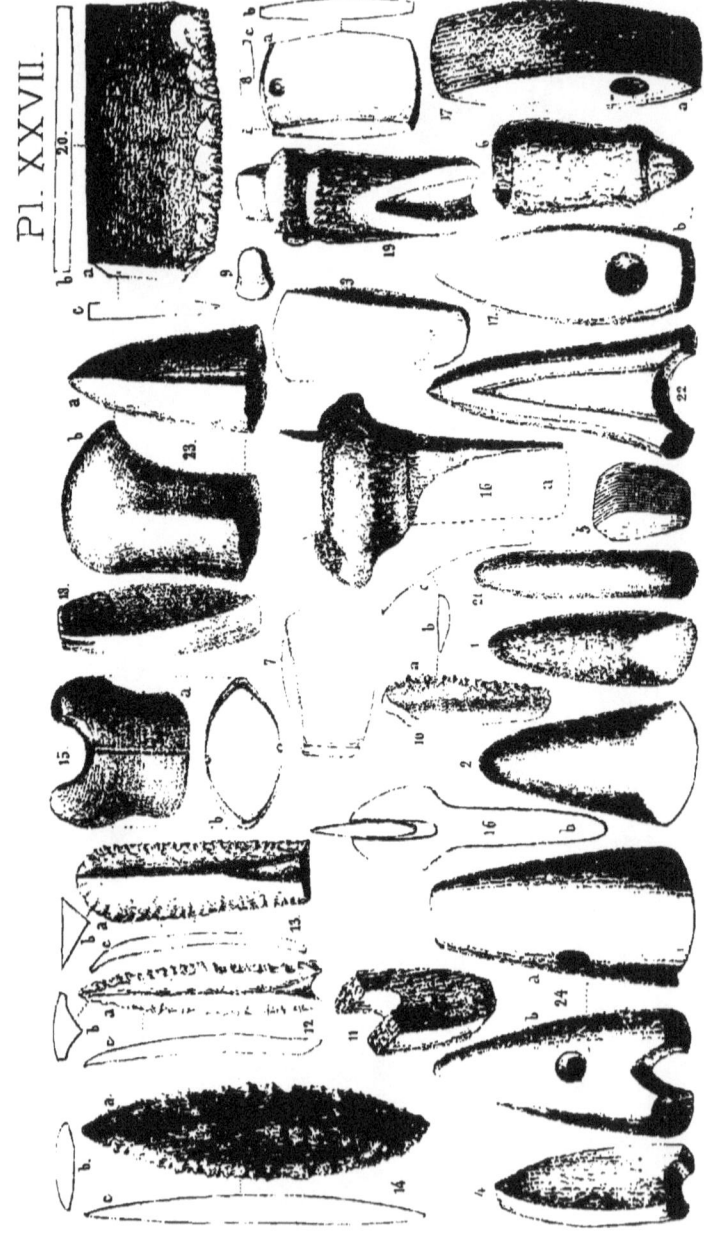

Pl. XXVII.

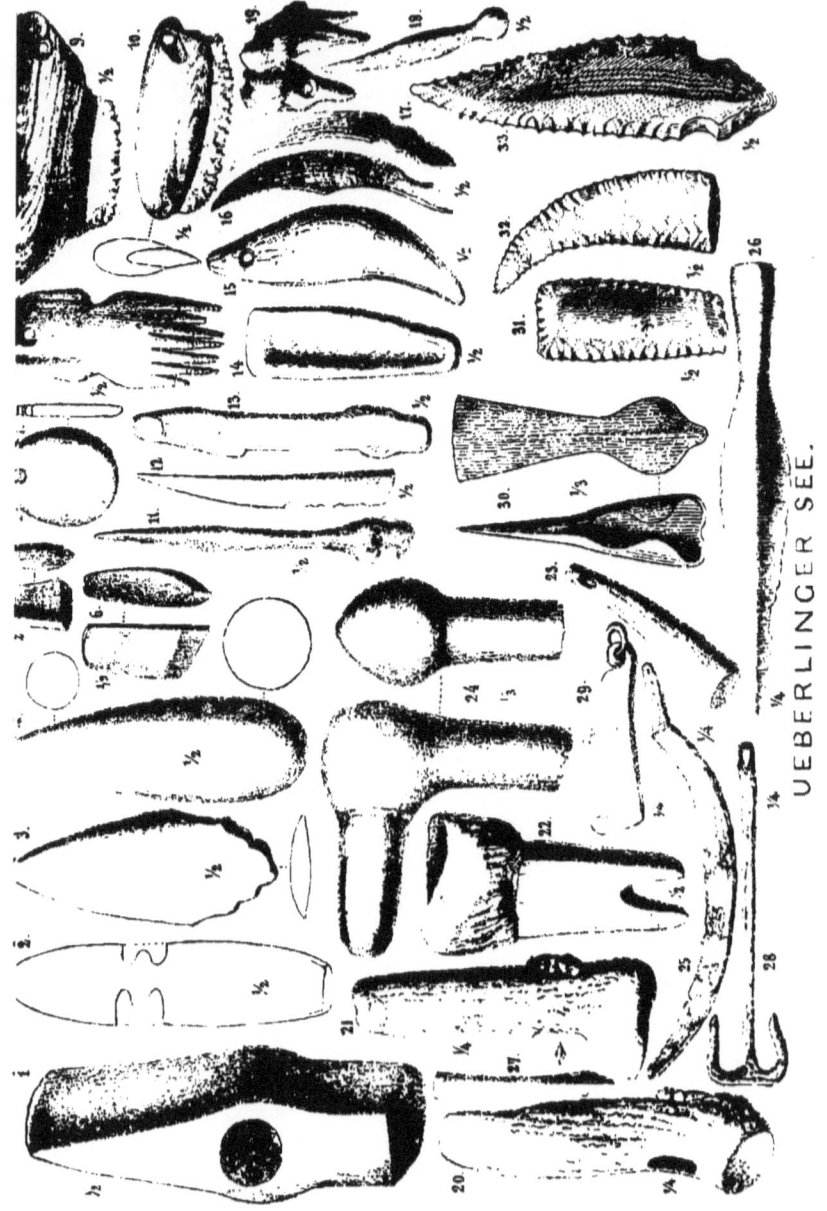

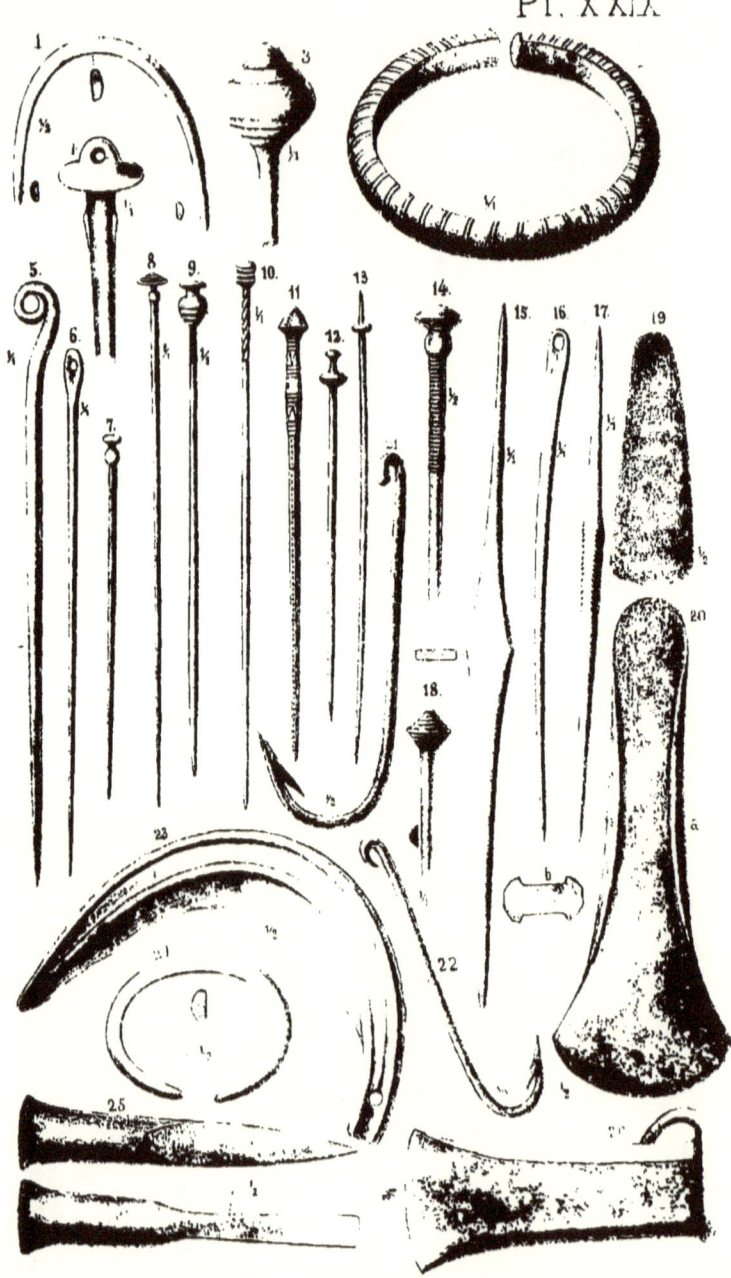

Pl. XXIX

UEBERLINGER SEE.

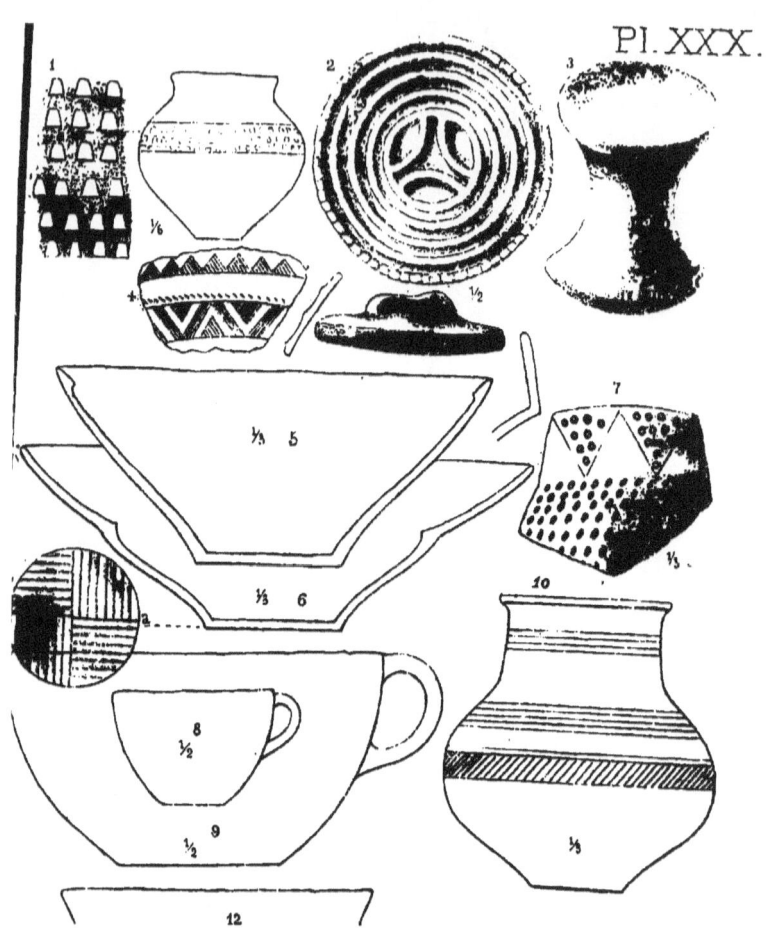

Pl. XXXI.

UEBERLINGER SEE.

Pl. XXXII.

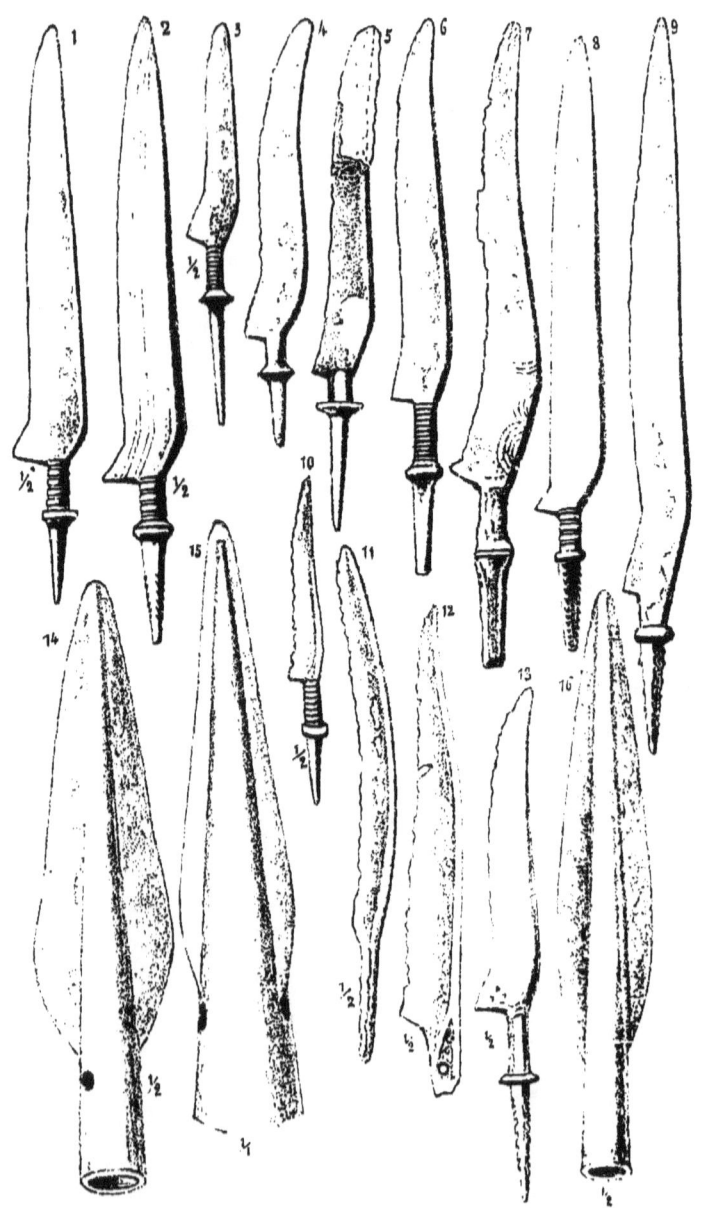

UEBERLINGER SEE

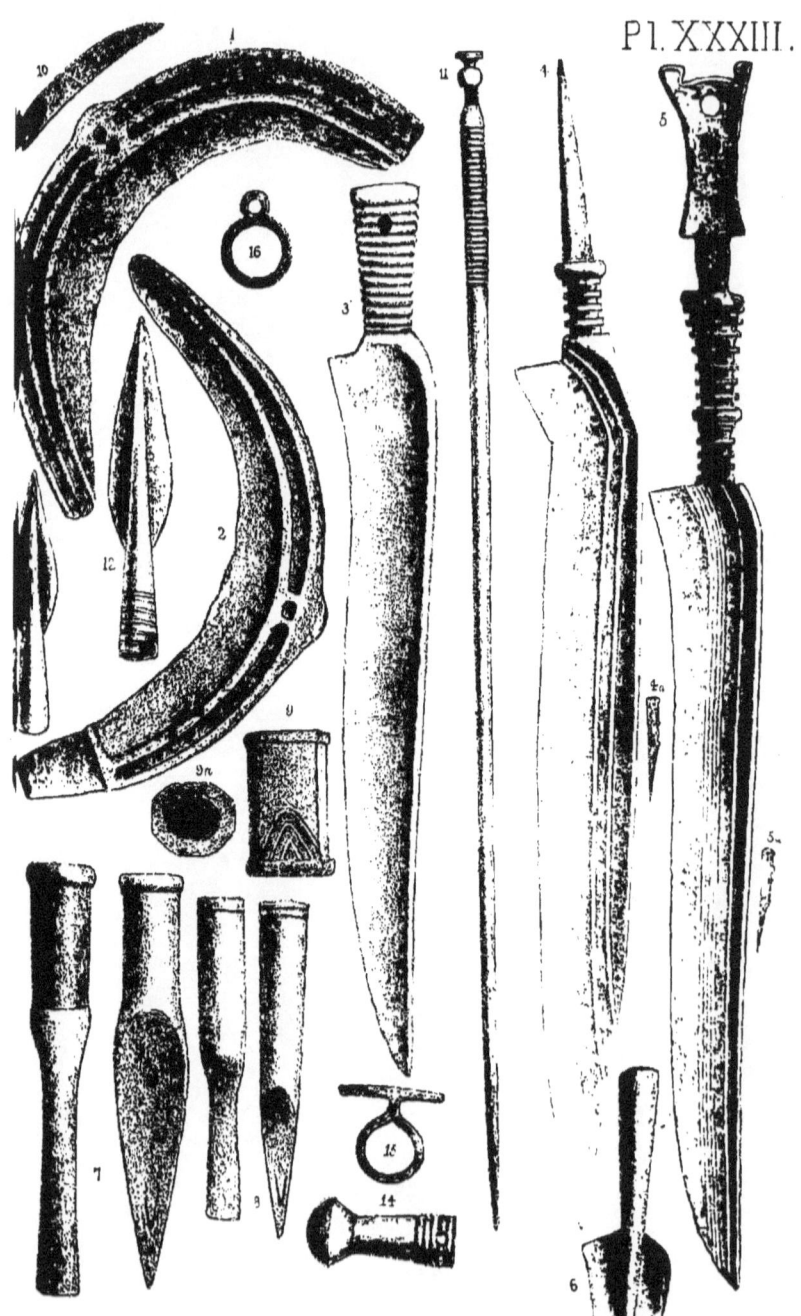

Pl. XXXIII.

NIDAU STEINBERG. *Bronze.*

Pl. XXXIV.

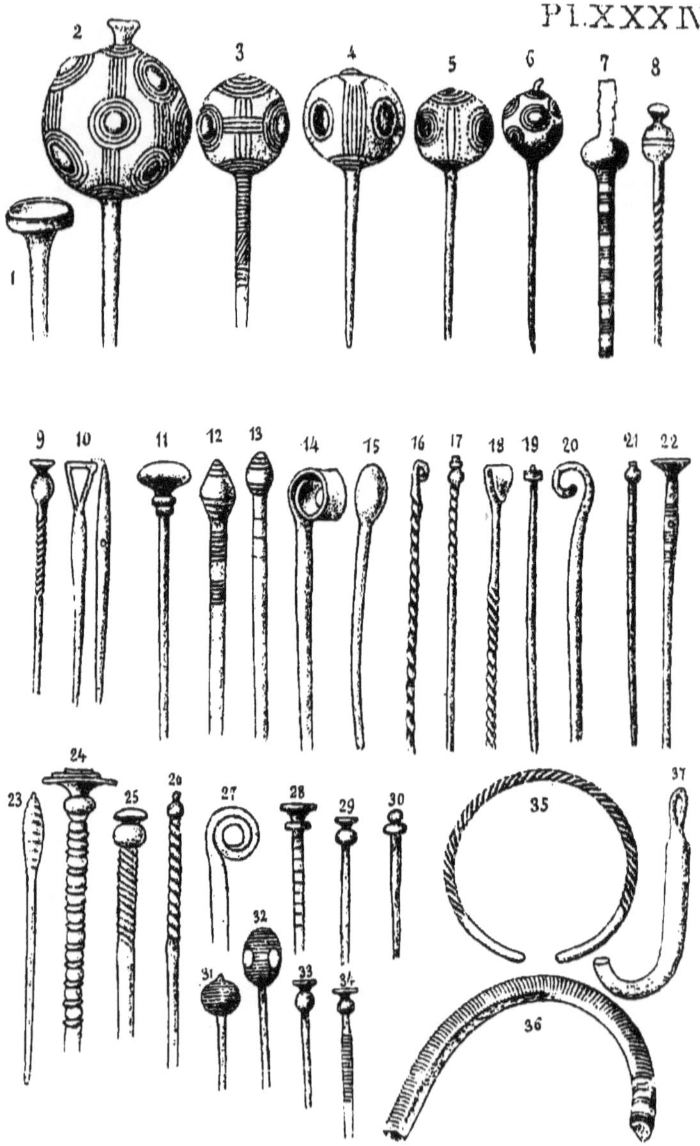

NIDAU — STEINBERG. Bronze.

Fig. 1-4. to 23. 28. to 30. 33 to 37. ½ size — 23. ⅓ size. 24 to 27. 31. 32. full size.

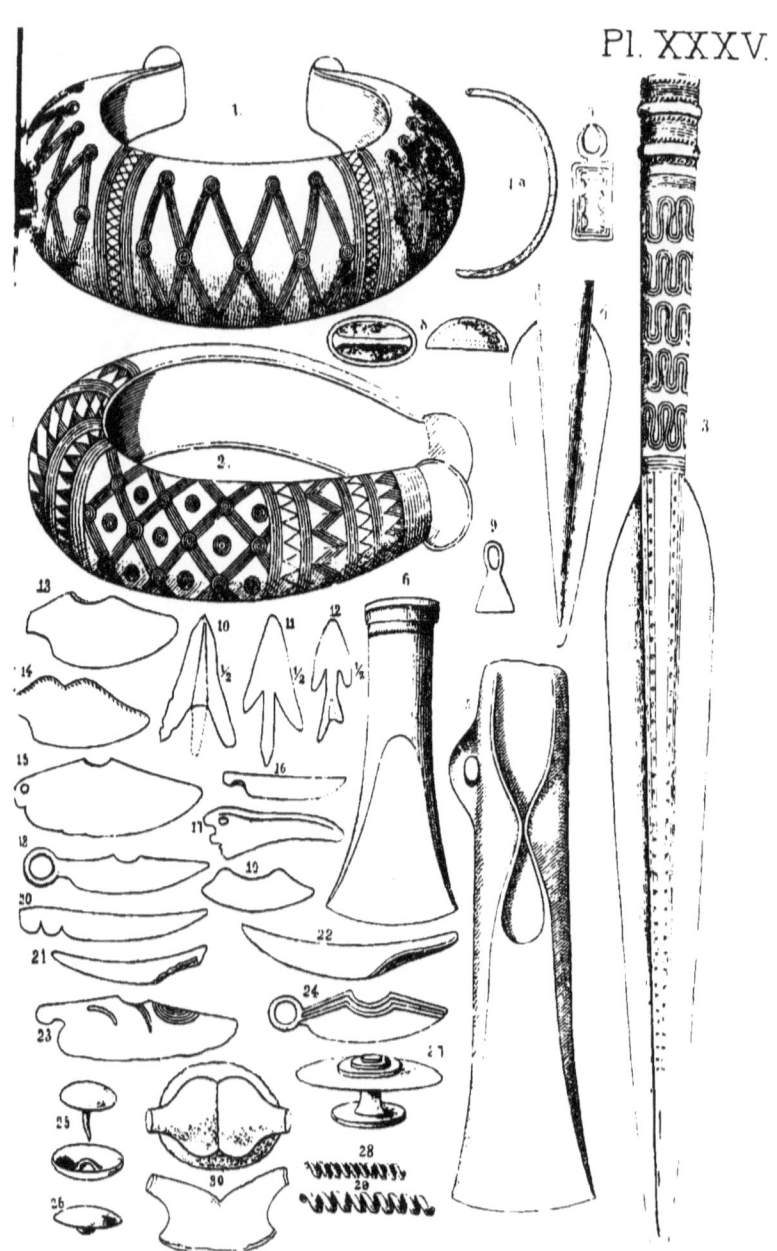

NIDAU- STEINBERG *Bronze.*
10 to 12. 25 to 27. 30 ½ size. 13 to 24 ⅓ size, Rem. full size.

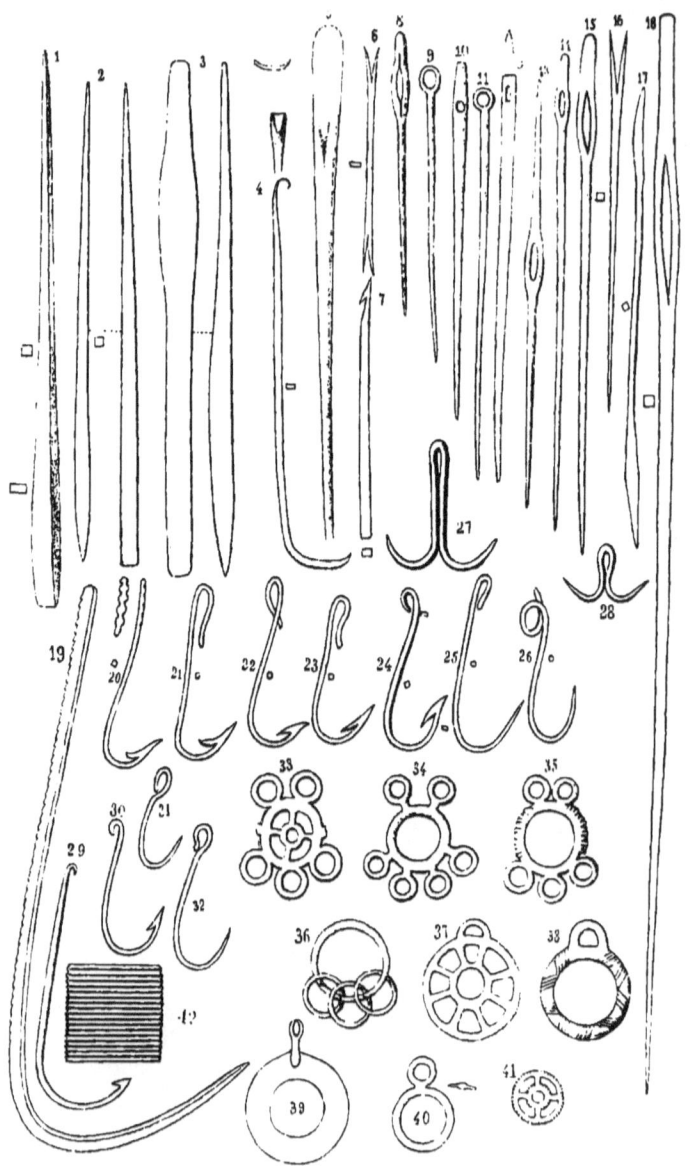

NIDAU-STEINBERG. Bronze & Gold
Figs. 1 to 18. 42 Full size 19. 33 to 41 ½. 20 to 32 ½ size.

Pl XXXVII.

NIDAU STEINBERG

Pl XXXVIII

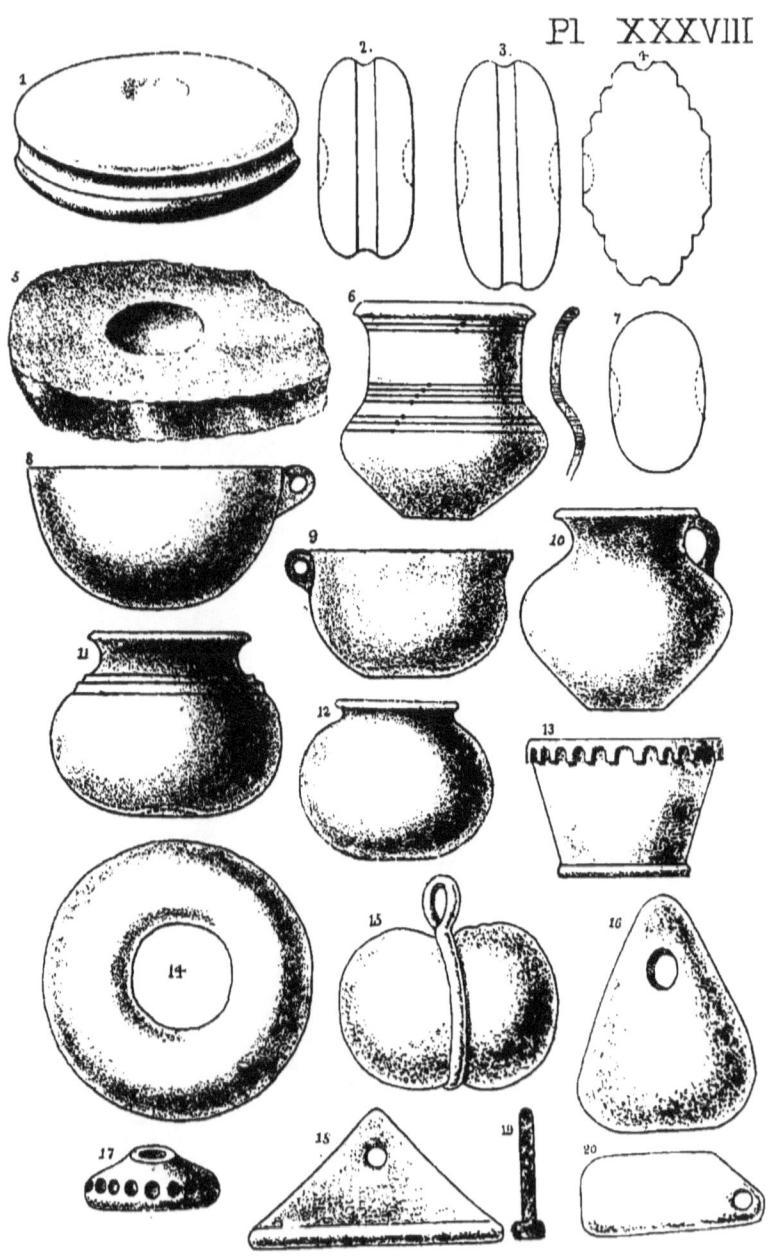

NIDAU STEINBERG &c.

PlXXXIX

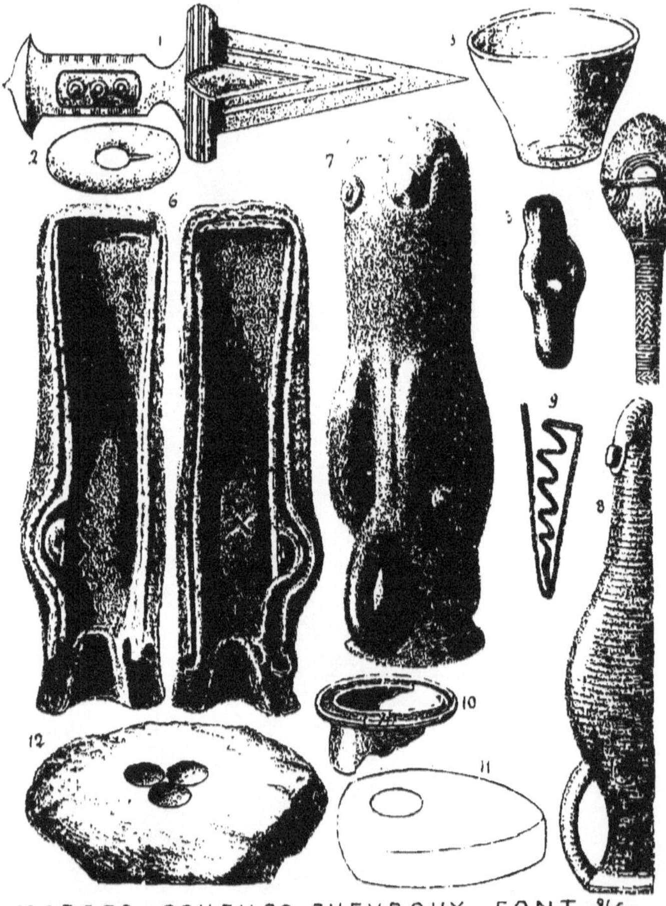

MORGES, SCHEUSS, CHEVROUX, FONT, &C

MAIN LAND   FOR COMPARISON

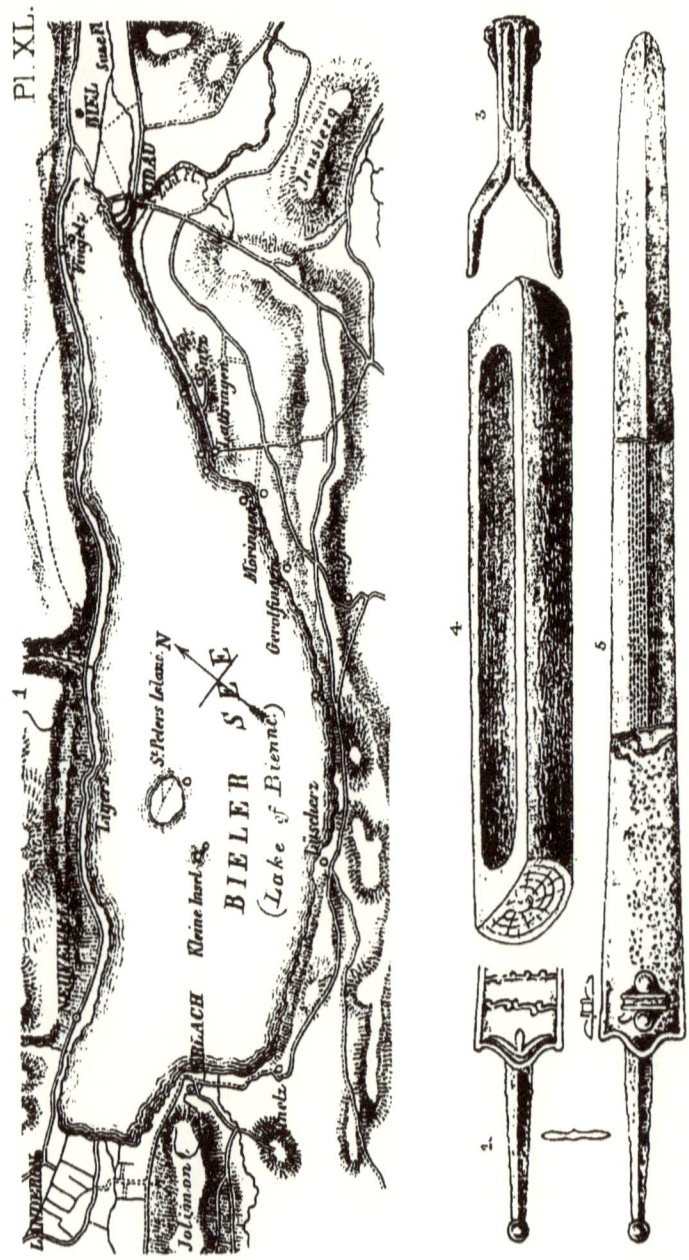

MÖRINGEN &c.

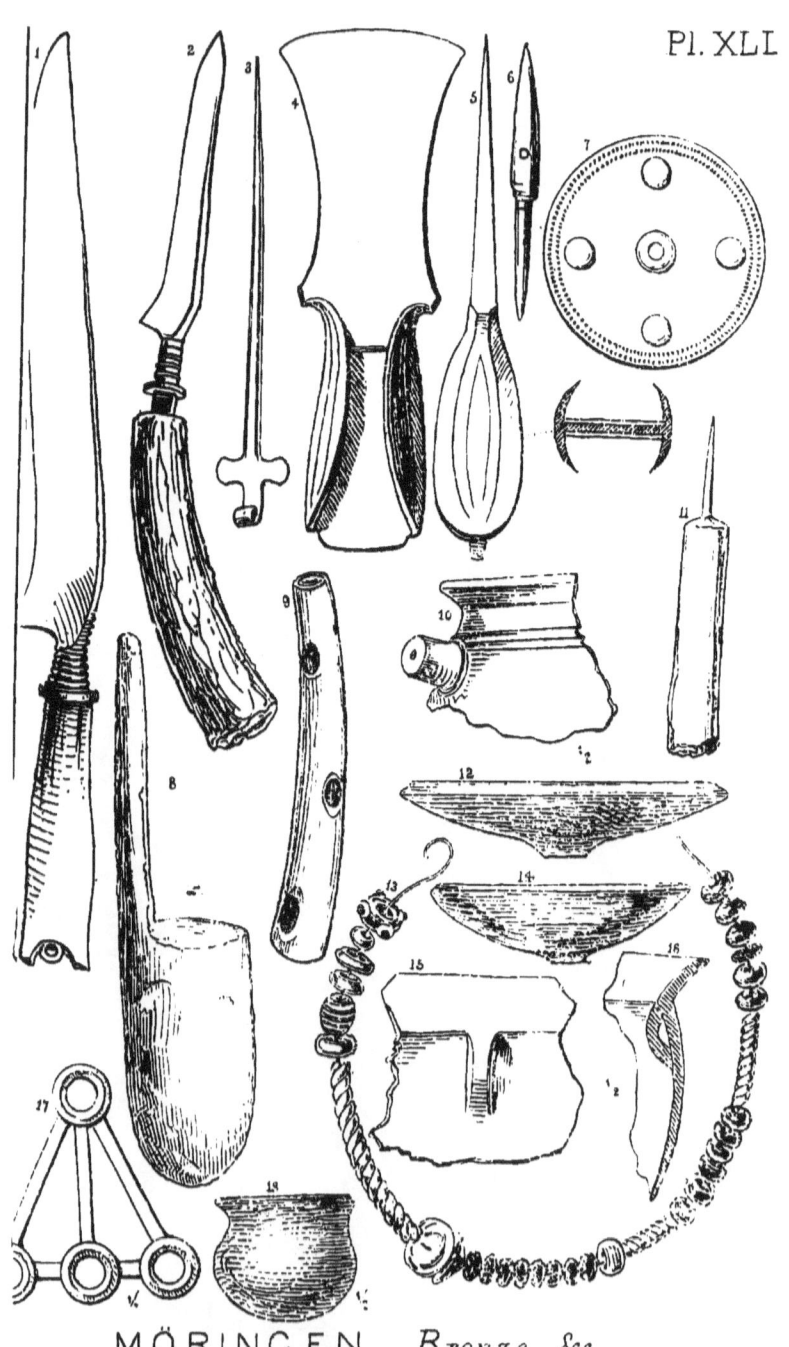

Pl. XLI

MÖRINGEN Bronze &c.

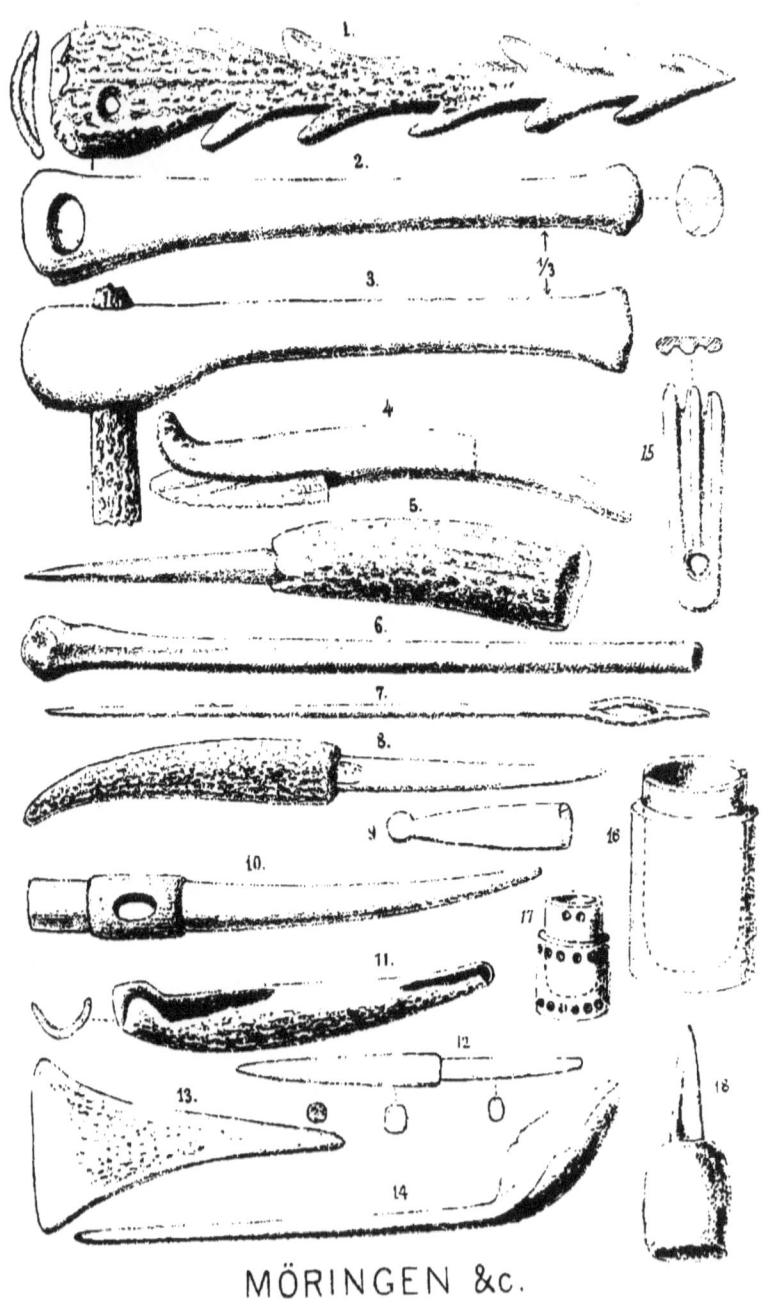

MÖRINGEN &c.

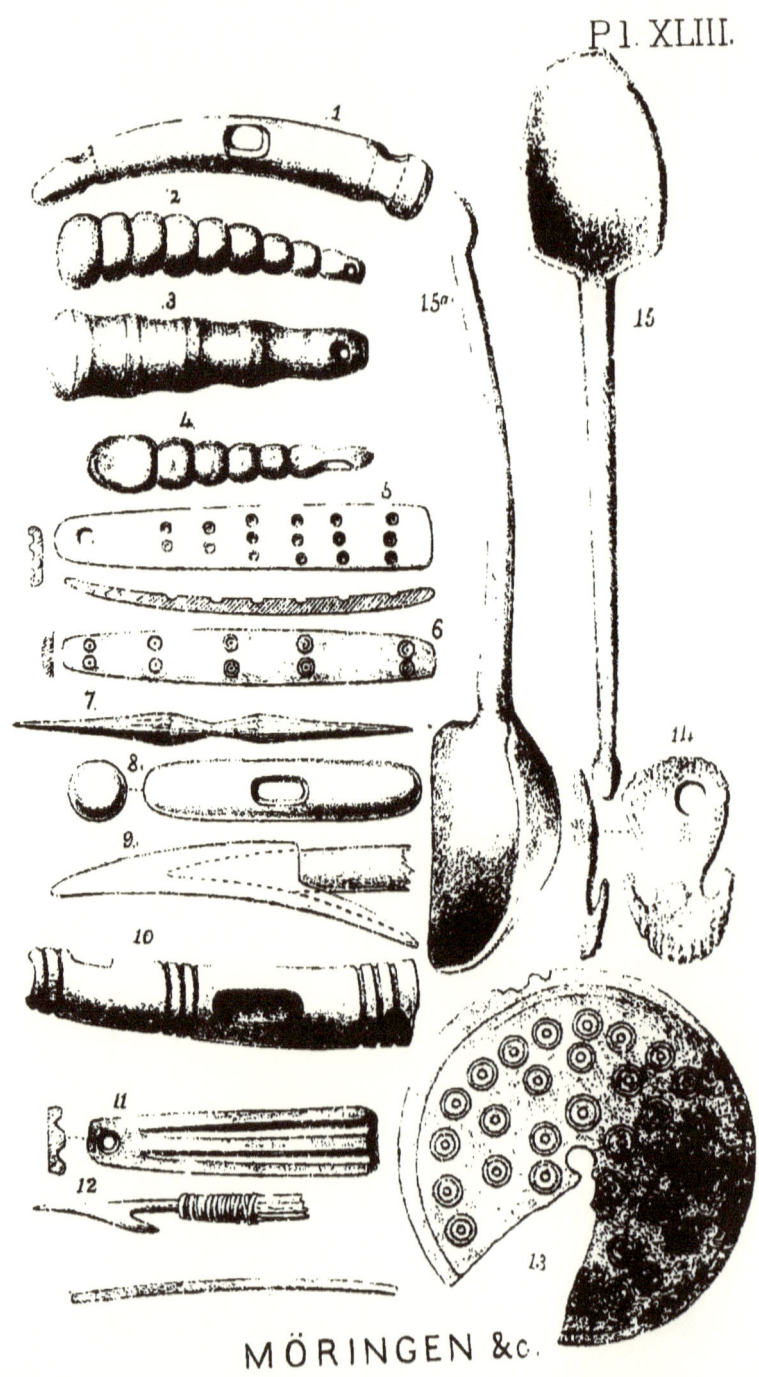

Pl. XLIII.

MÖRINGEN &c.

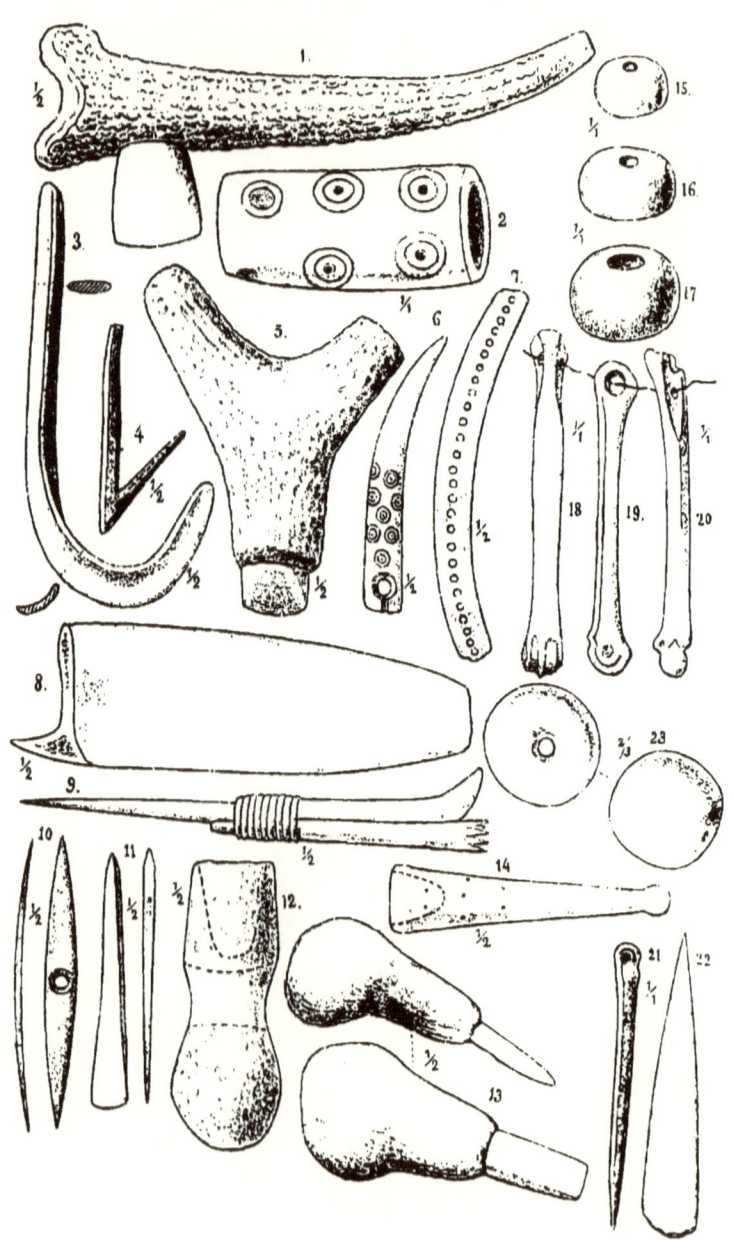

ST AUBIN &c.

Pl. XLV.

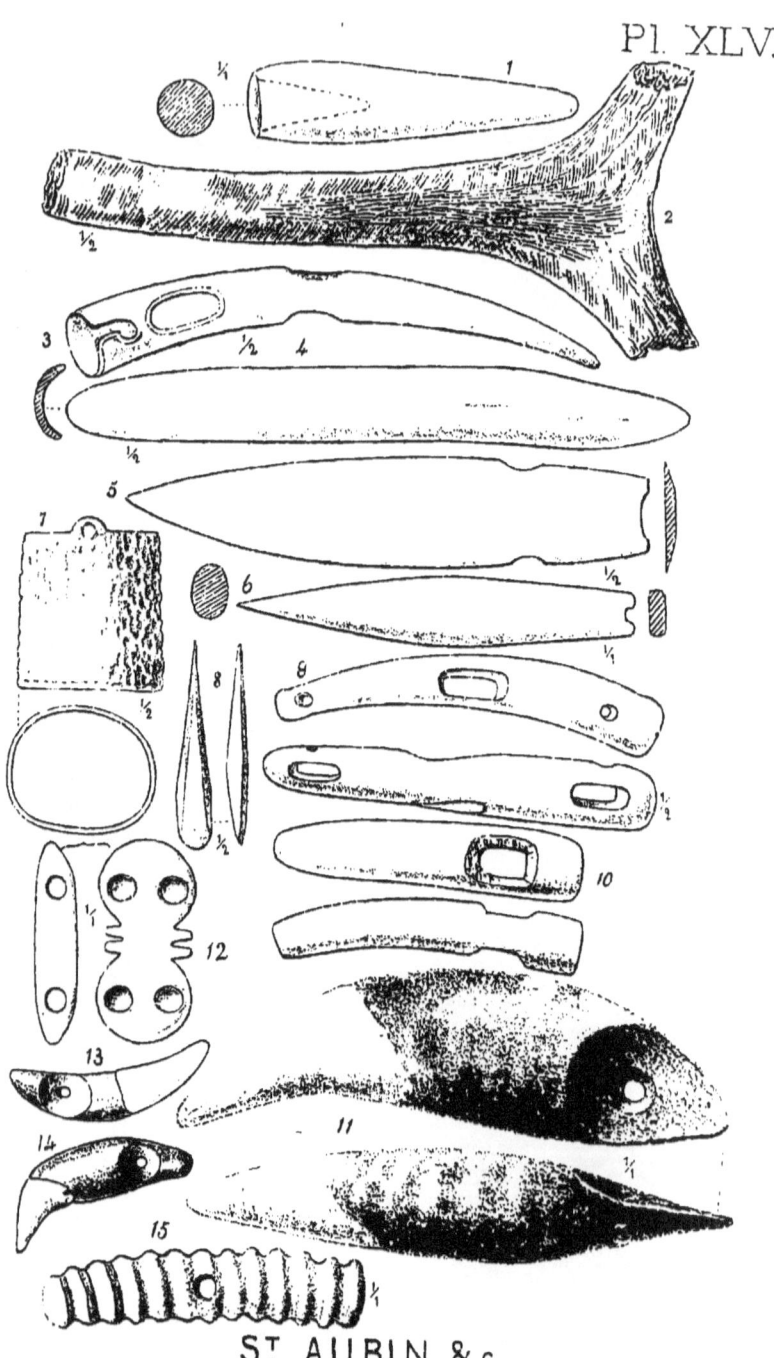

ST AUBIN &c.

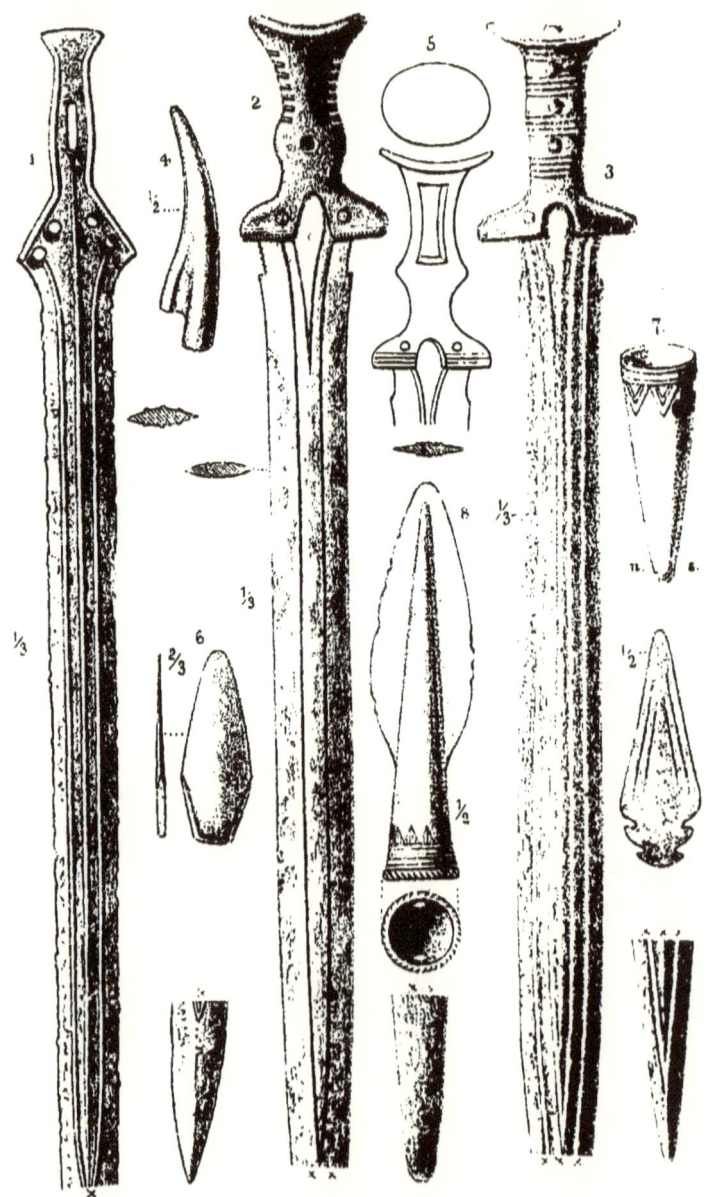

Pl. XLVI.

ESTAVAYER &c.

Pl XLVII

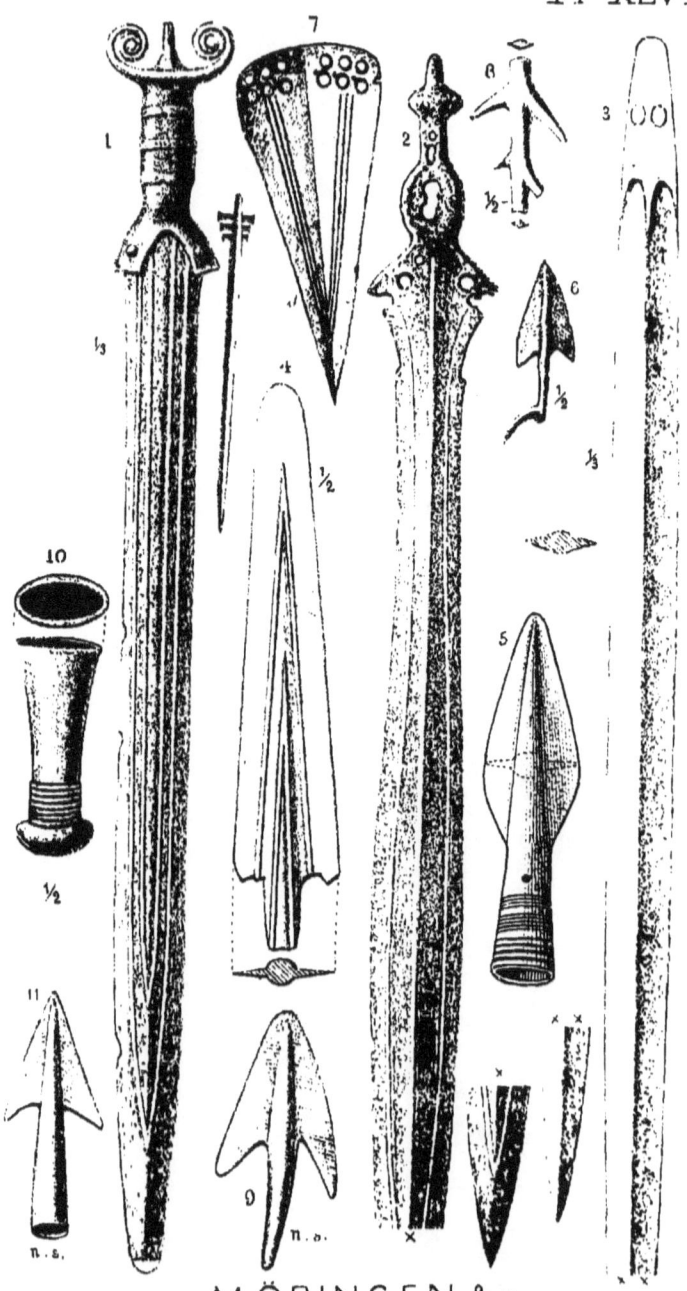

MÖRINGEN &c.

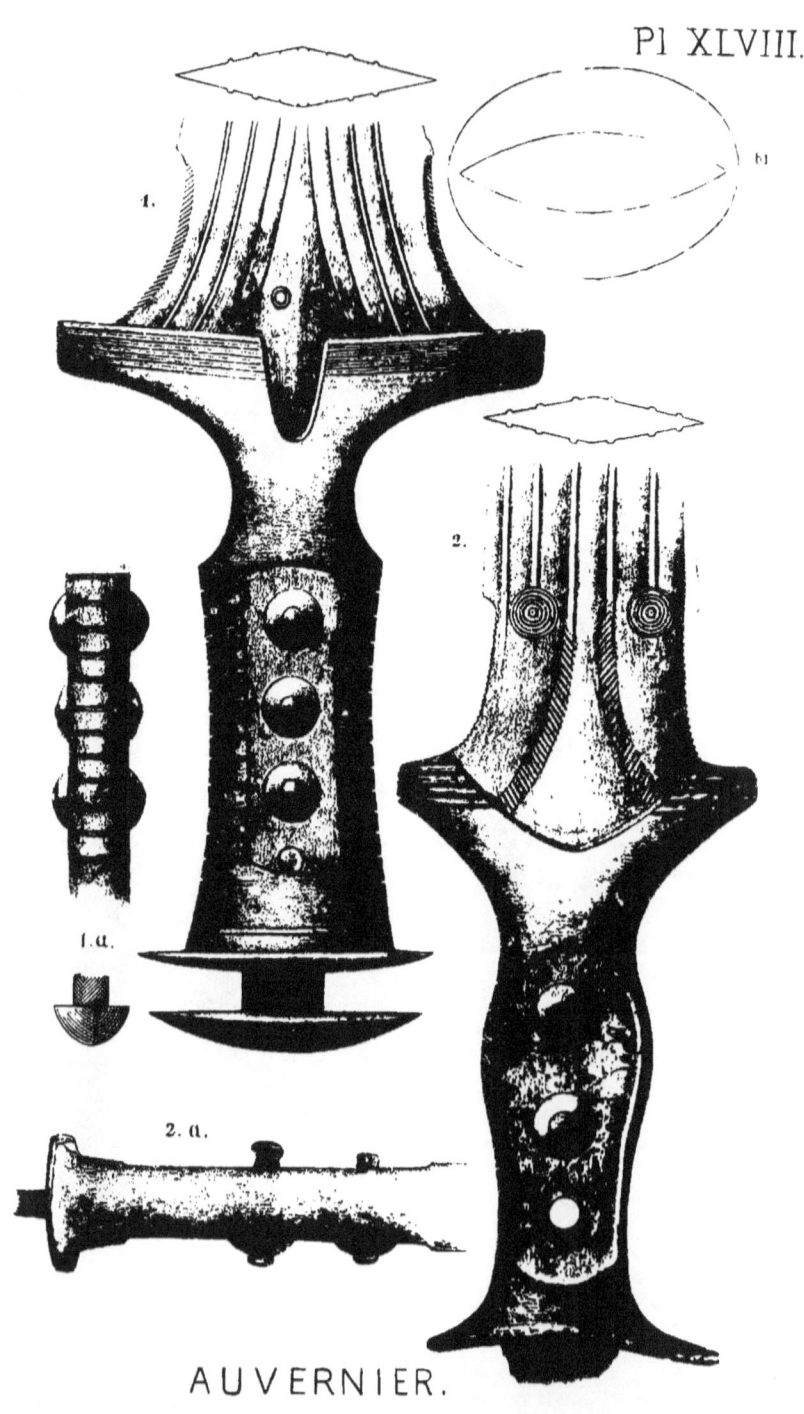

Pl XLVIII.

AUVERNIER.

MÖRINGEN &c.

AUVERNIER &c.

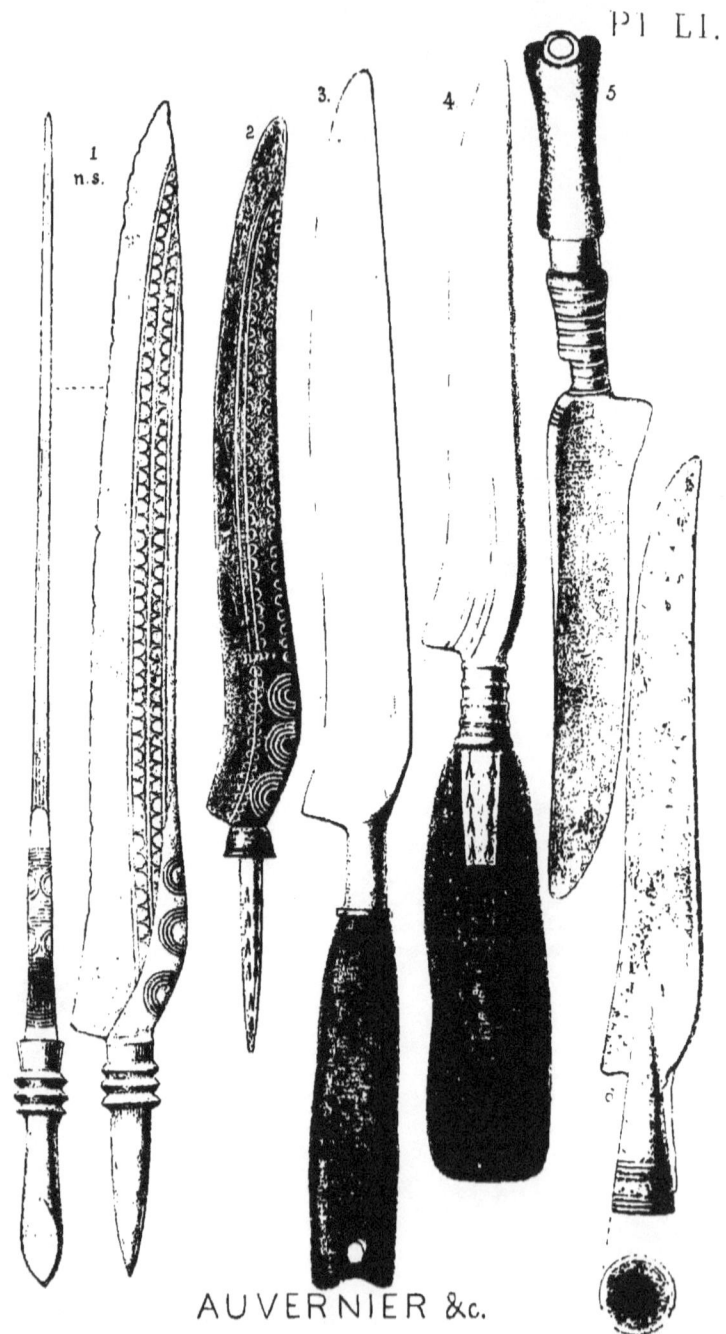

AUVERNIER &c.

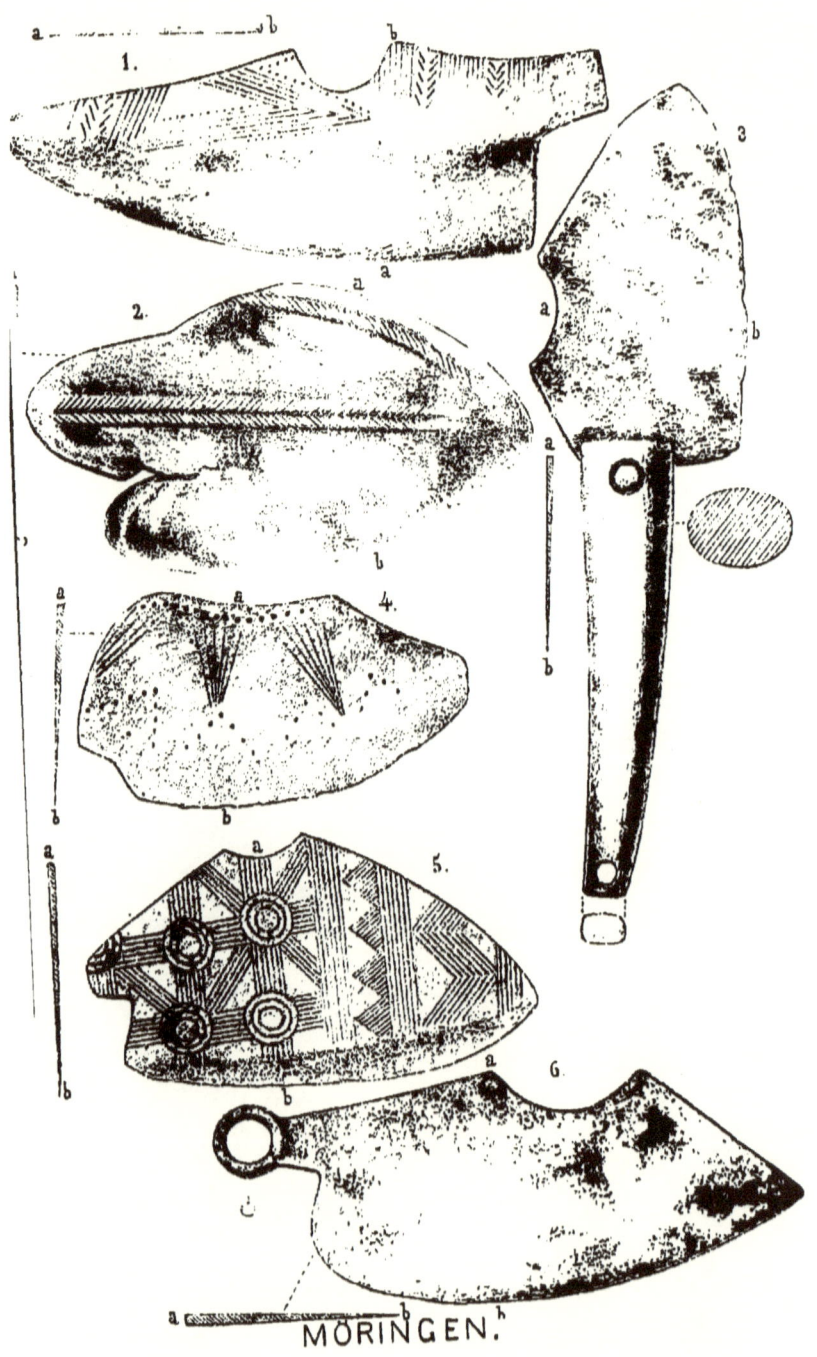

MÖRINGEN.

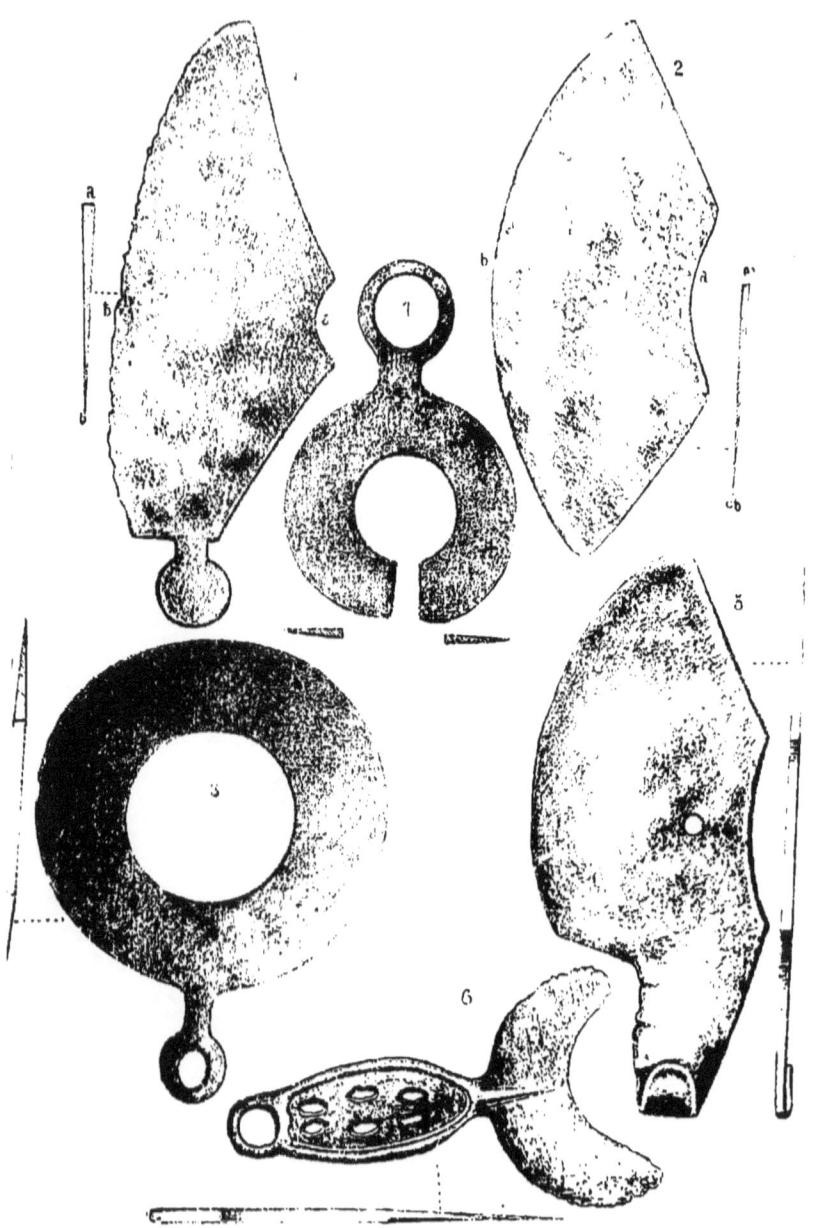

Pl. LIV.

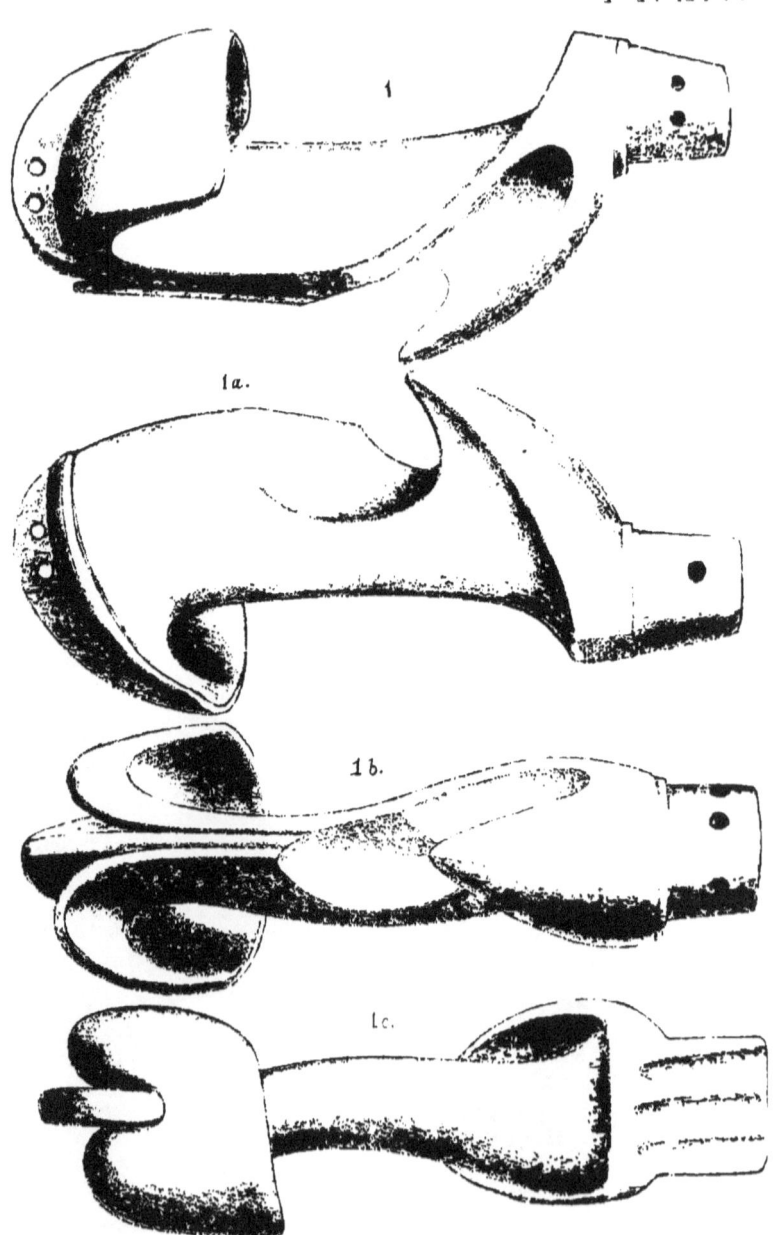

Pl LV.

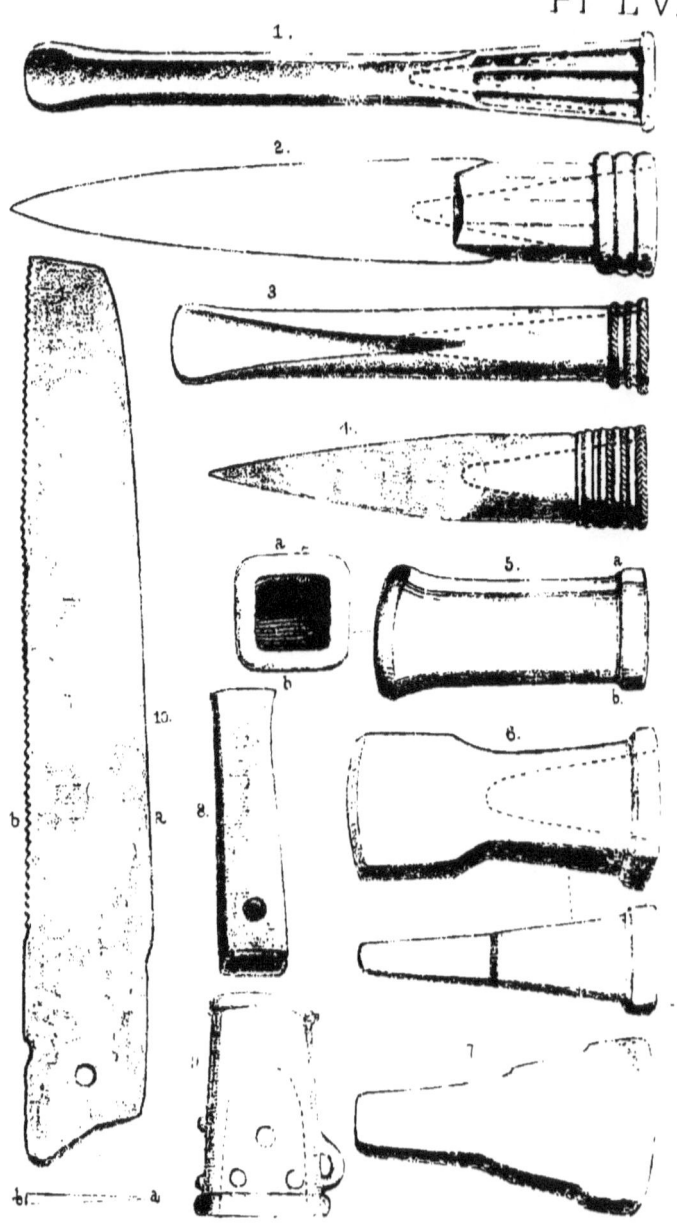

AUVERNIER &c.

Pl. LVI

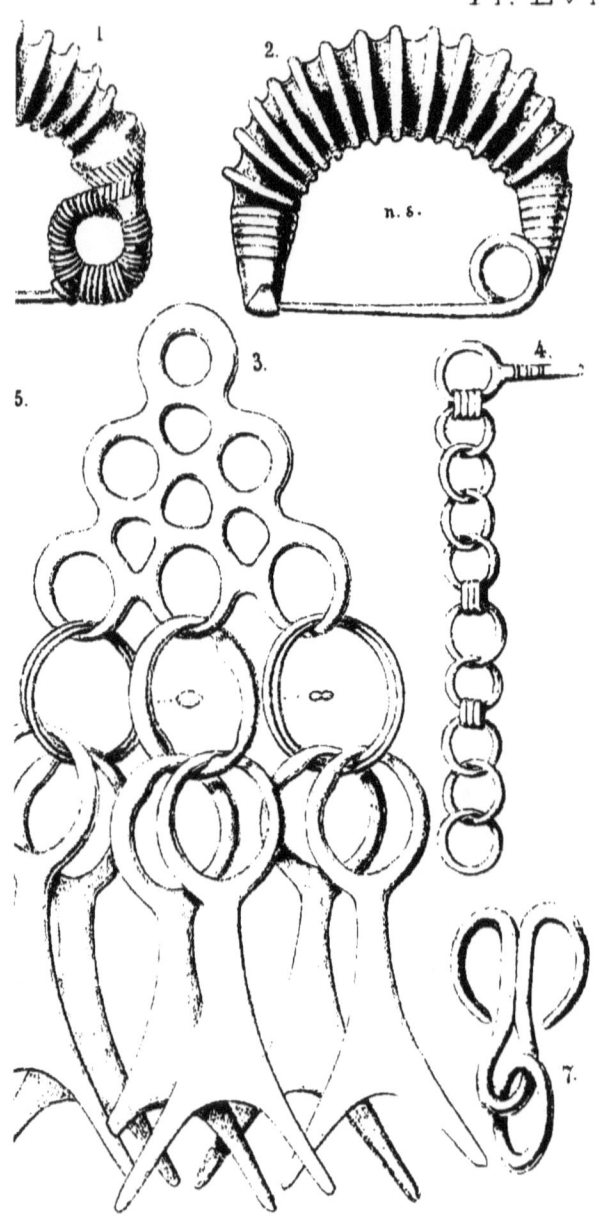

MÖRINGEN &c.

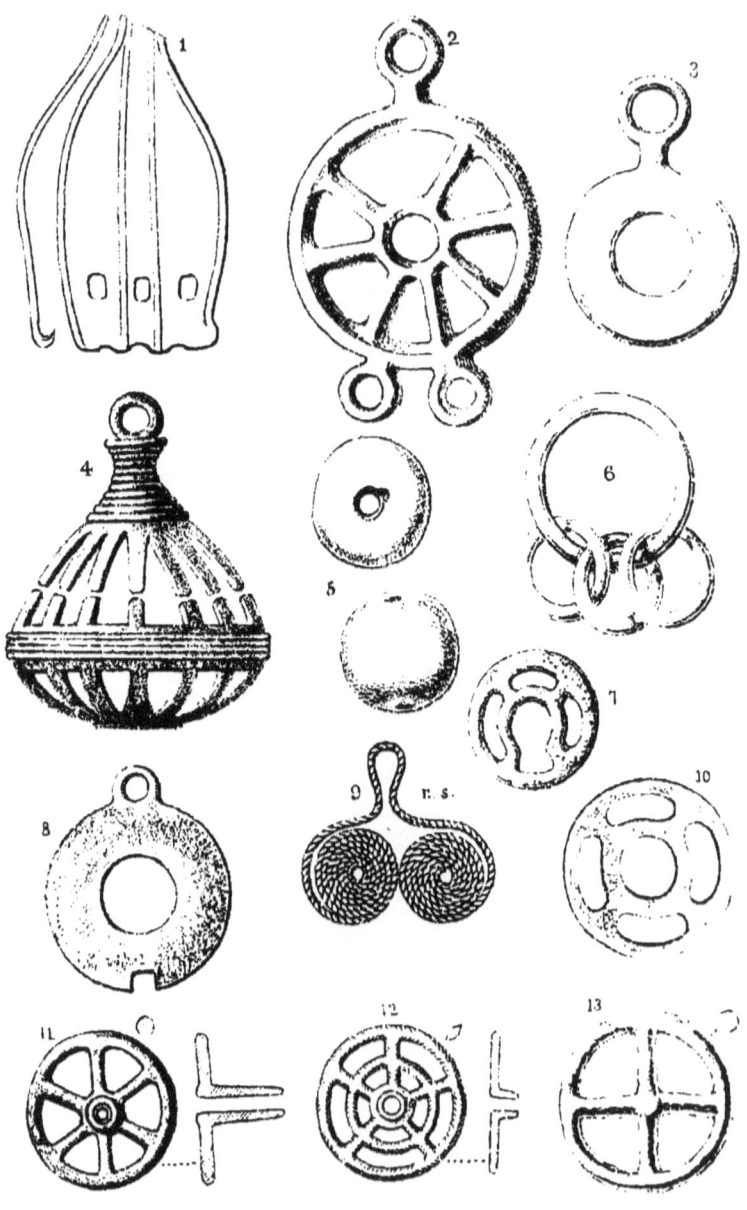

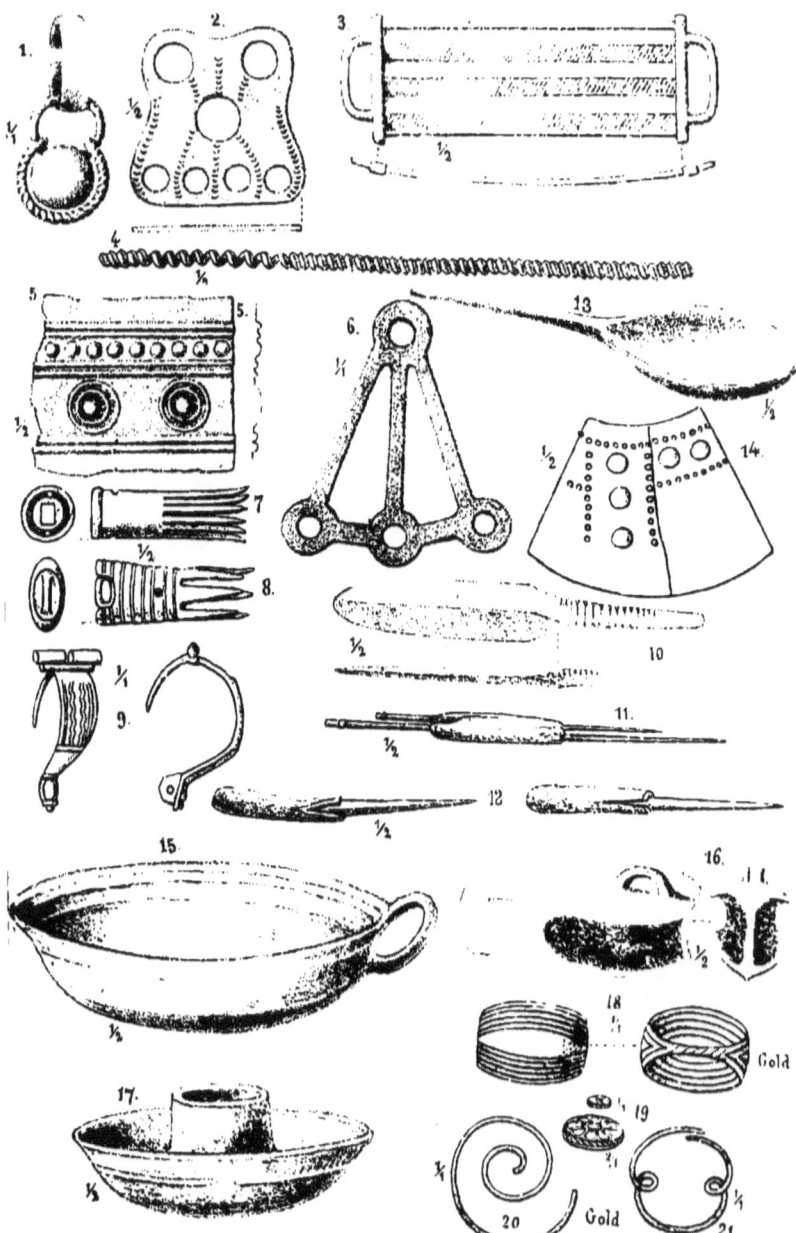

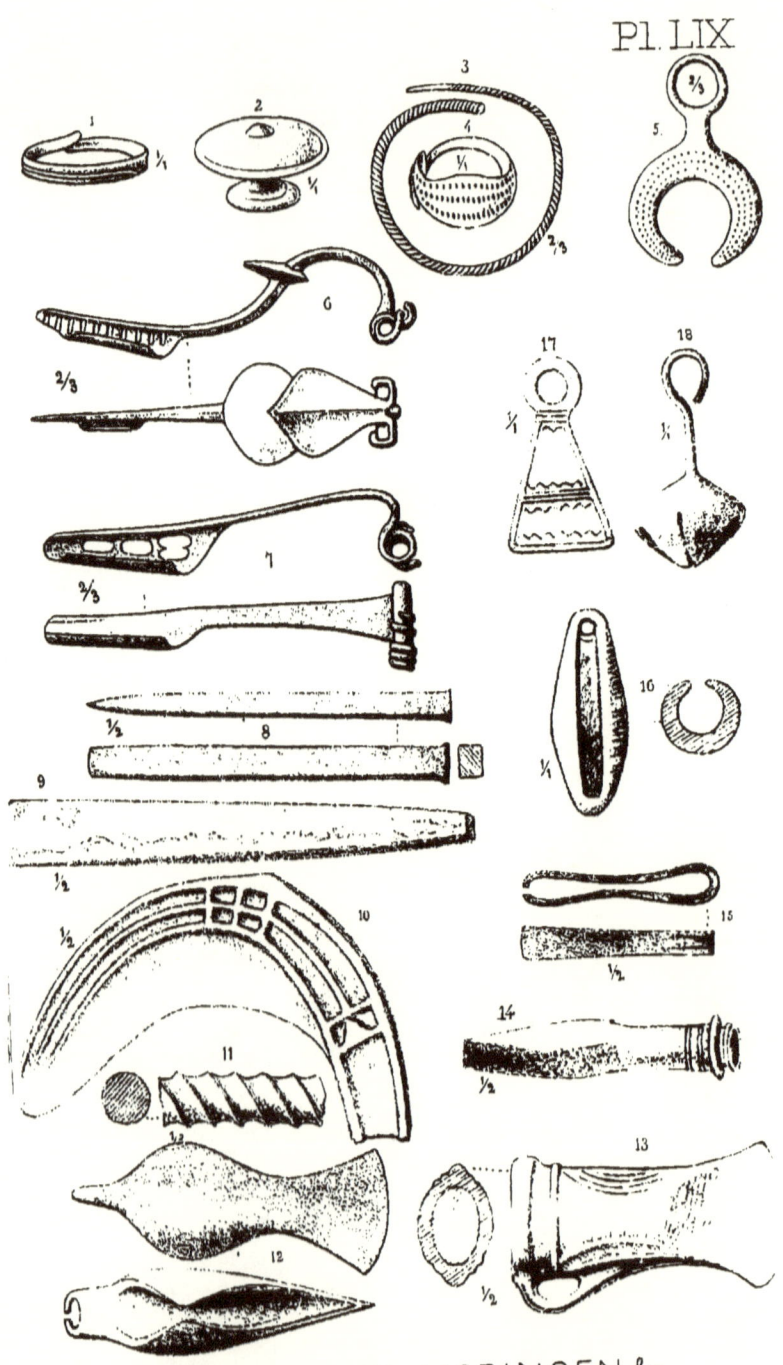

Pl. LIX

AUVERNIER, MORINGEN &c.

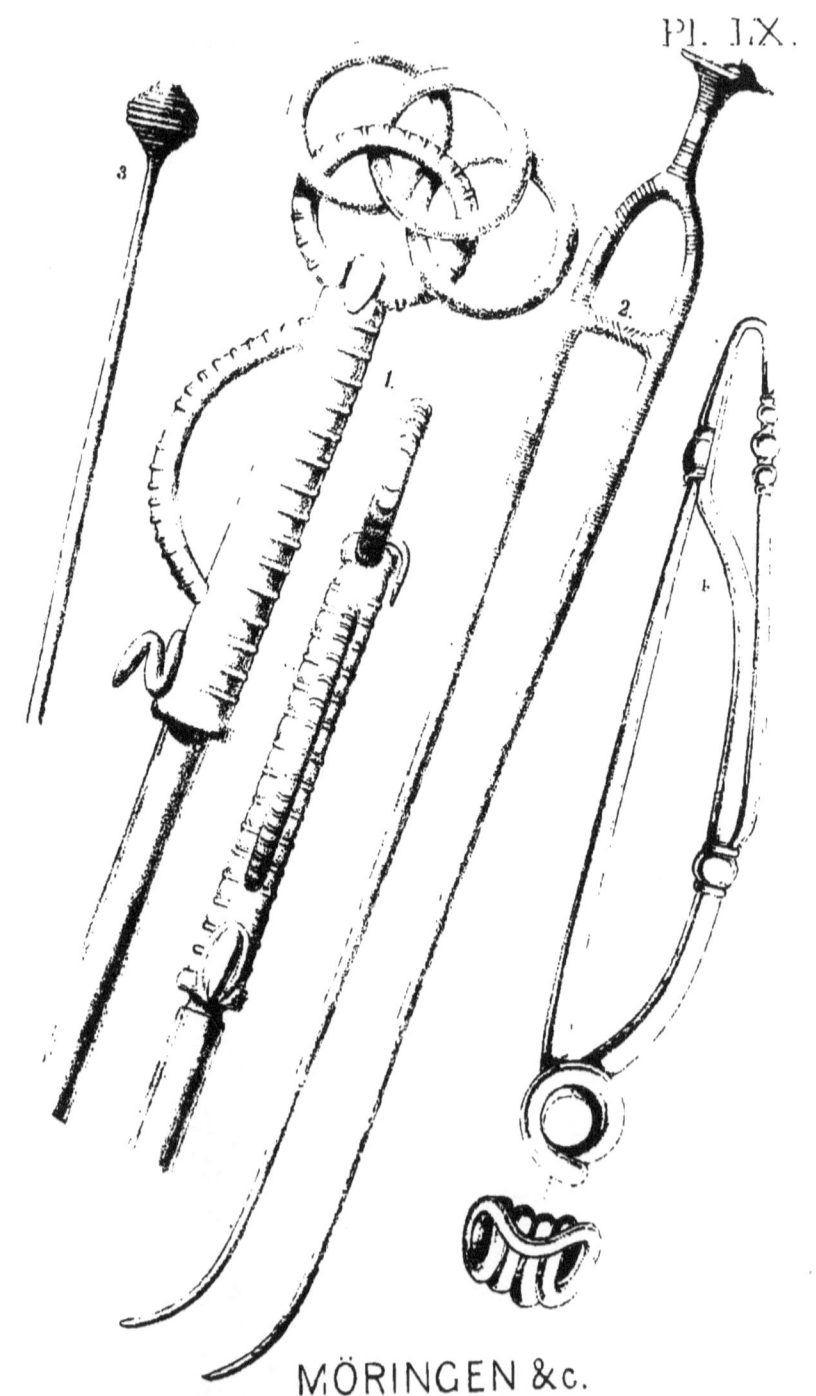

Pl. LX.

MÖRINGEN &c.

Pl. LXI.

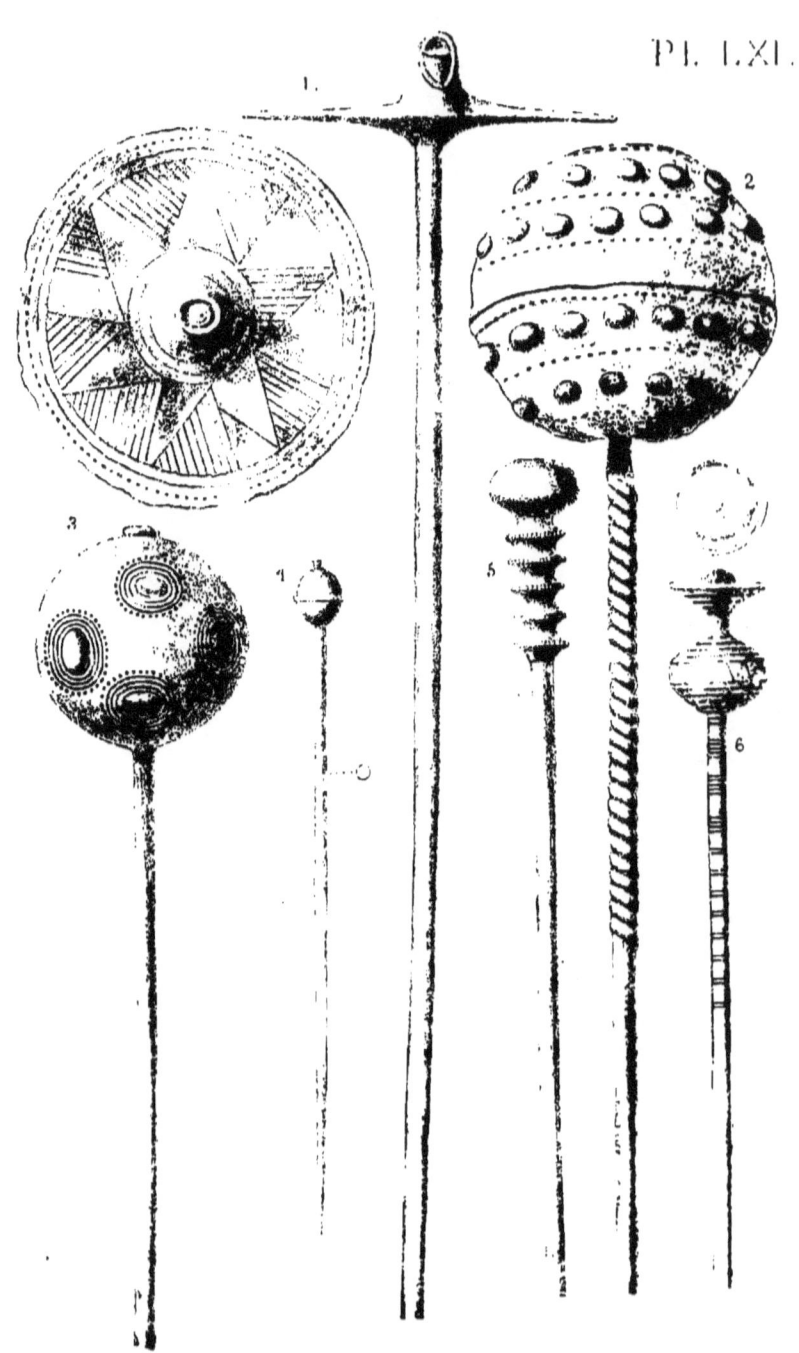

AUVERNIER &c.

PL. LXII.

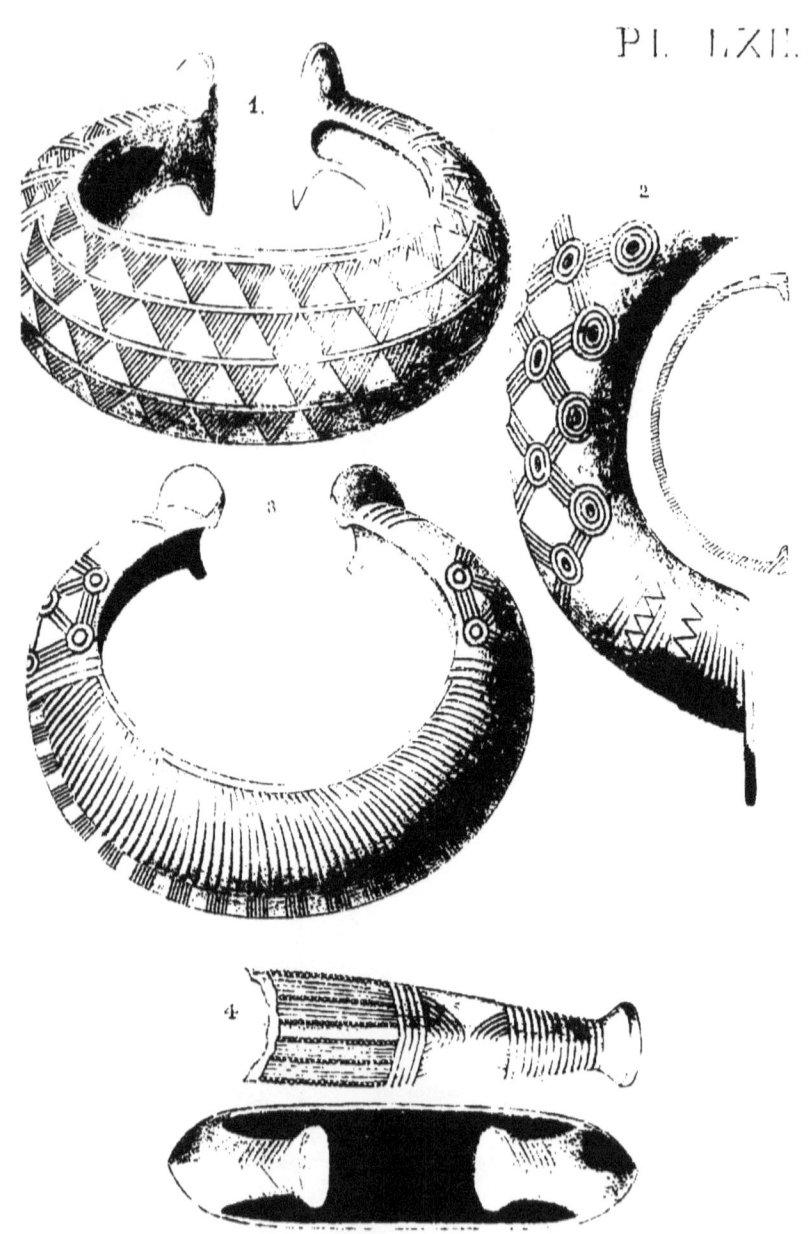

MÖRINGEN & AUVERNIER.

Pl. LXIII.

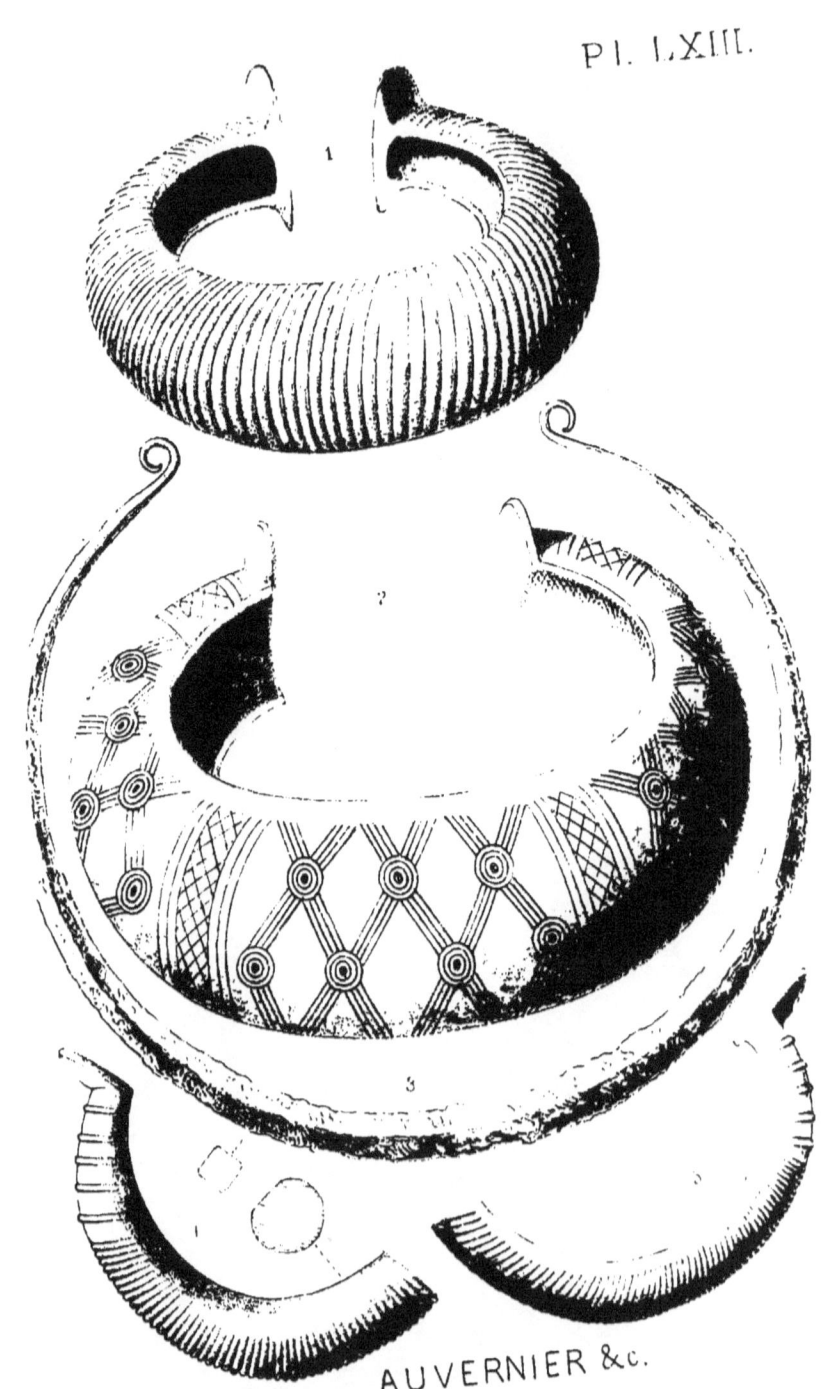

AUVERNIER &c.

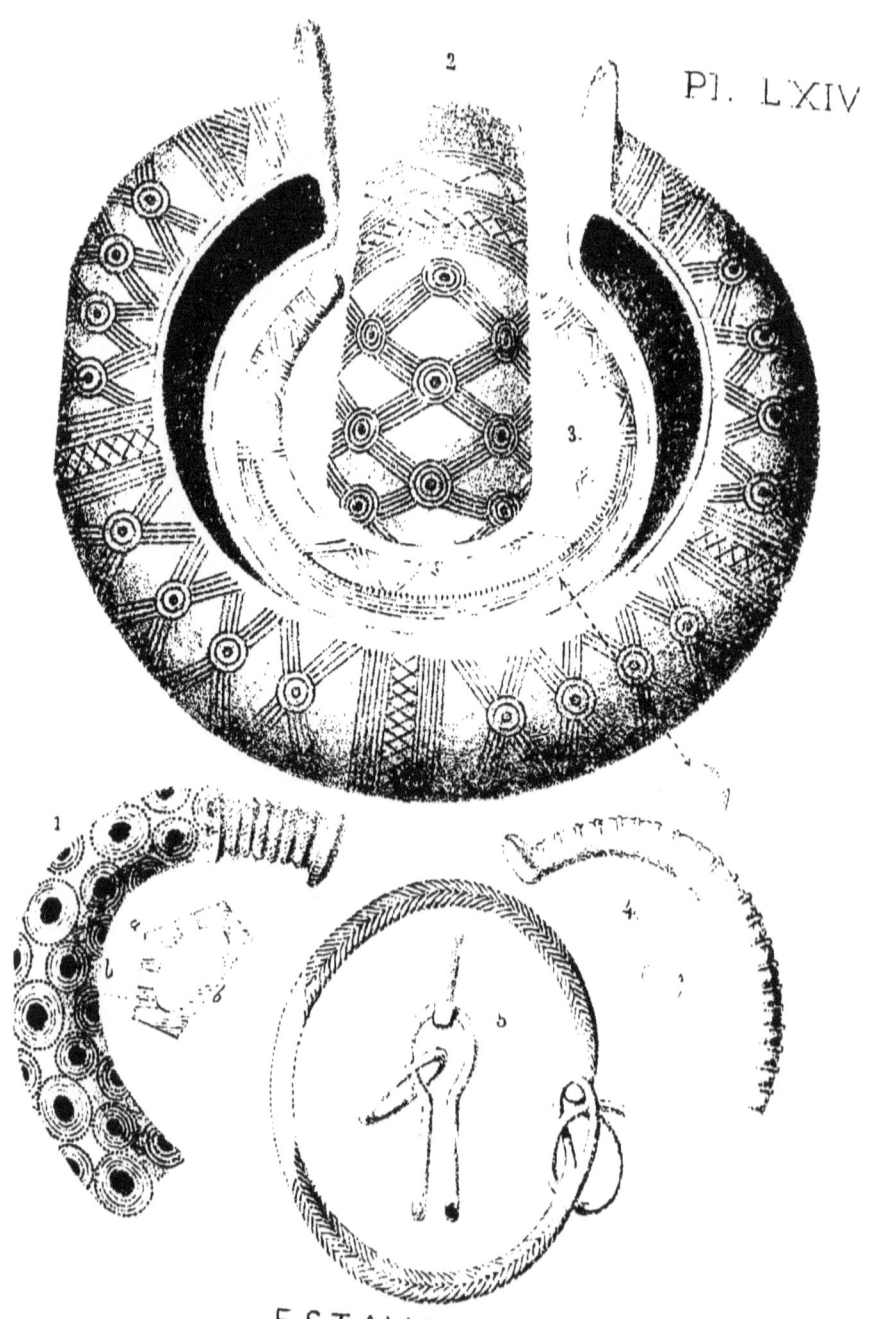

Pl. LXIV

ESTAVAYER &c.

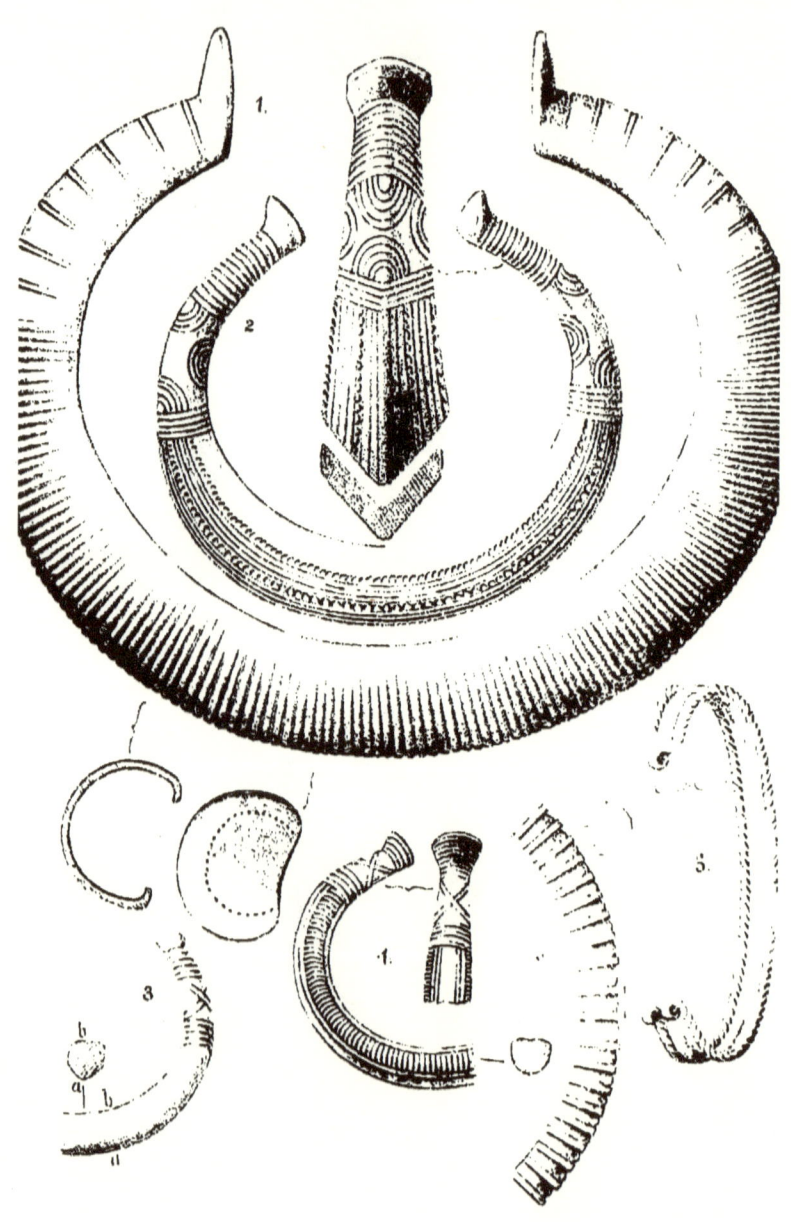

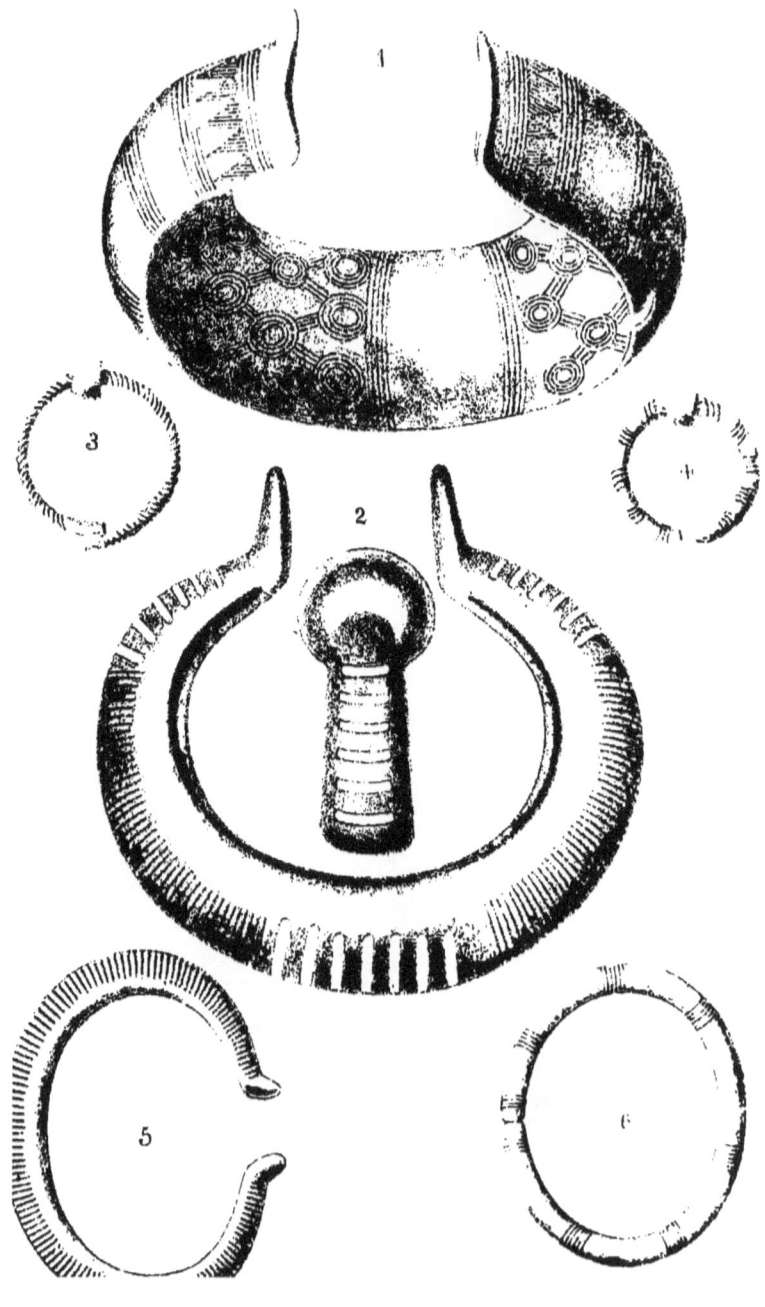

Pl. LXVII.

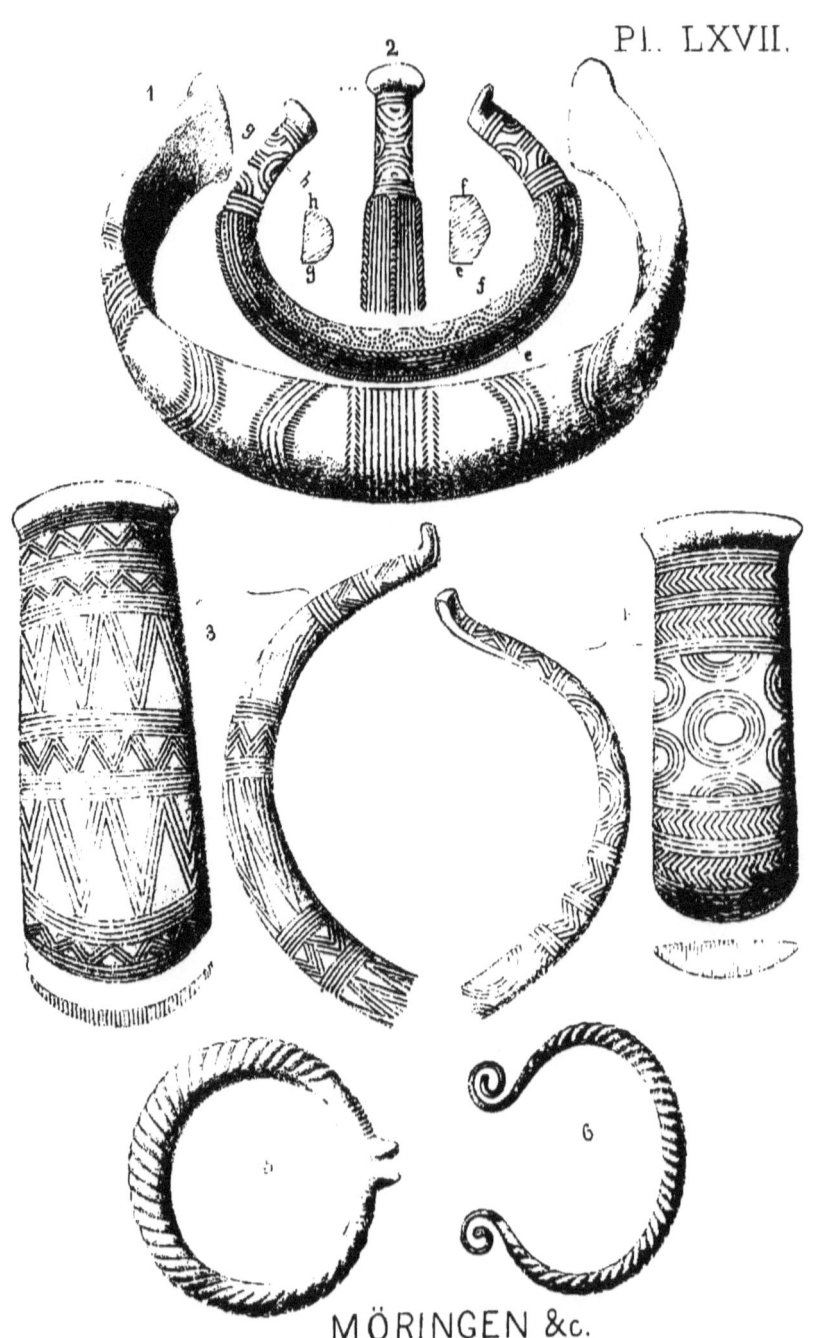

MÖRINGEN &c.

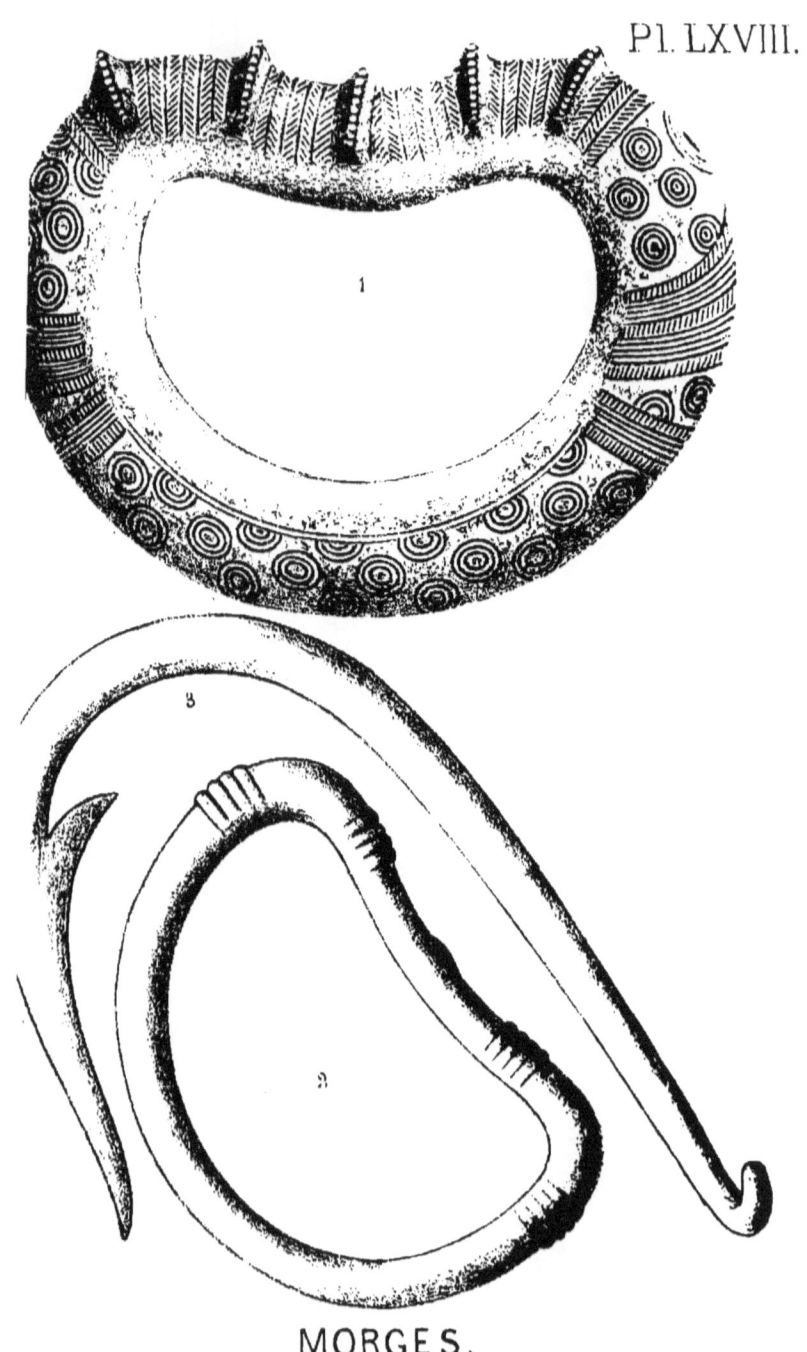

Pl. LXVIII.

MORGES.

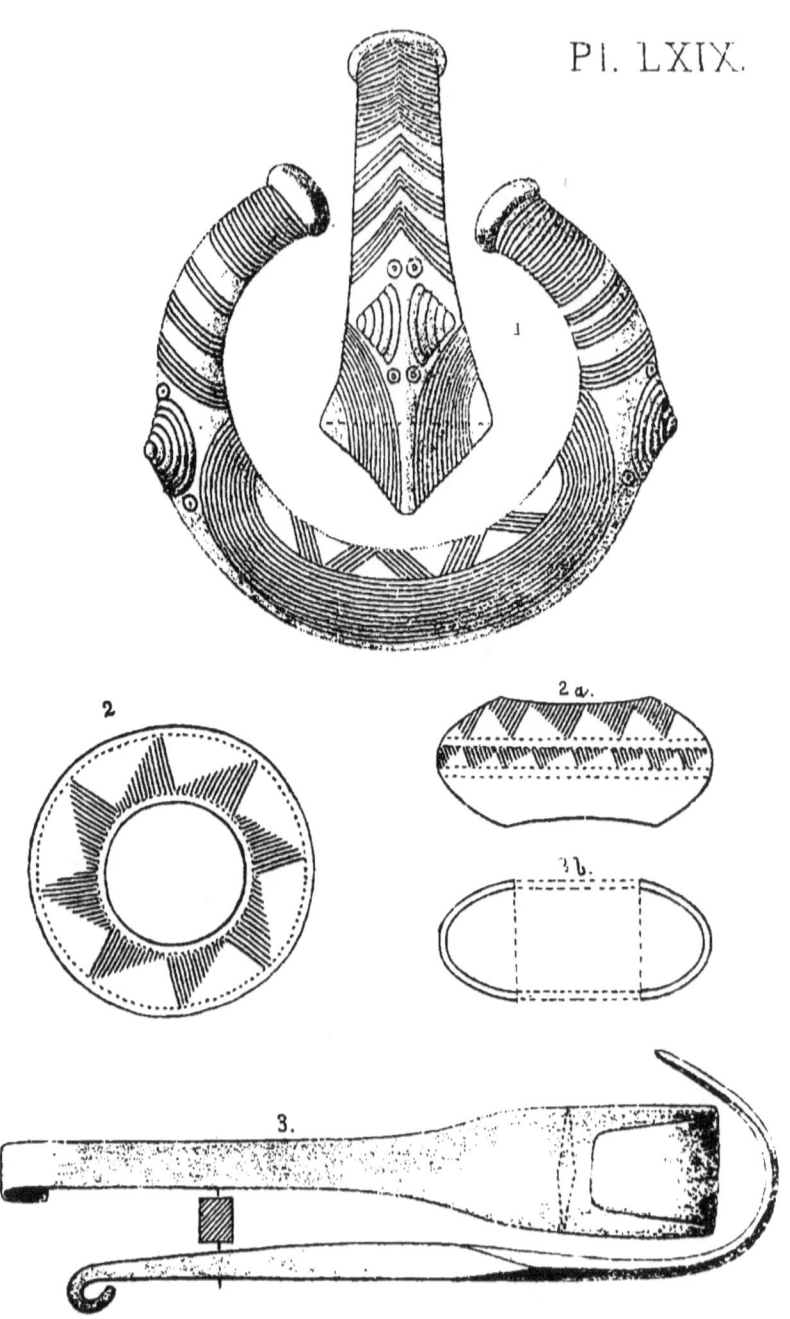

Pl. LXIX.

MORGES AUVERNIER.

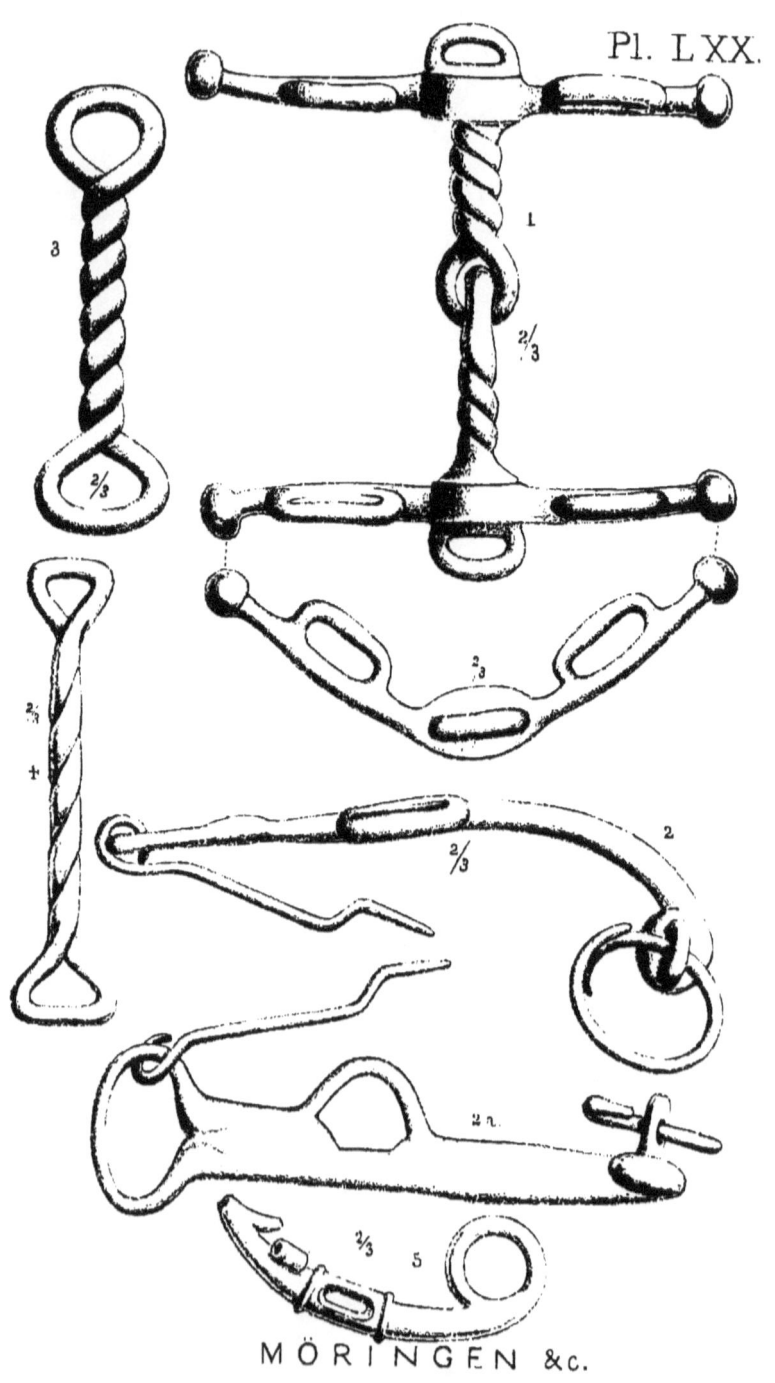

Pl. LXX.

MÖRINGEN &c.

Pl. LXXI.

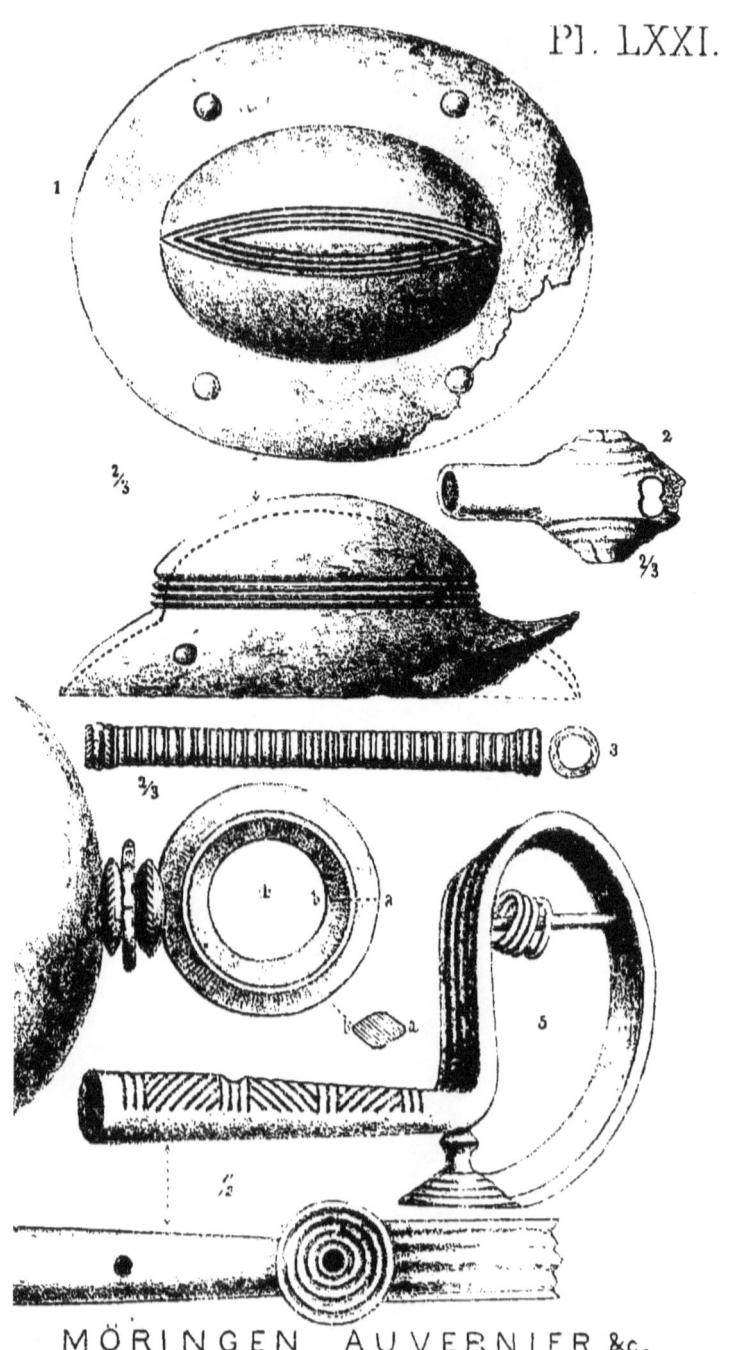

MÖRINGEN AUVERNIER &c.

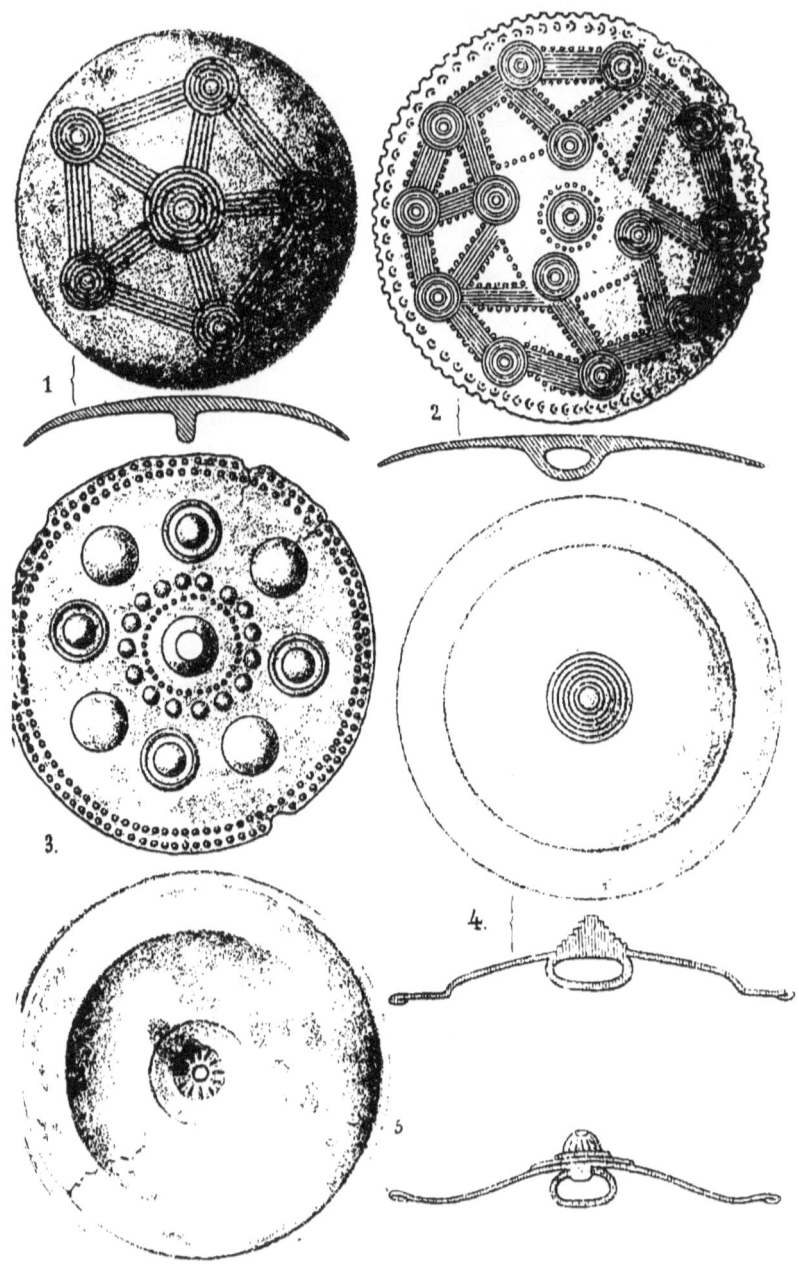

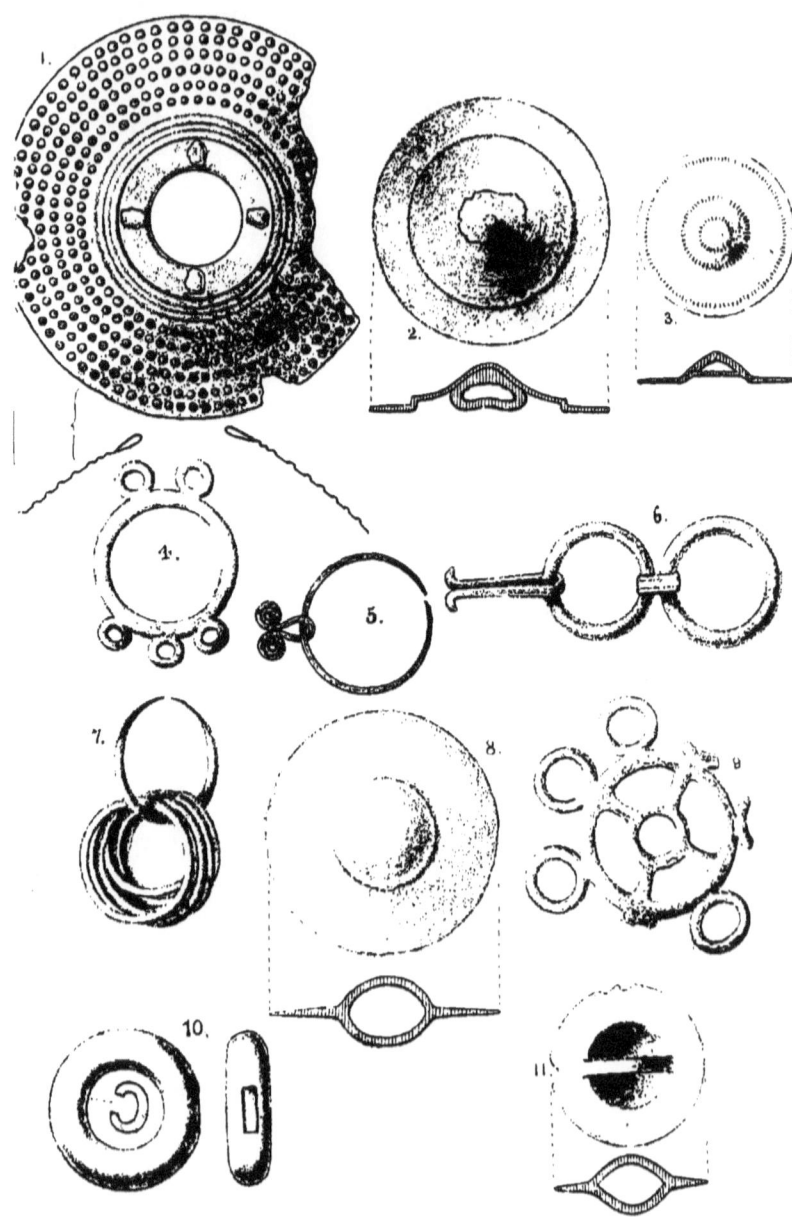

MÖRINGEN. AUVERNIER &c

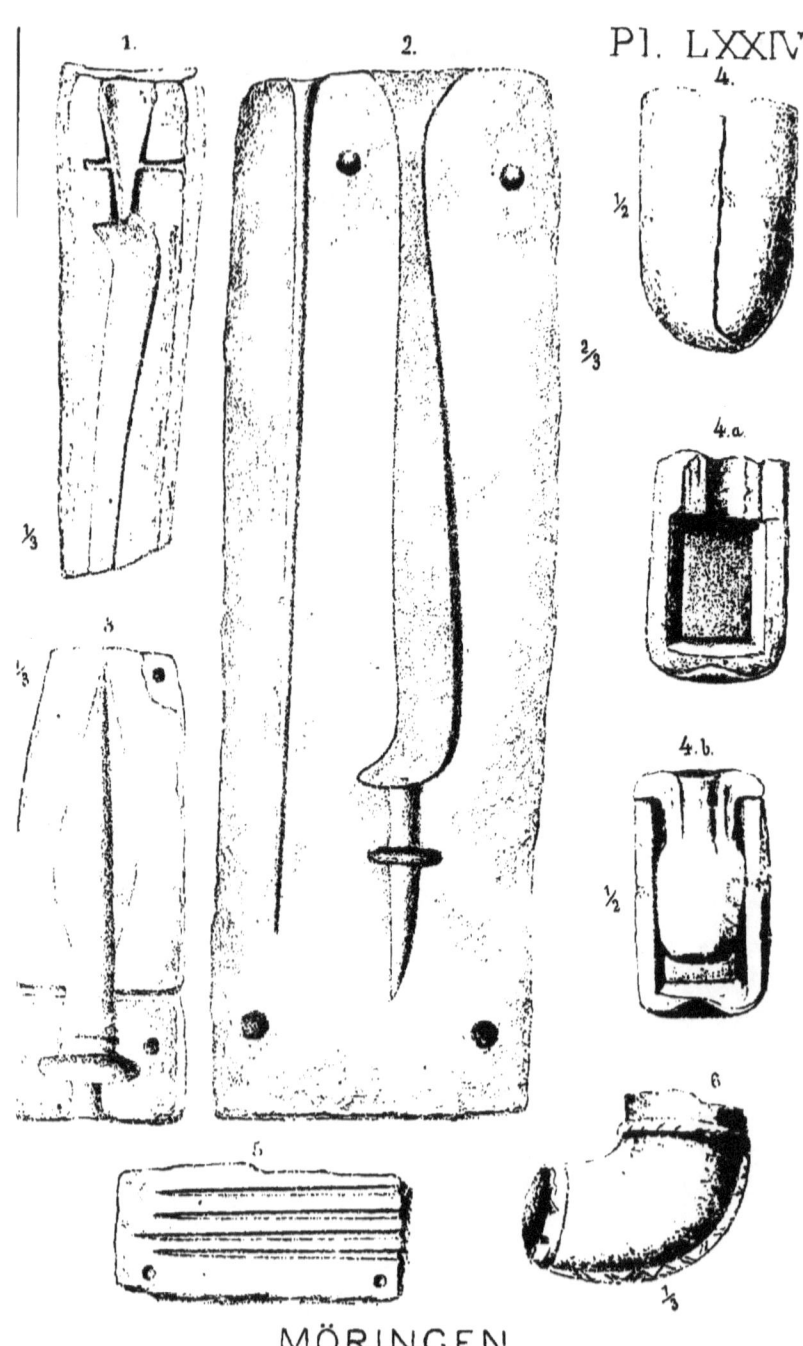

Pl. LXXIV.

MÖRINGEN.

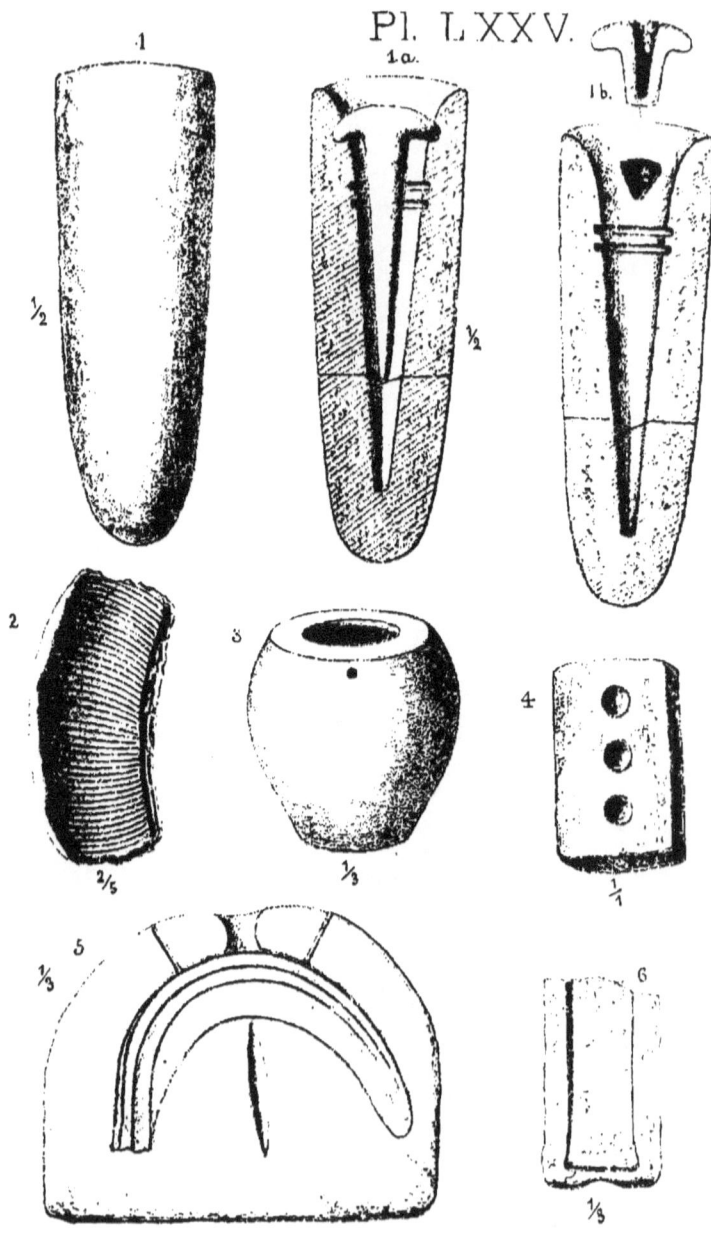

Pl. LXXV.

MÖRINGEN & AUVERNIER.

Pl. LXXVI.

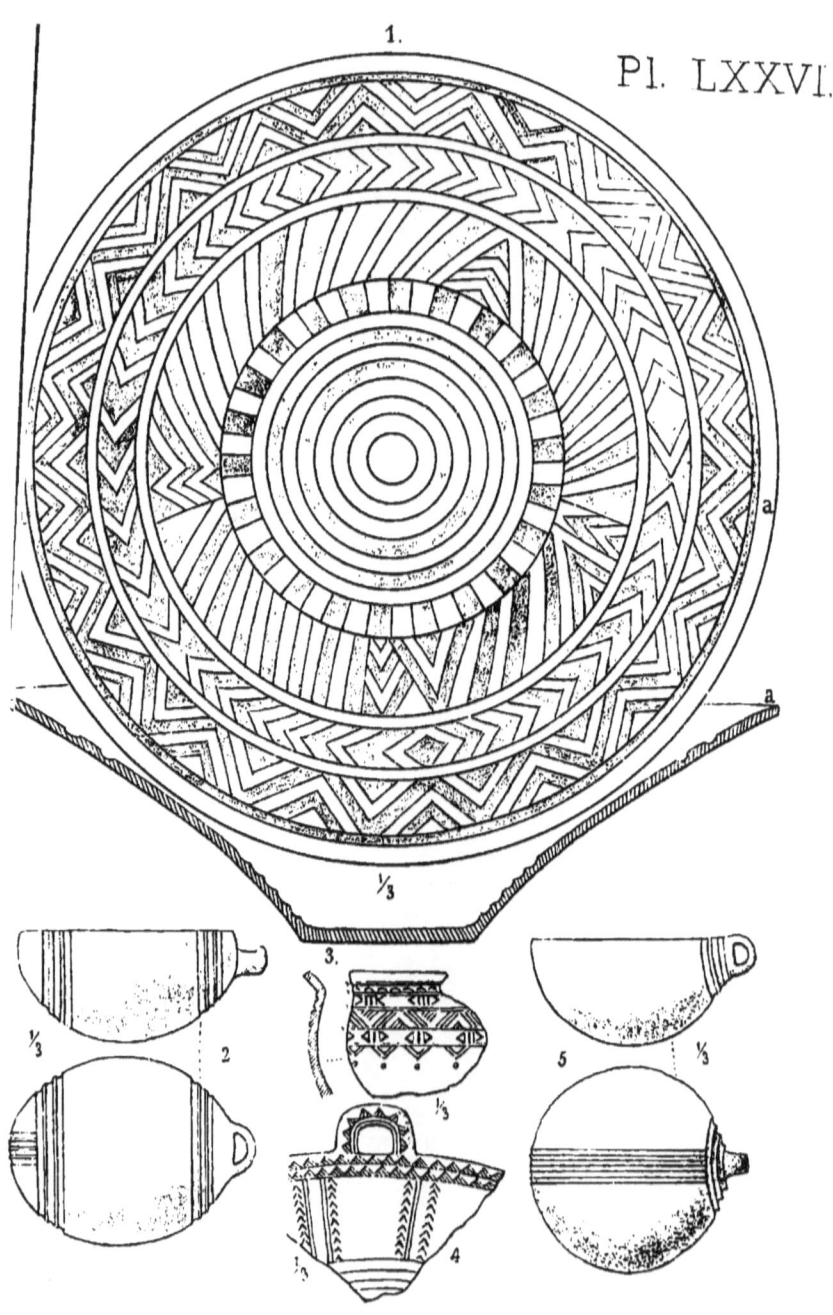

MÖRINGEN & AUVERNIER.

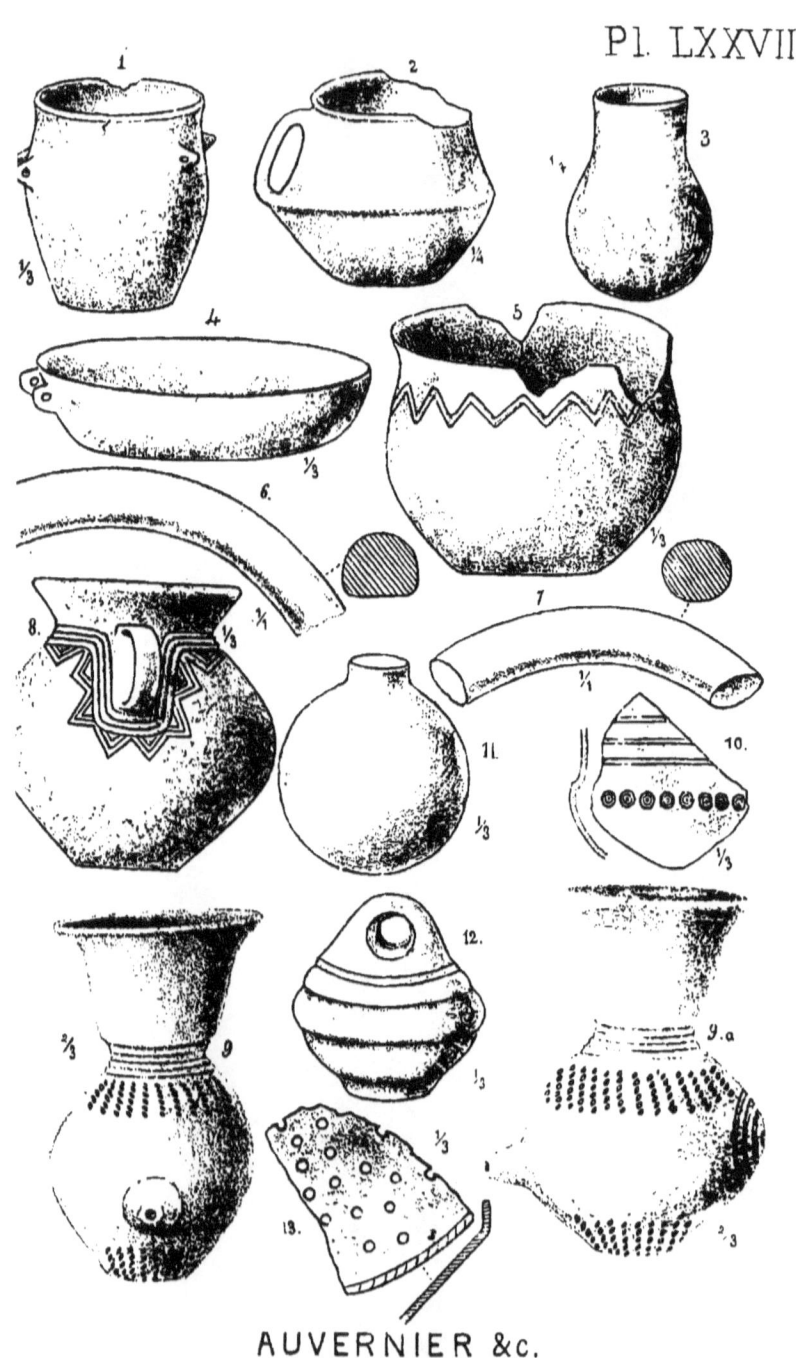

Pl. LXXVII.

AUVERNIER &c.

Pl. LXXVIII.

Pl. LXXIX.

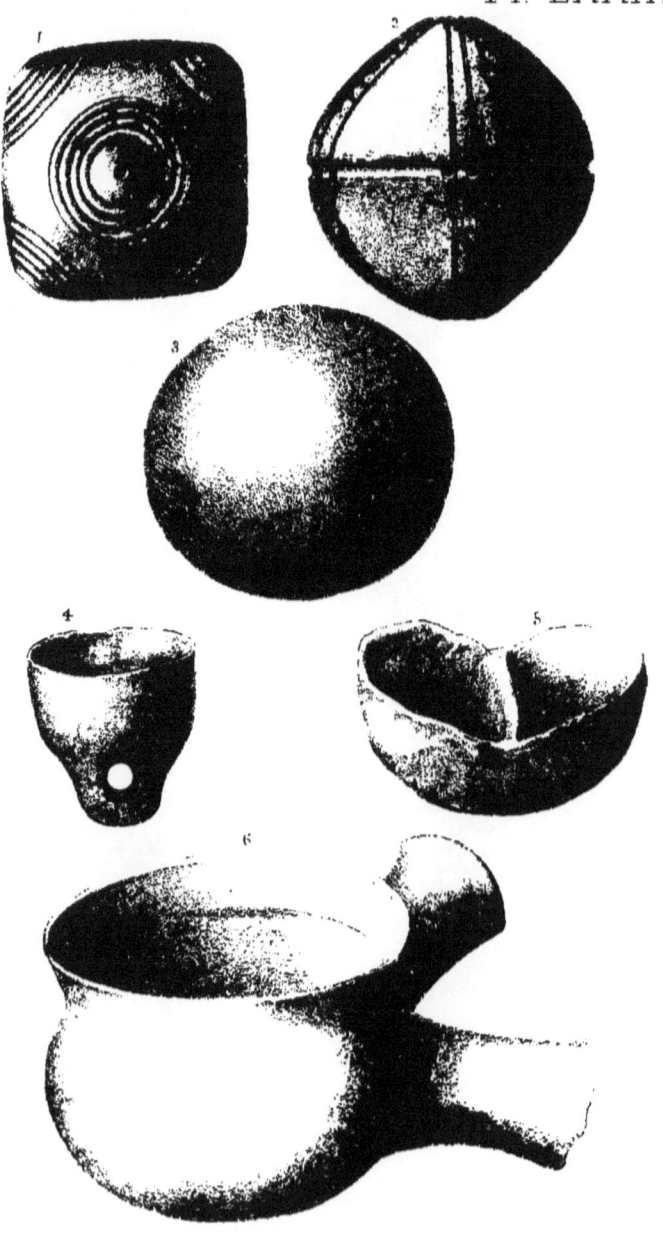

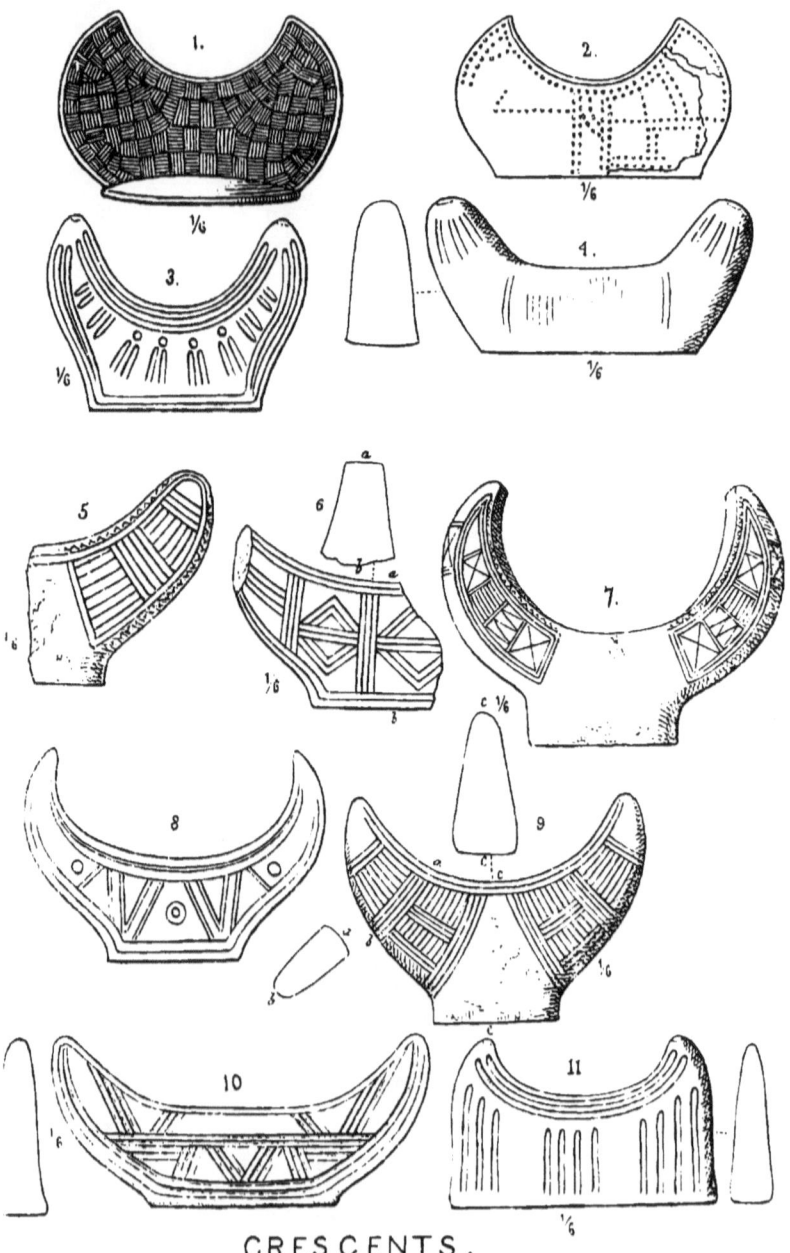

CRESCENTS.

Figs 5 & 7 from Ebersberg in the Mainland - The remainder from L.D

Pl. LXXXI.

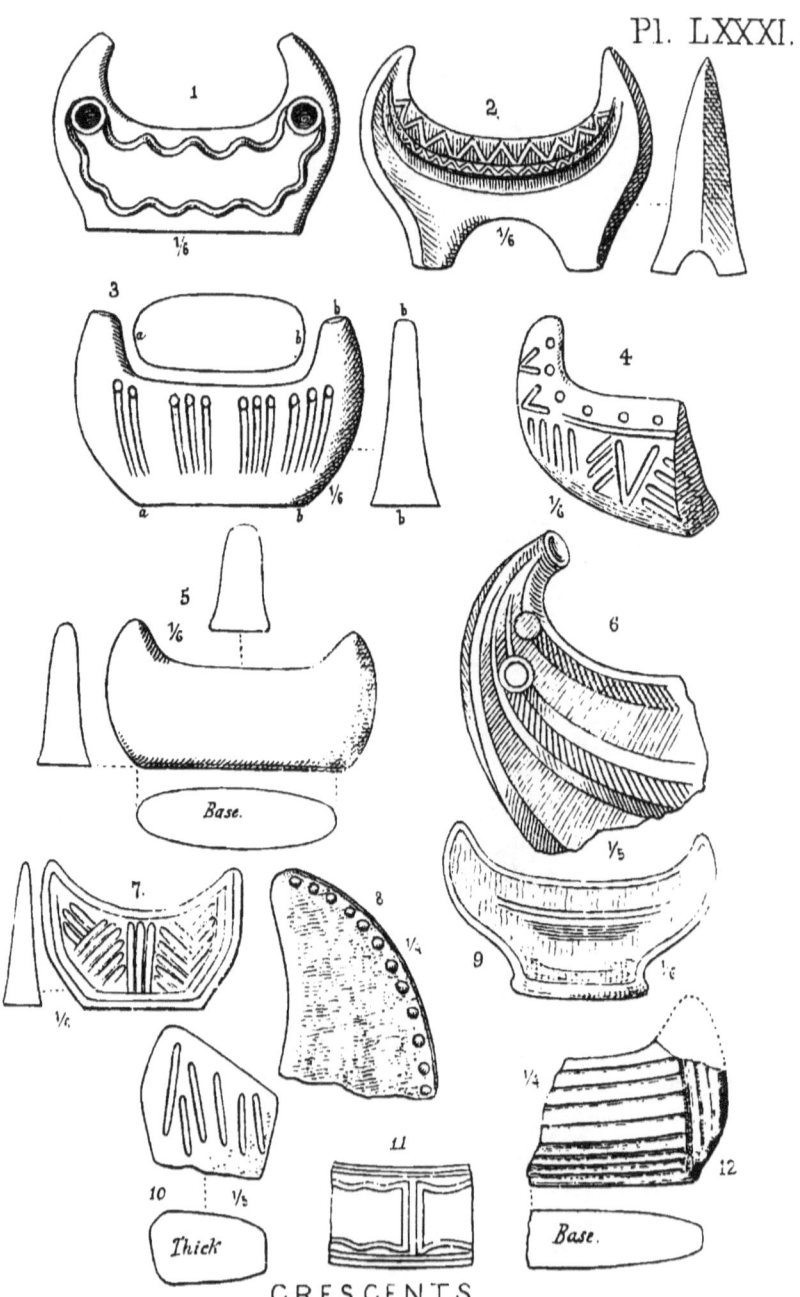

CRESCENTS.

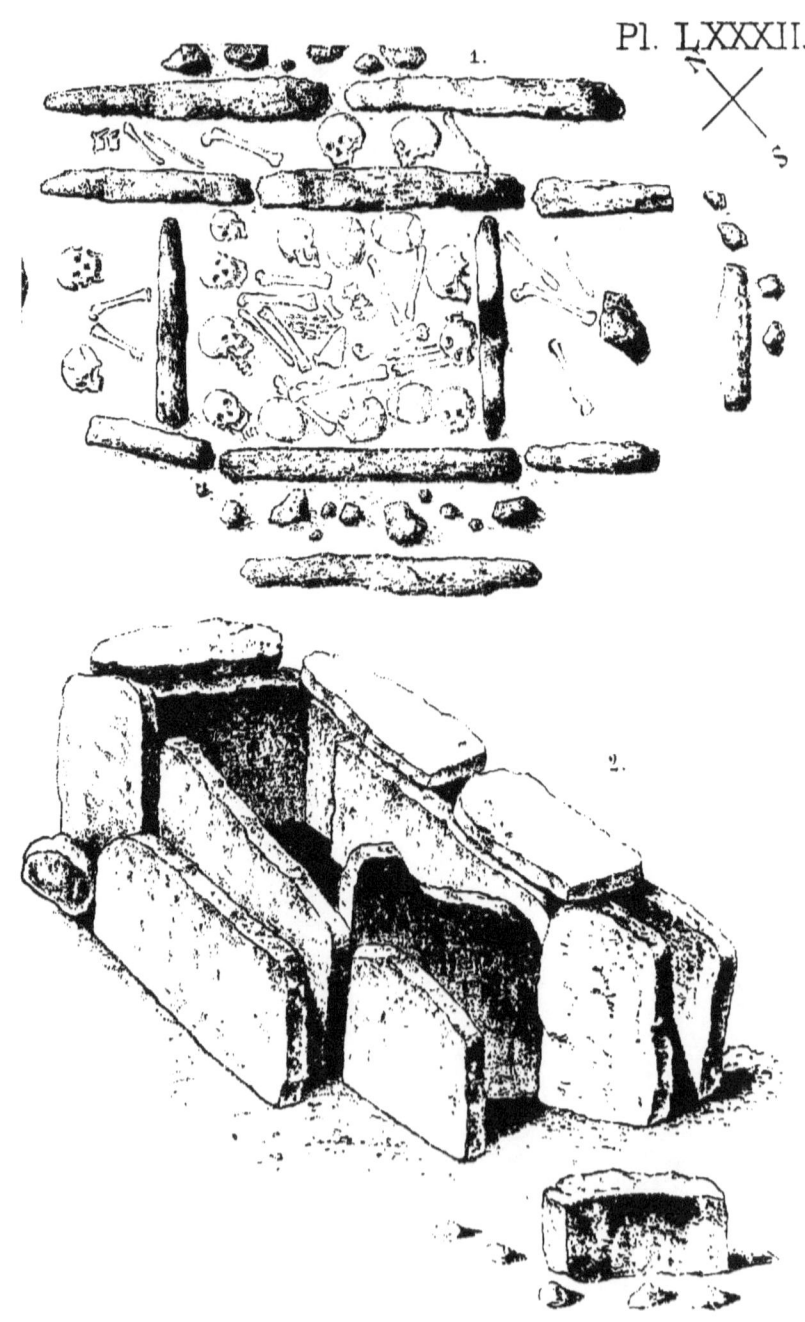

Pl. LXXXII.

Pl. LXXXIII.

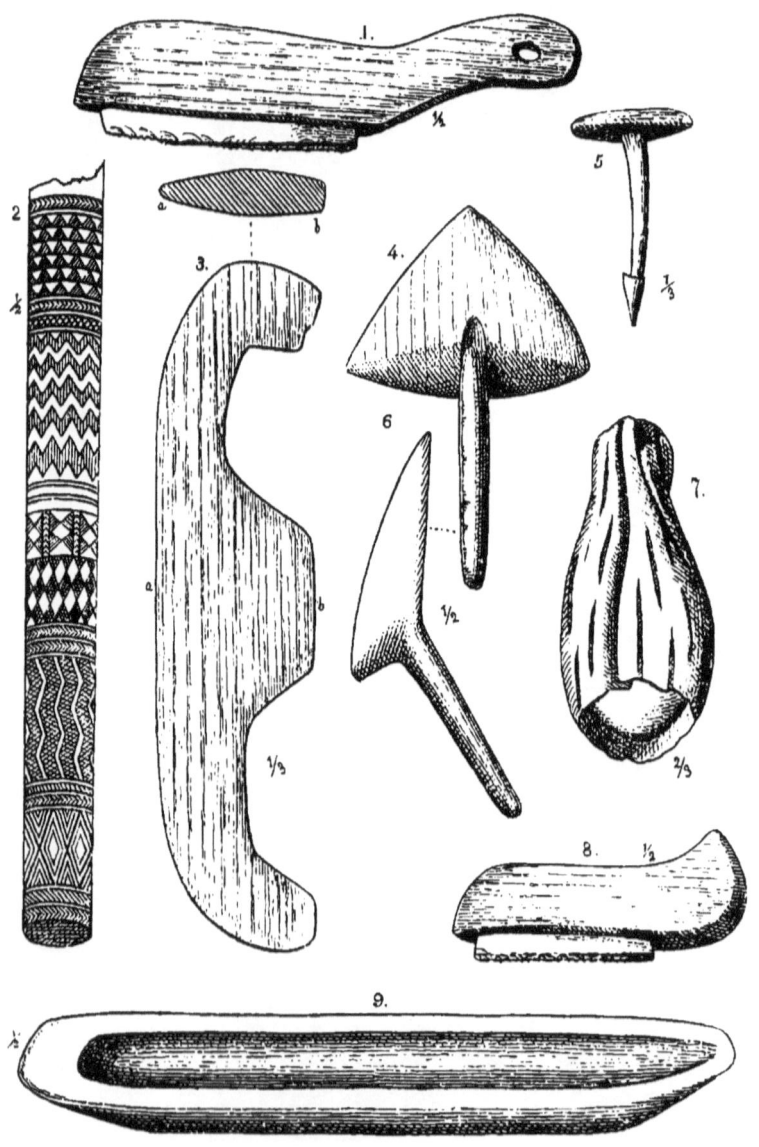

AUVERNIER &c.

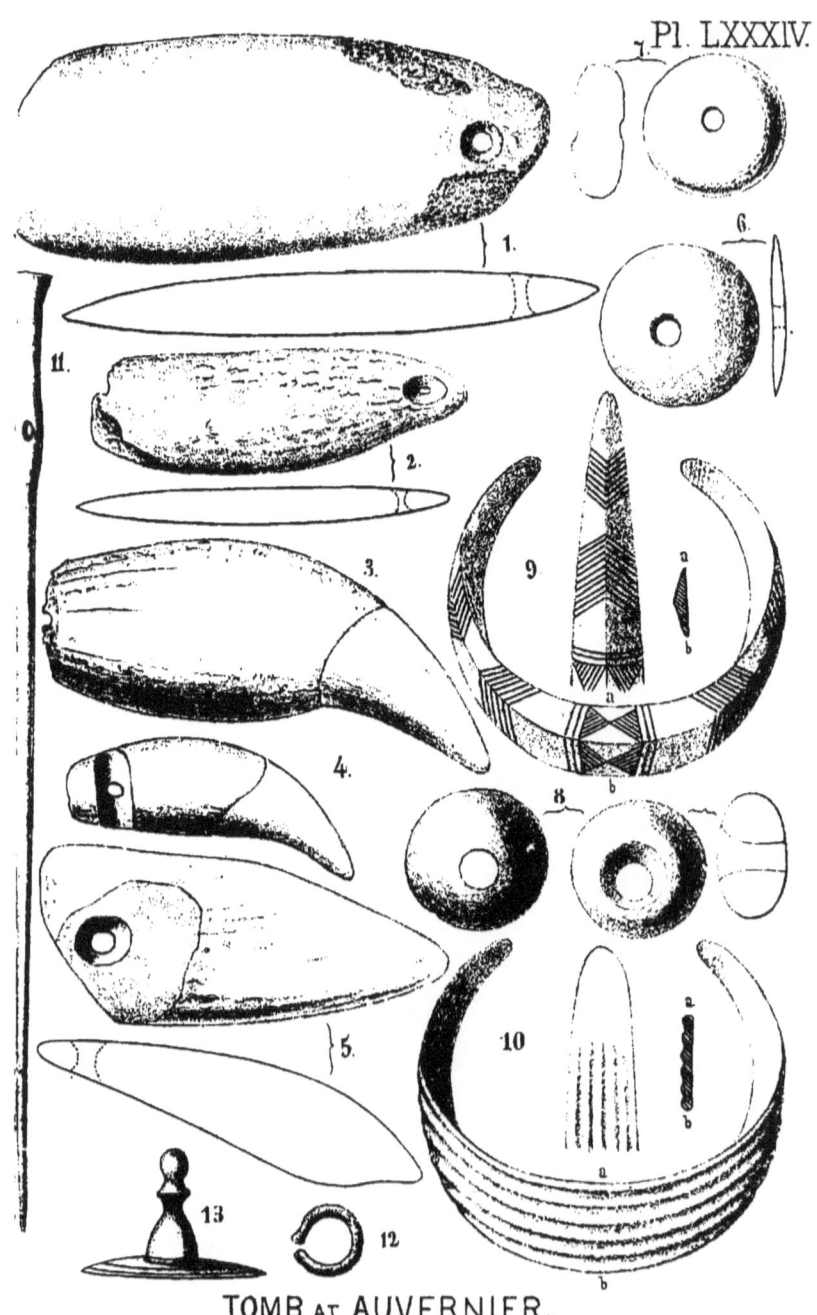

Pl. LXXXIV.

TOMB at AUVERNIER.

MÖRINGEN & AUVERNIER.
Spindle-whorls.

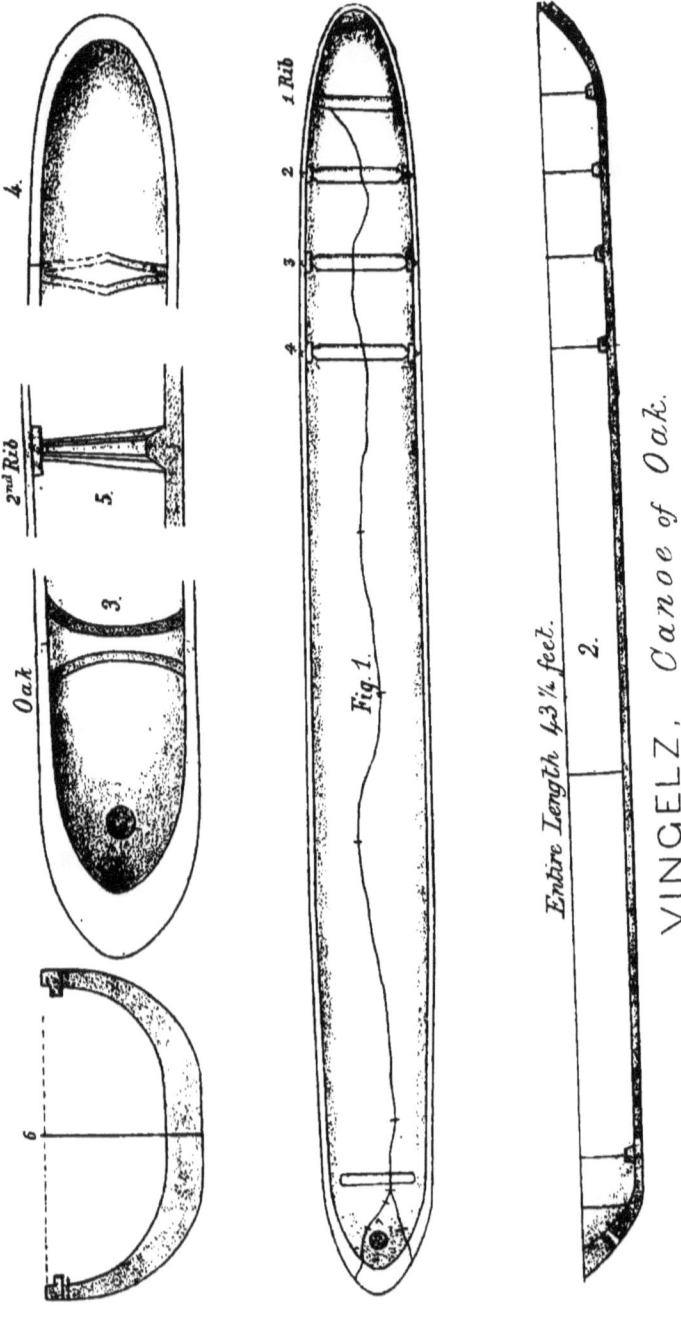

VINGELZ. Canoe of Oak.

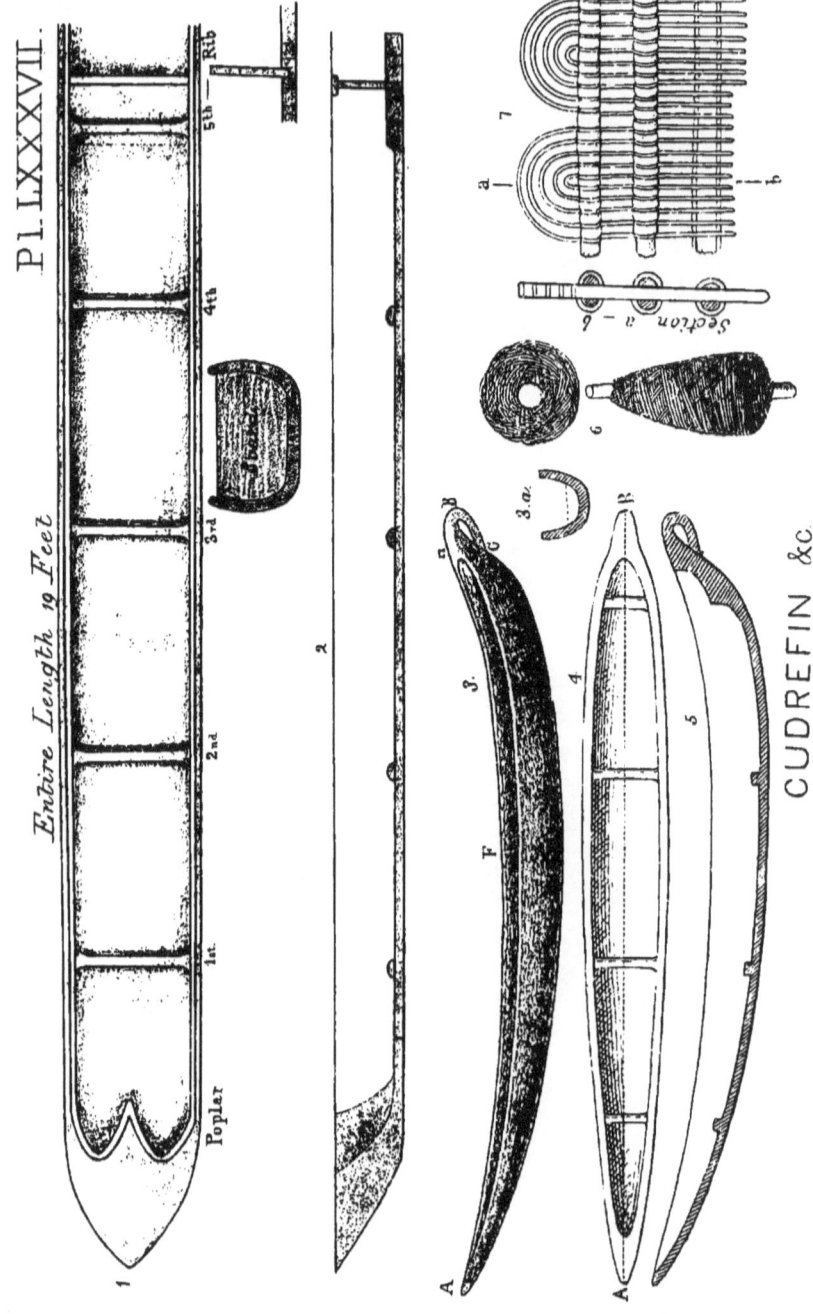

Pl LXXXVIII

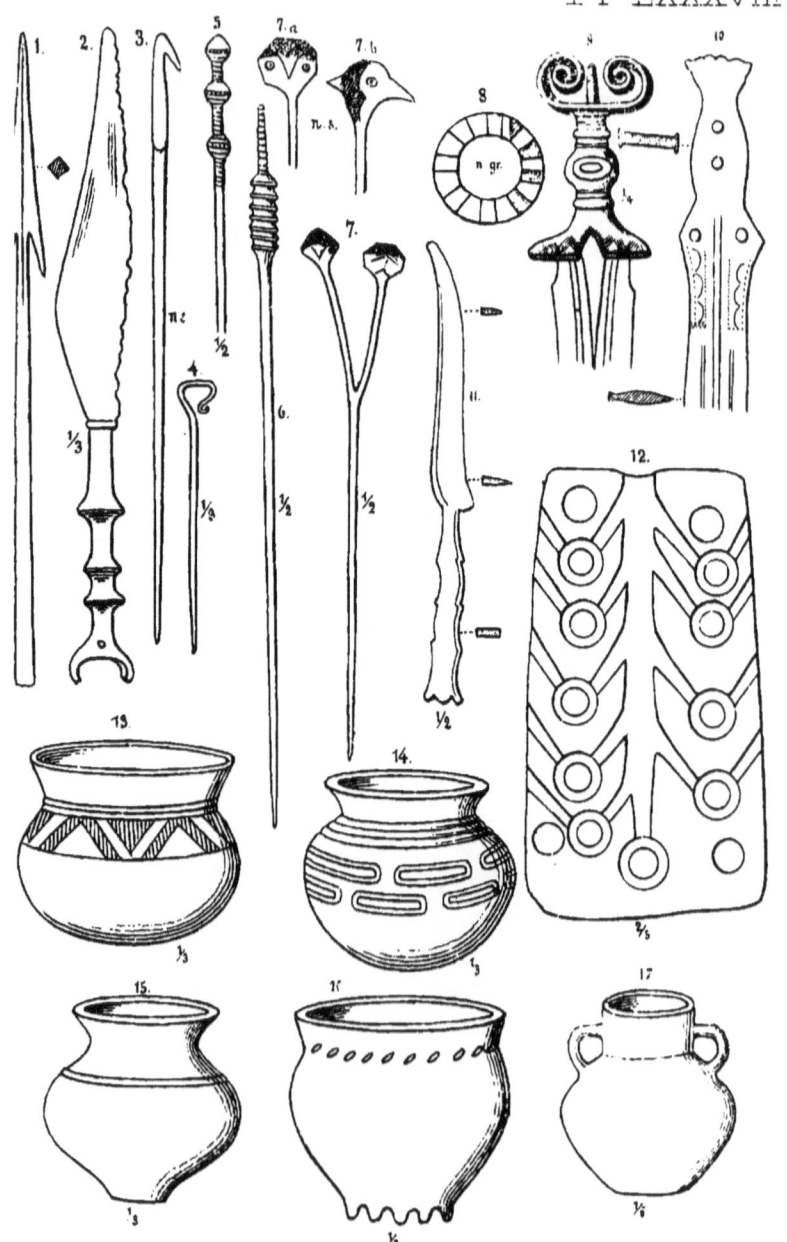

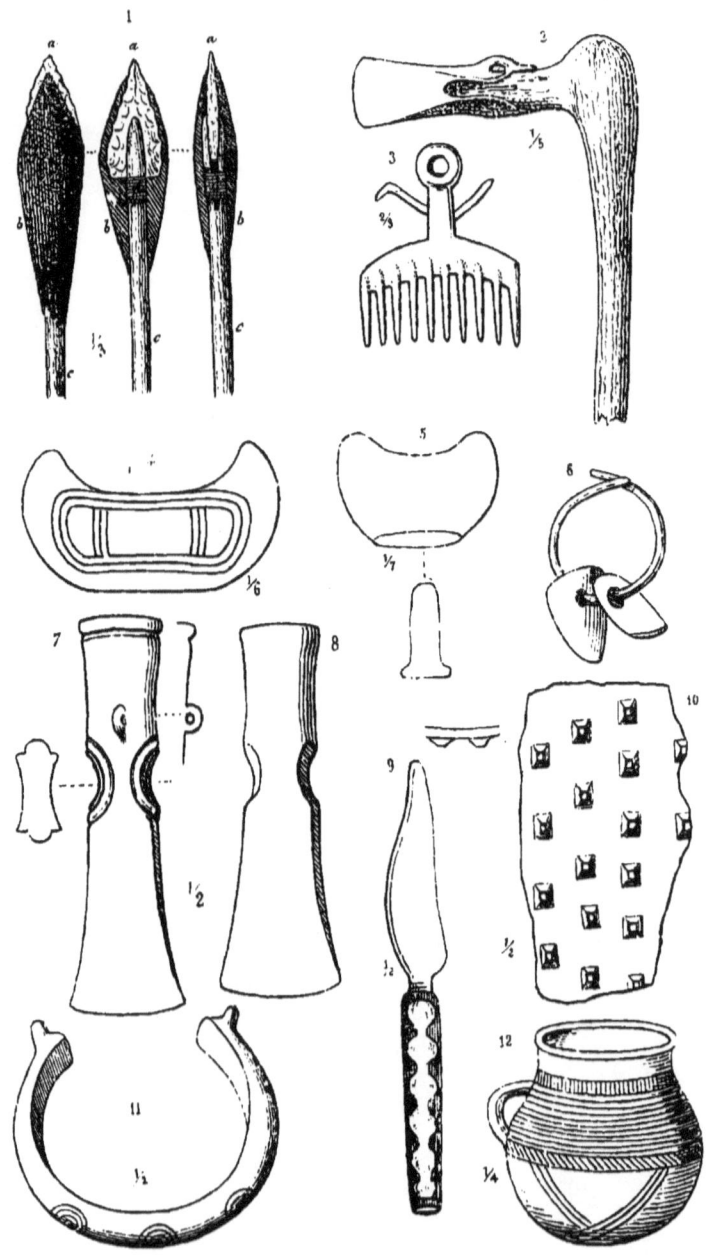

GENEVA, MÖRINGEN, &c.

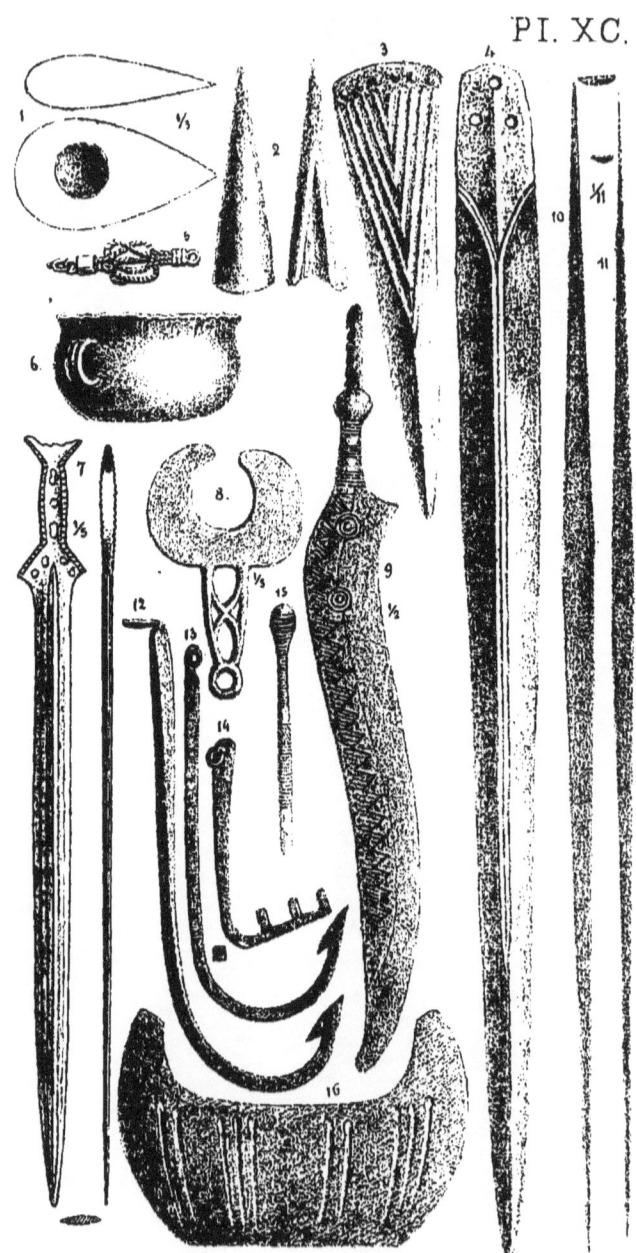

SUTZ, LATTRINGEN &c.

CORTAILLOD &c.

Pl. XCI.

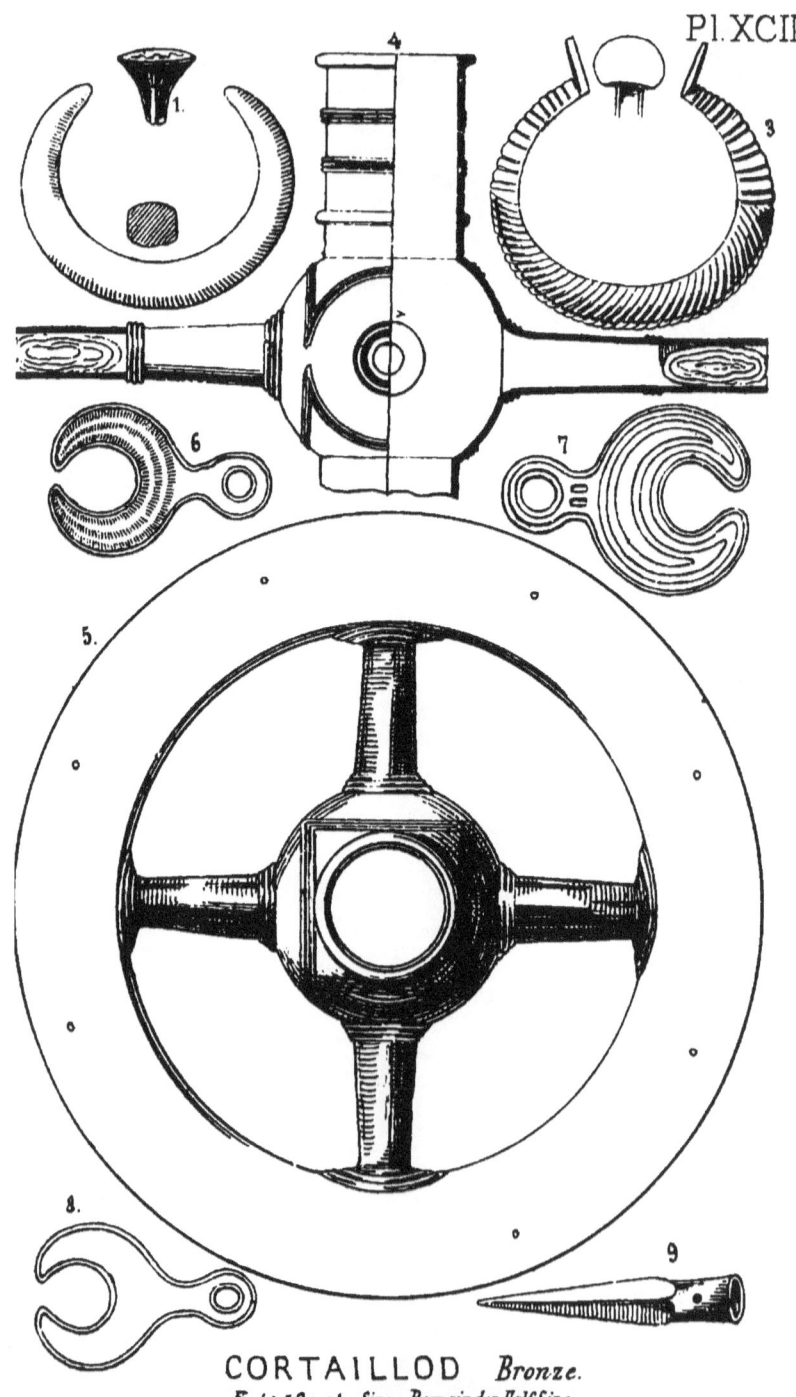

CORTAILLOD *Bronze.*
Fig 4 & 5 Quarter Size - Remainder Half Size.

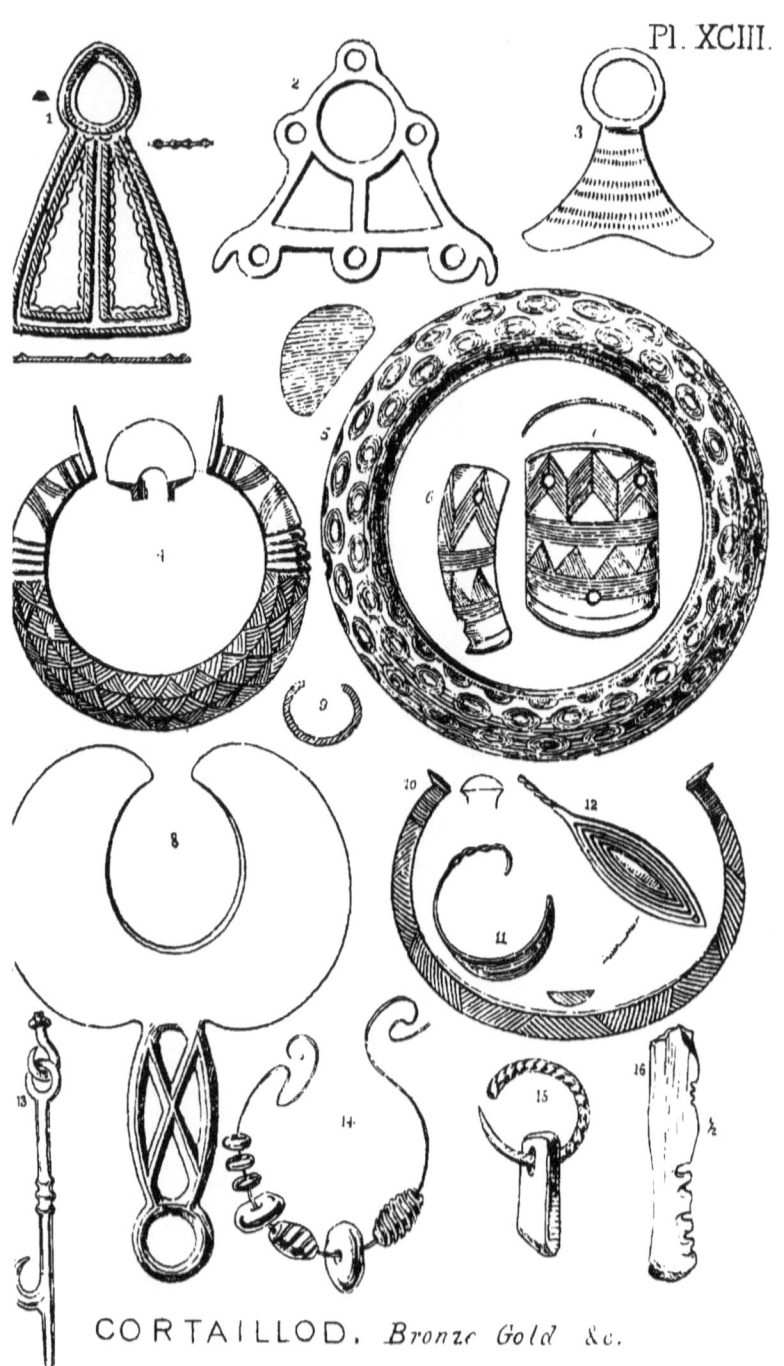

Pl. XCIII.

CORTAILLOD. *Bronze Gold &c.*

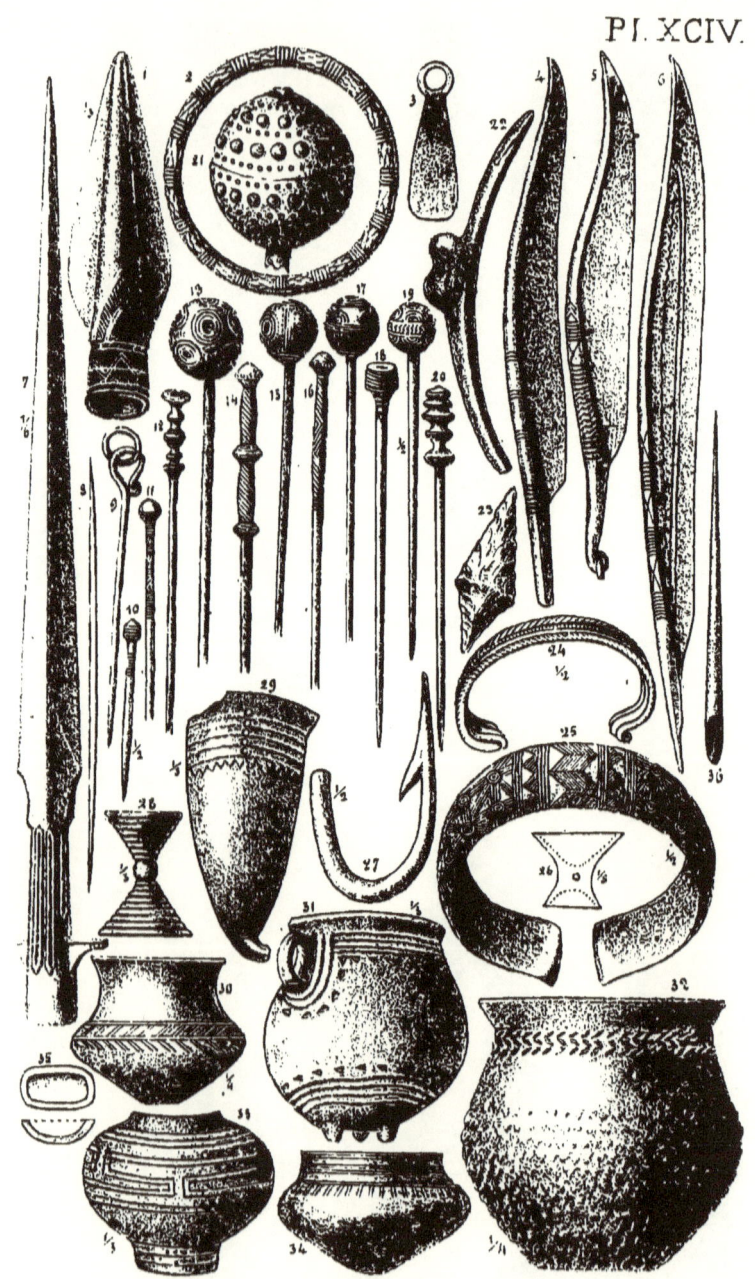

PL. XCIV.

AUVERNIER &c.

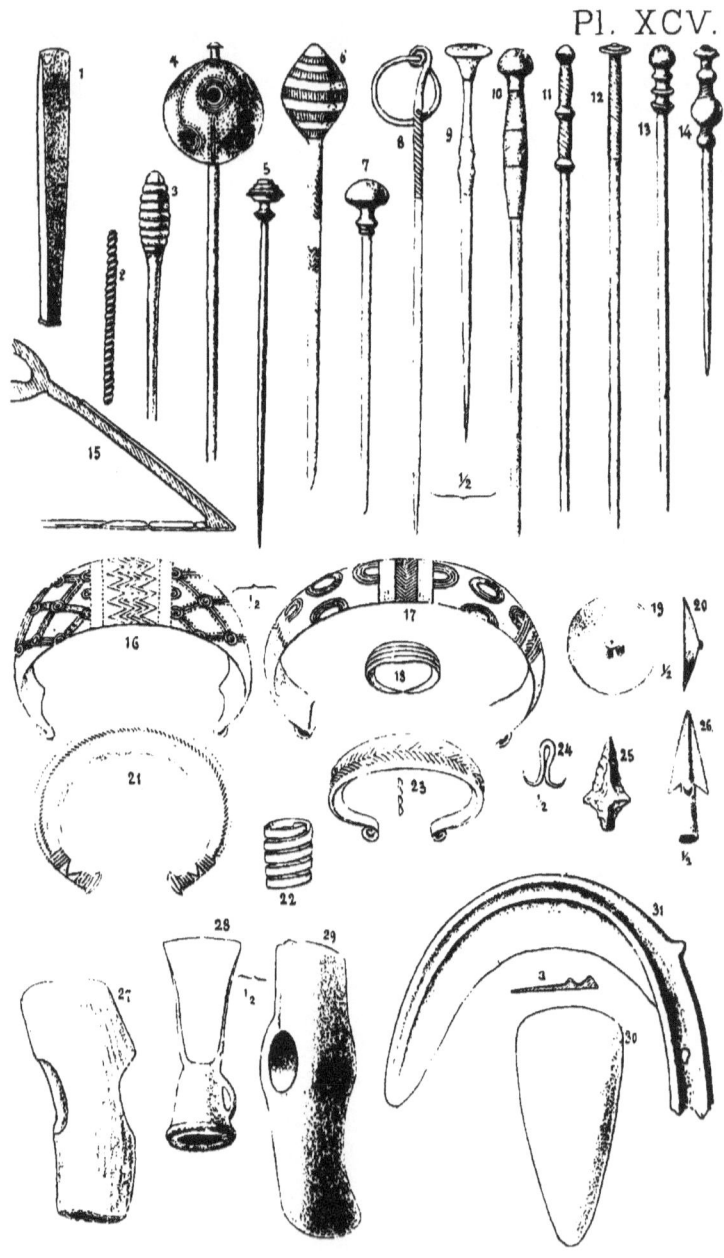

Pl. XCV.

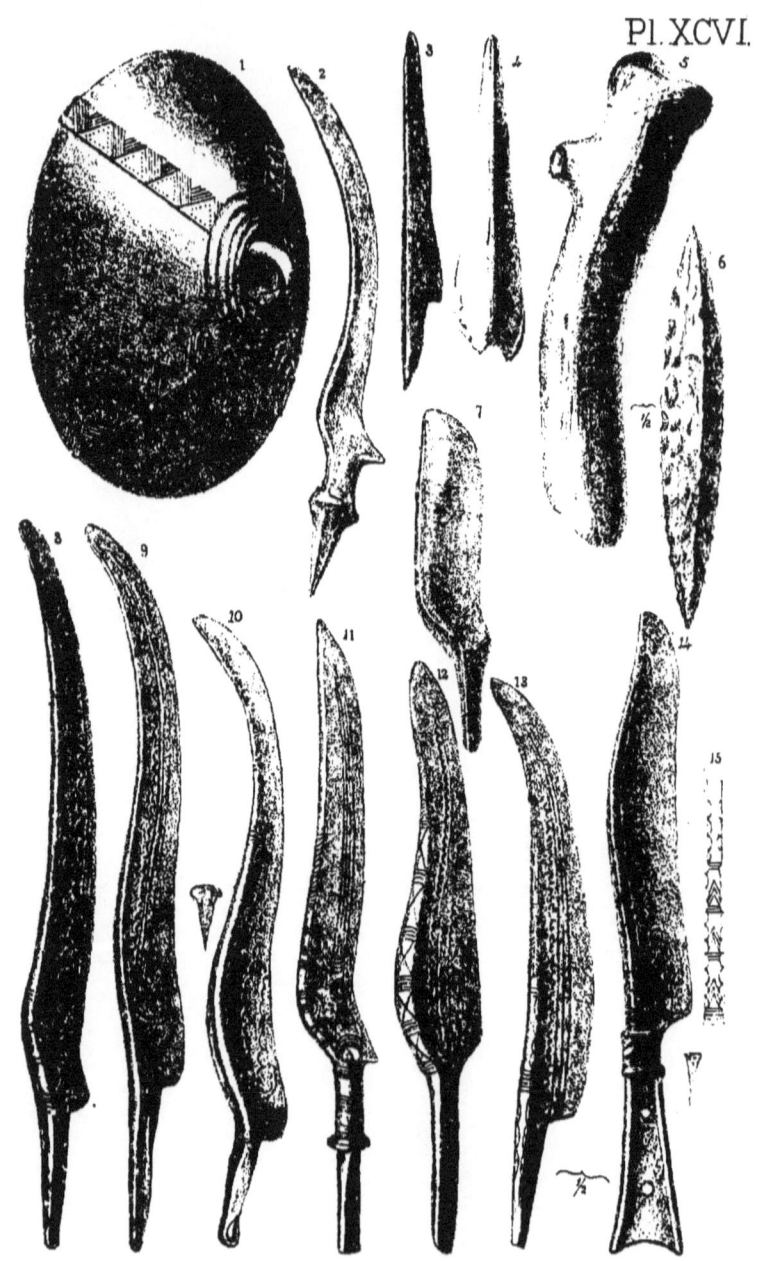

Pl. XCVI.

Pl. XCVII

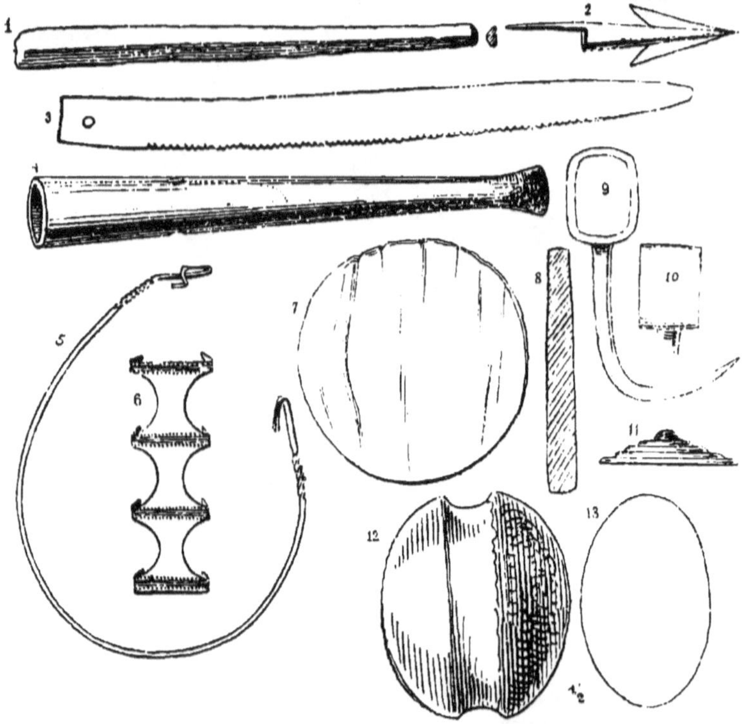

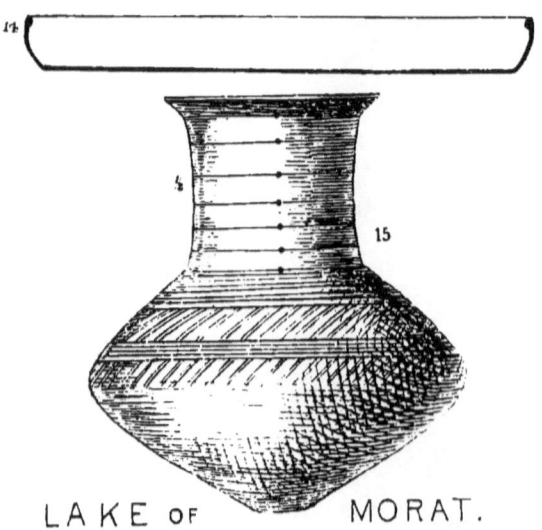

ESTAVAYER. Tin, Bronze &c.

LAKE OF MORAT.

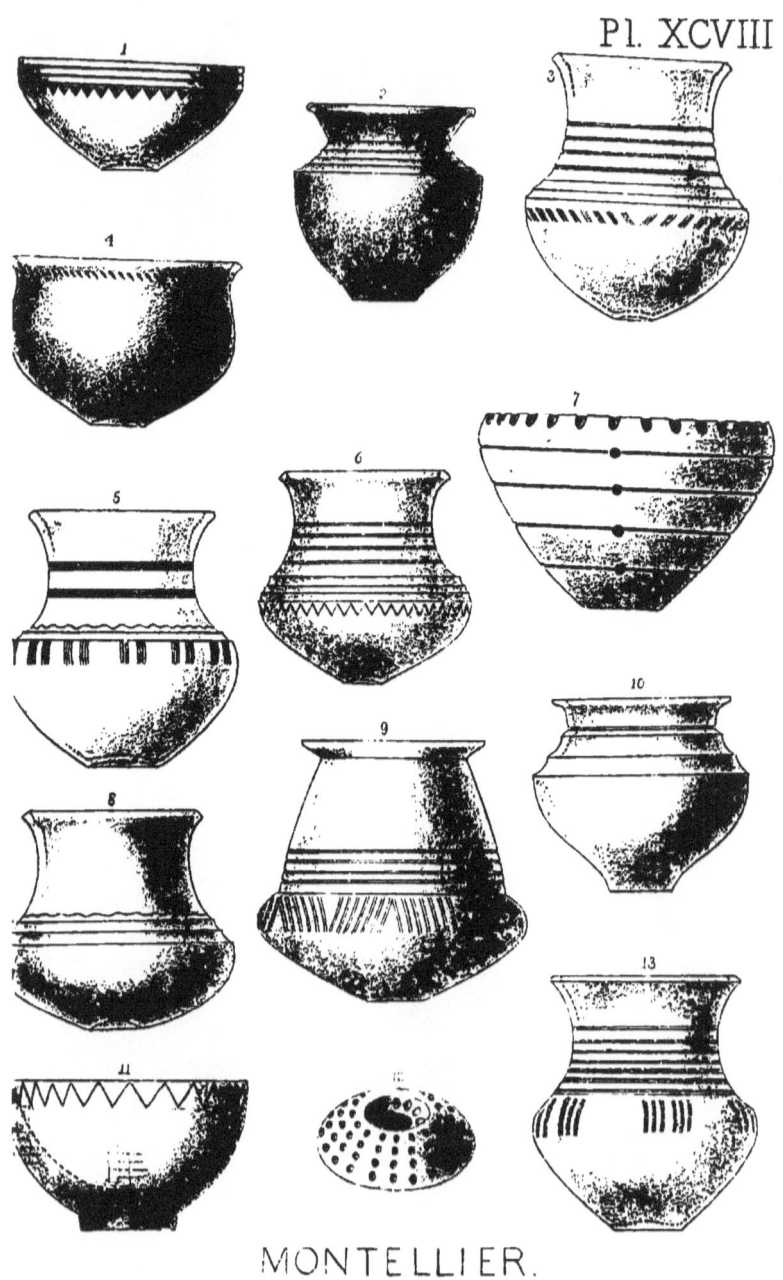

Pl. XCVIII

MONTELLIER.

Pl XCIX.

MONTELLIER.
all ⅗ except Figure Eight.

Pl. C.

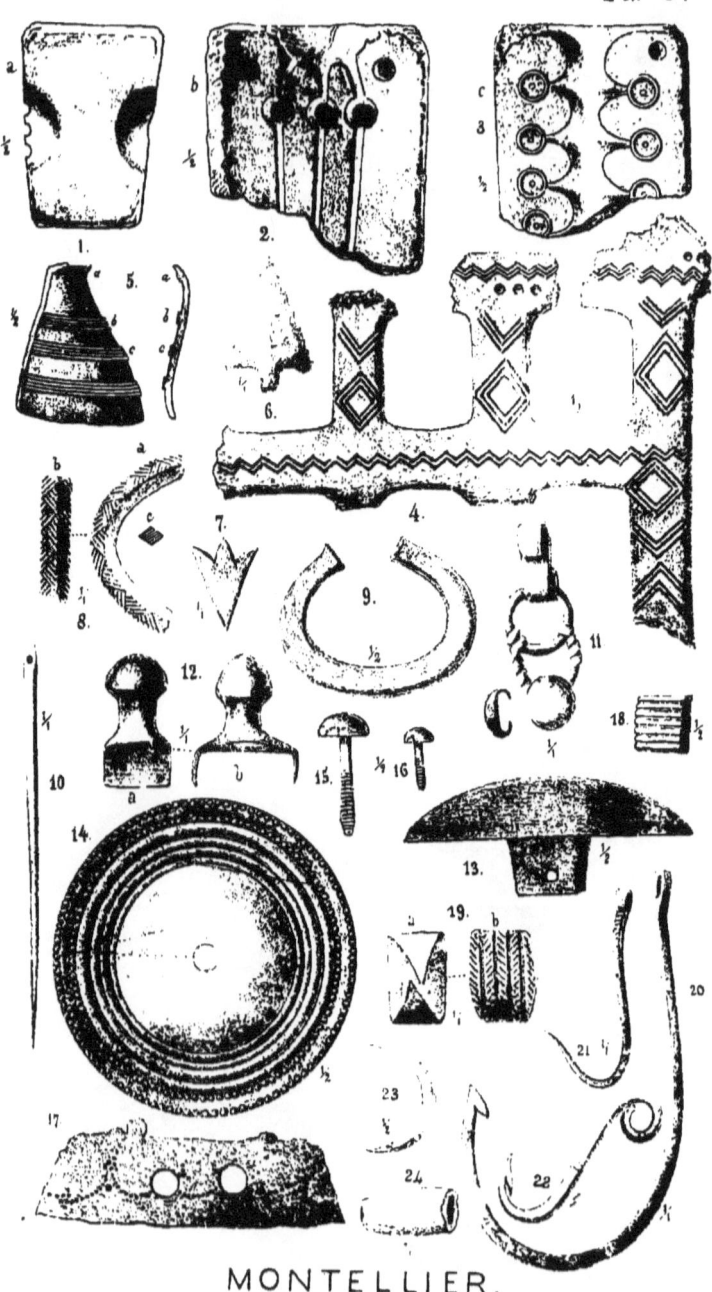

MONTELLIER.

Pl. CI.

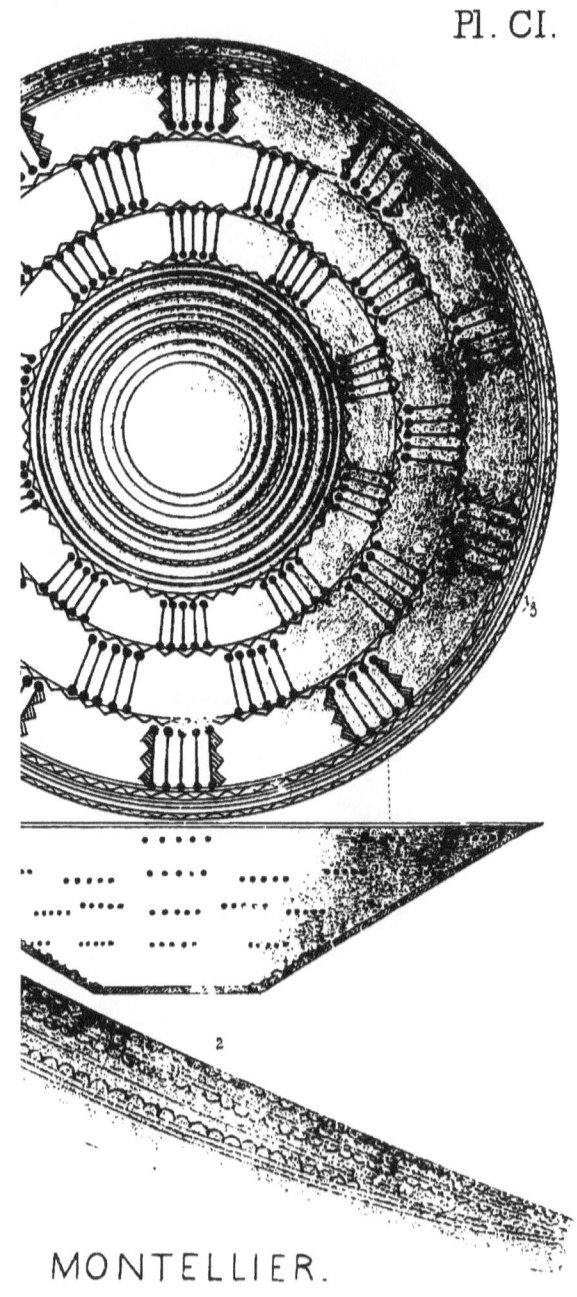

MONTELLIER.

Pl. CII.

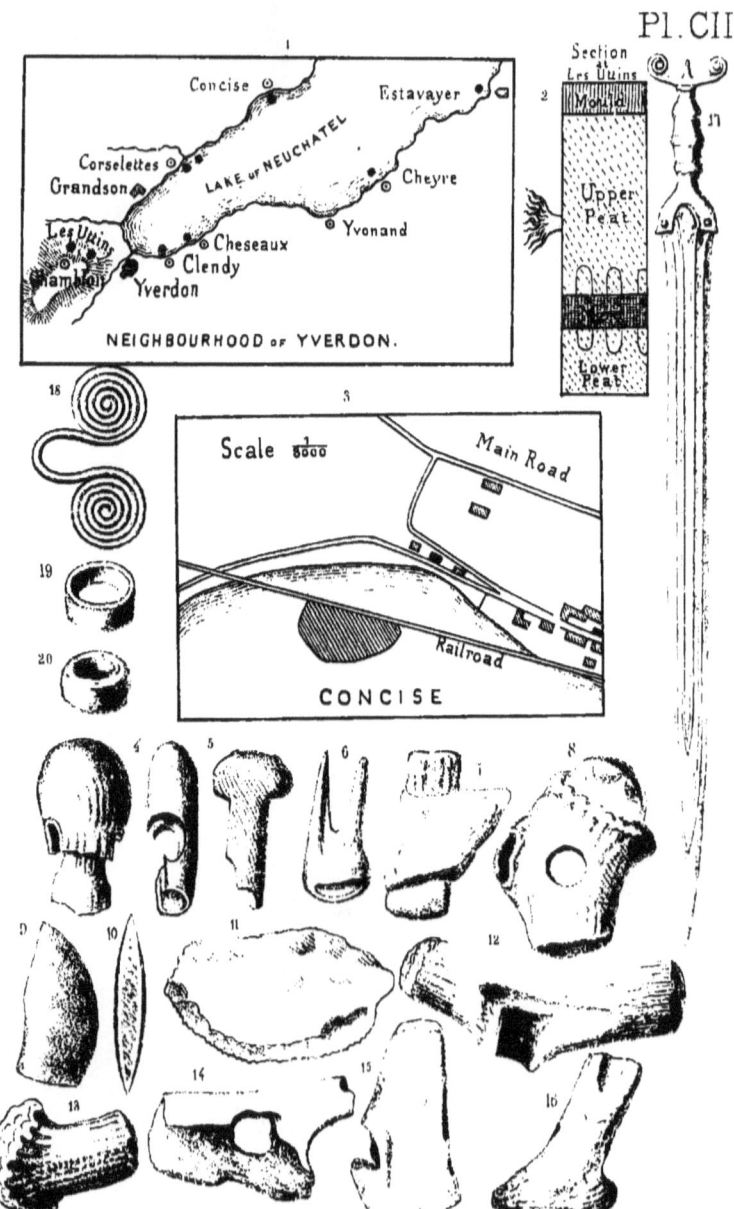

CONCISE &c.

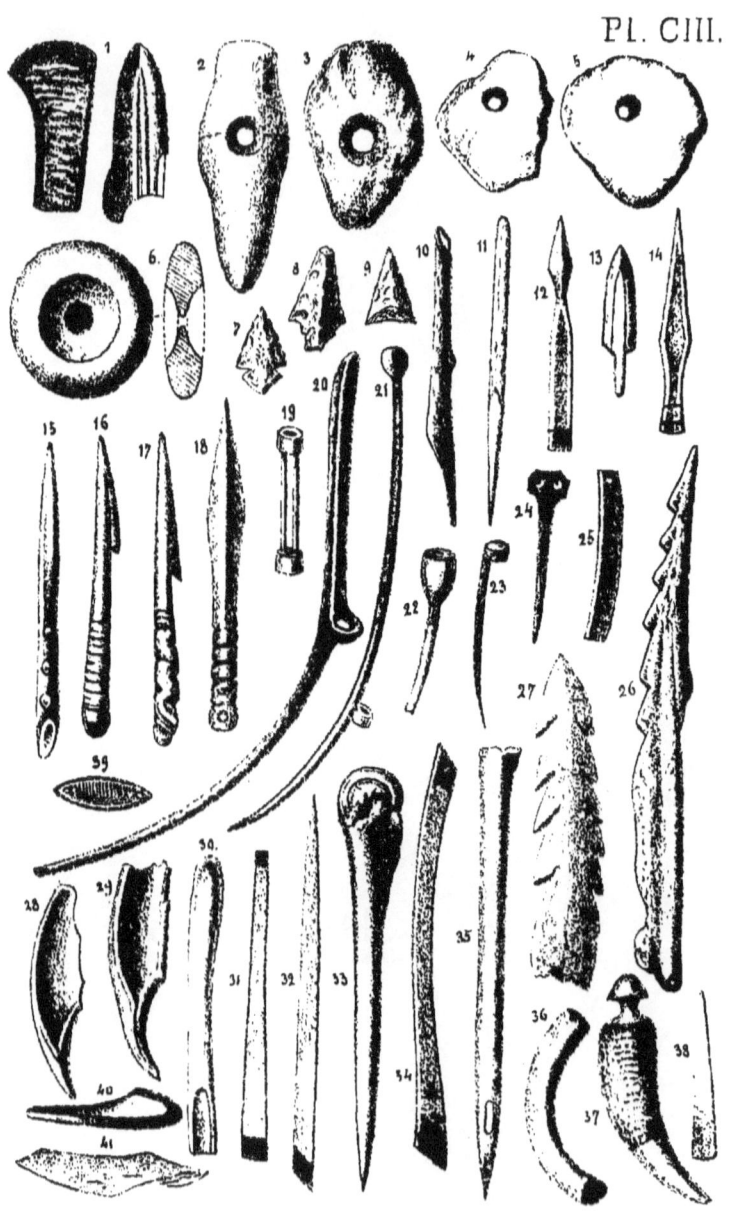

Pl. CIII.

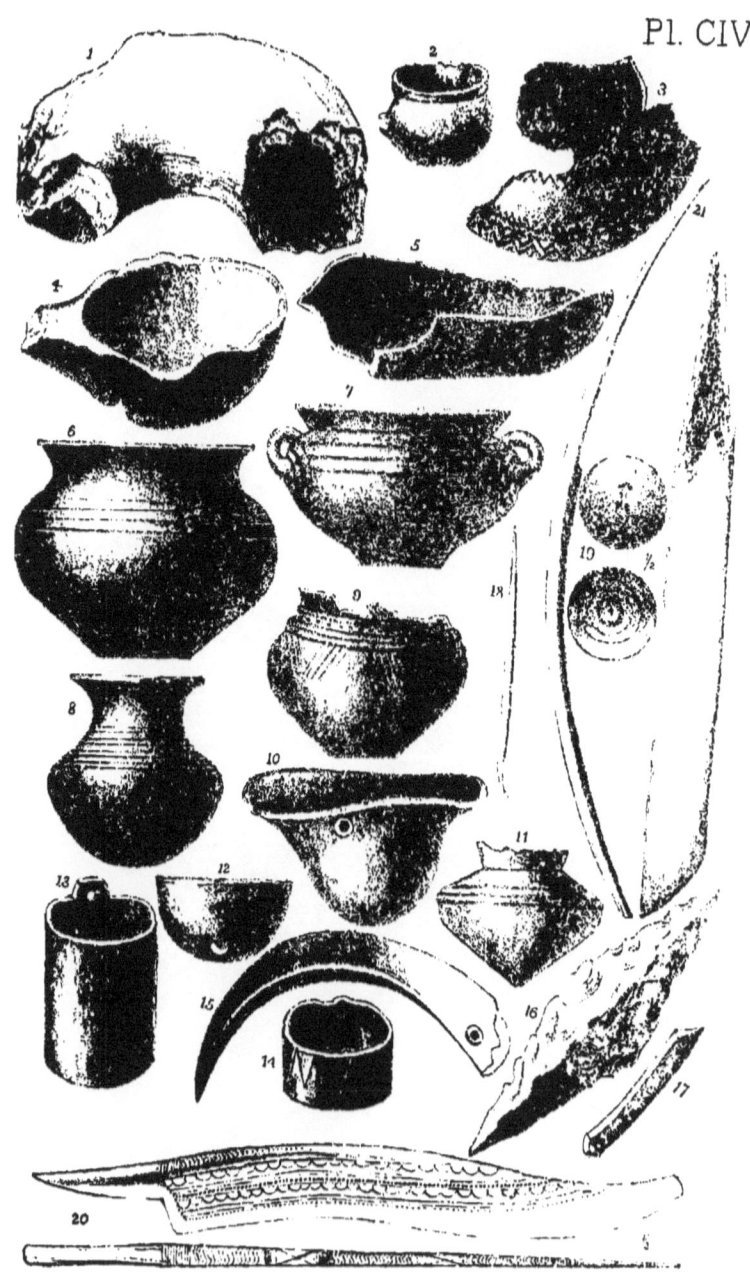

Pl. CIV.

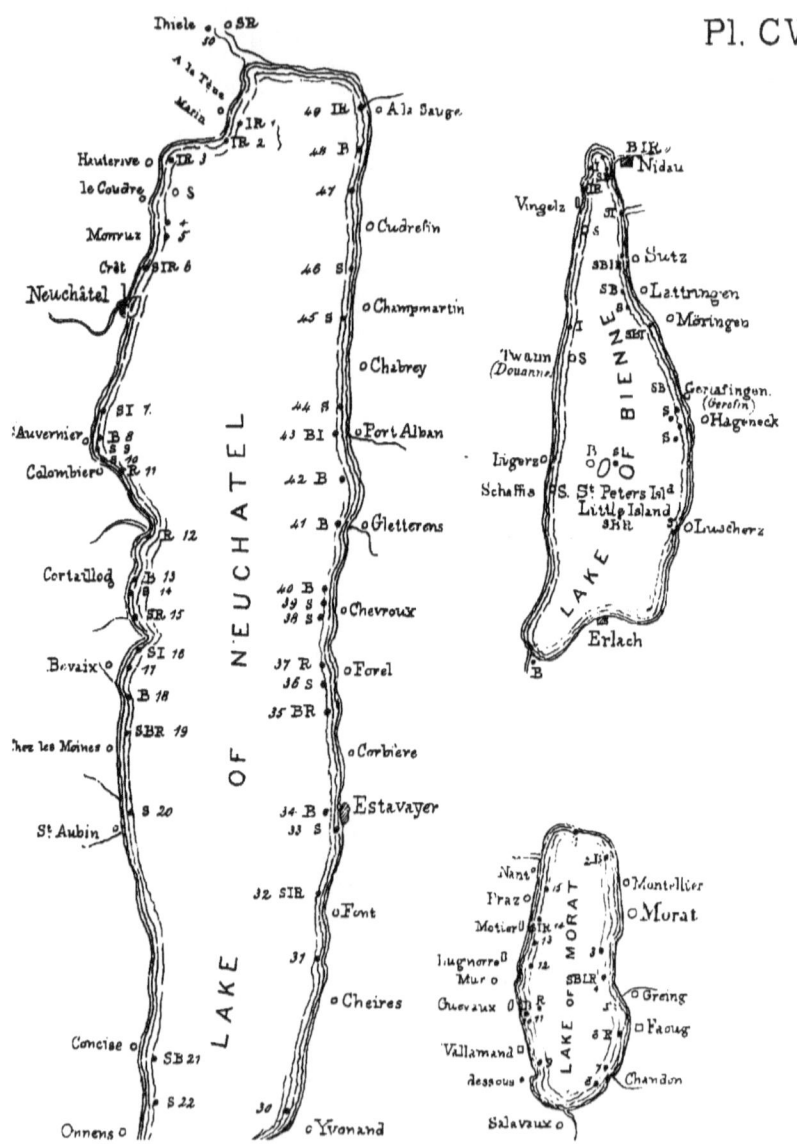

Pl. CV.

Pl. CVI.

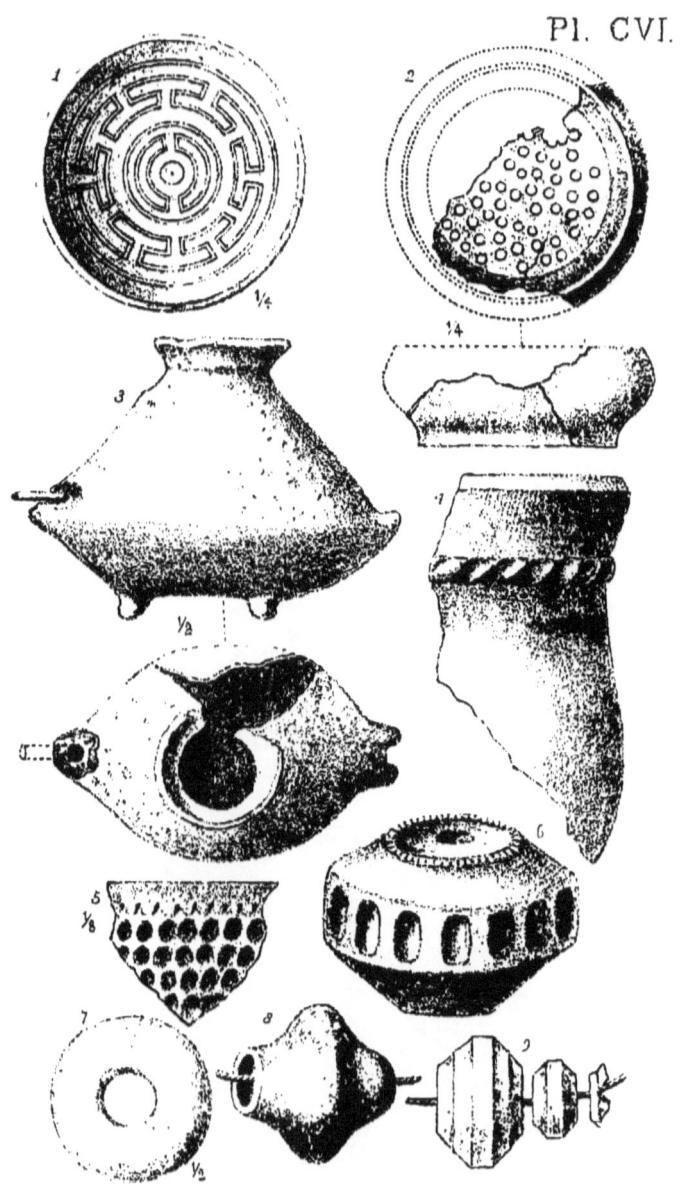

LAKE OF BOURGET.

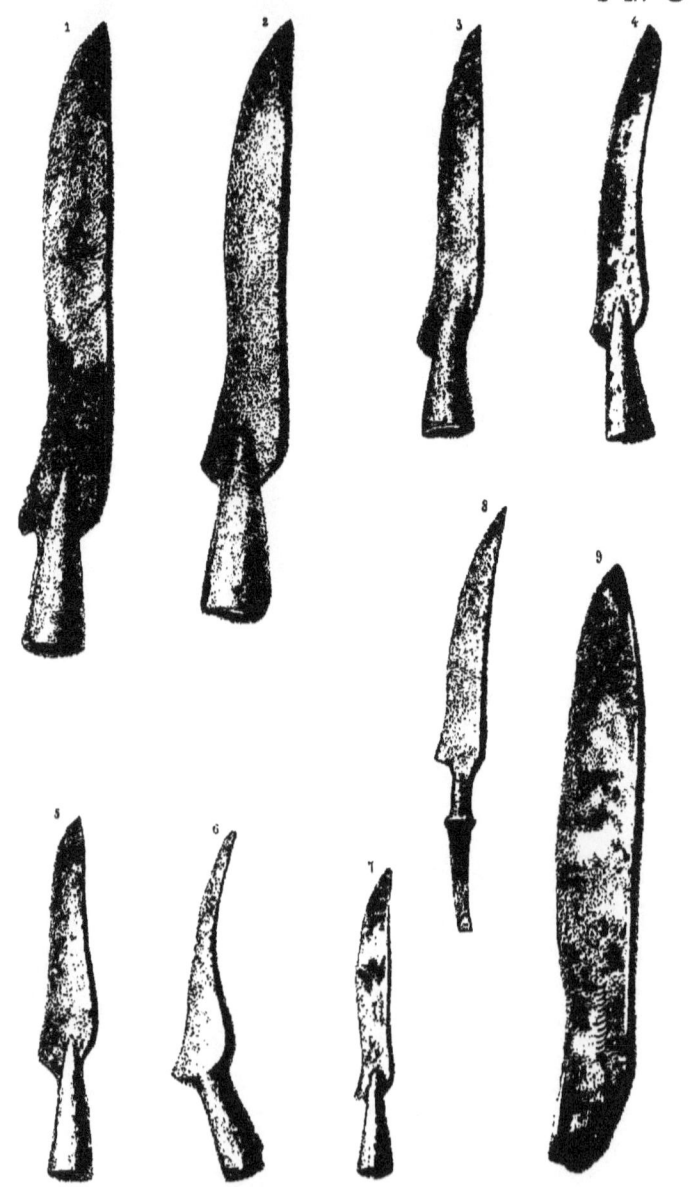

Pl. CVII.

LAKE OF BOURGET, *Bronze.*

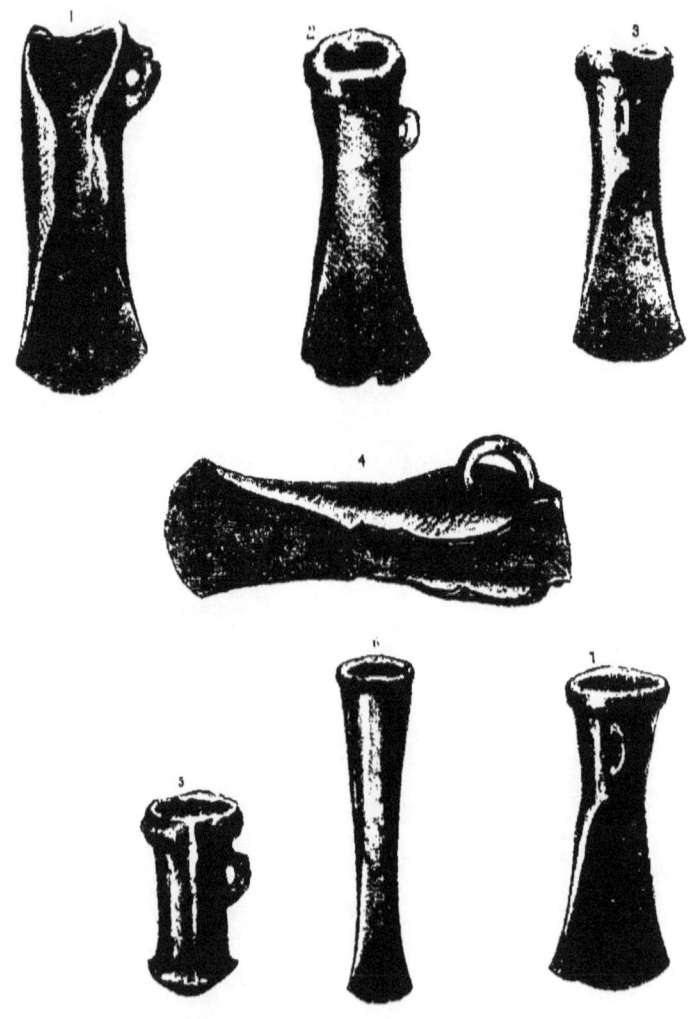

LAKE OF BOURGET. *Bronze.*

Pl CIX

LAKE OF BOURGET *Pottery*

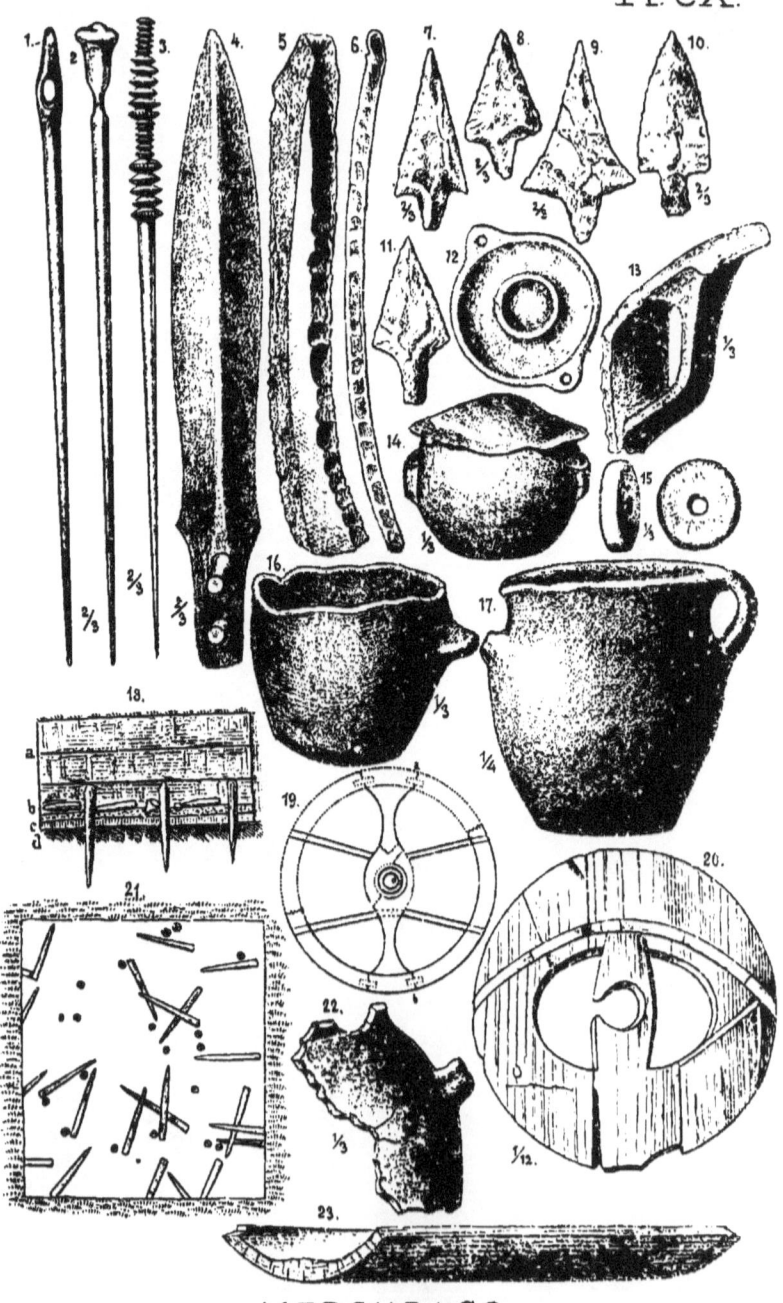

Pl. CX.

MERCURAGO.

Pl. CXI.

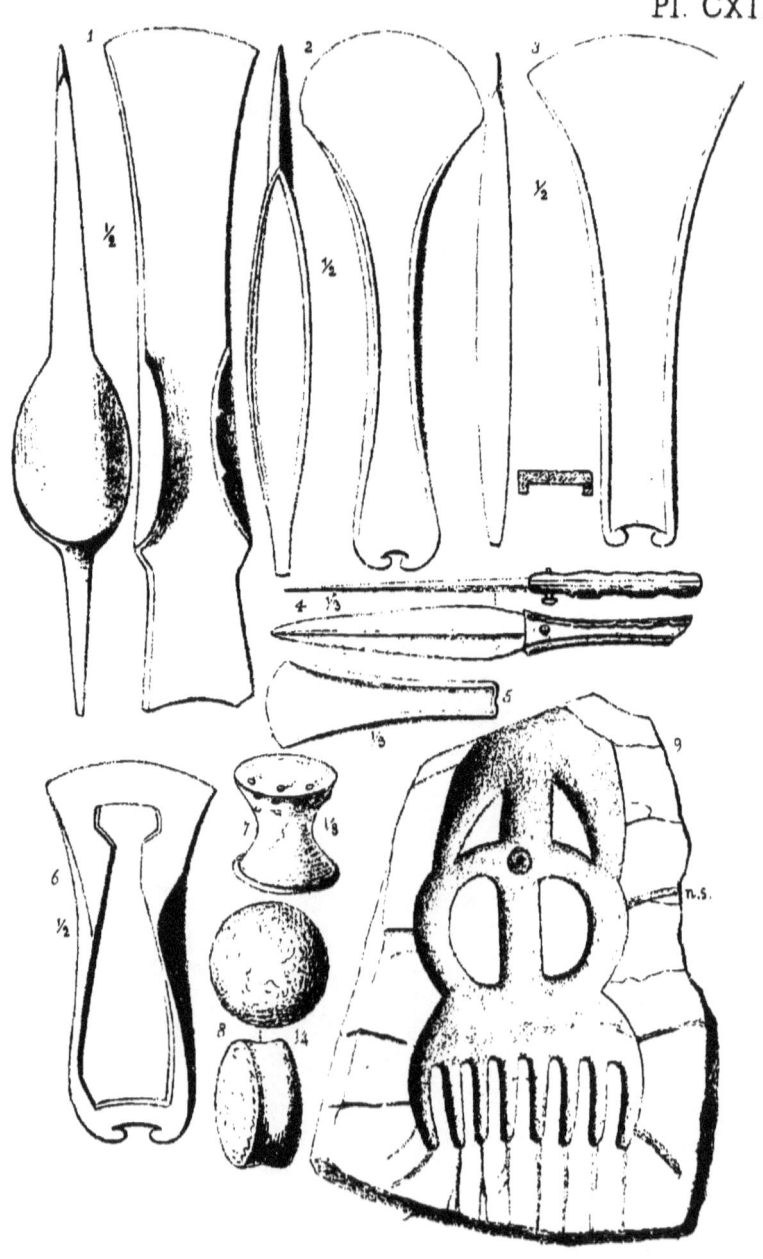

TERRAMARA.

Pl CXII

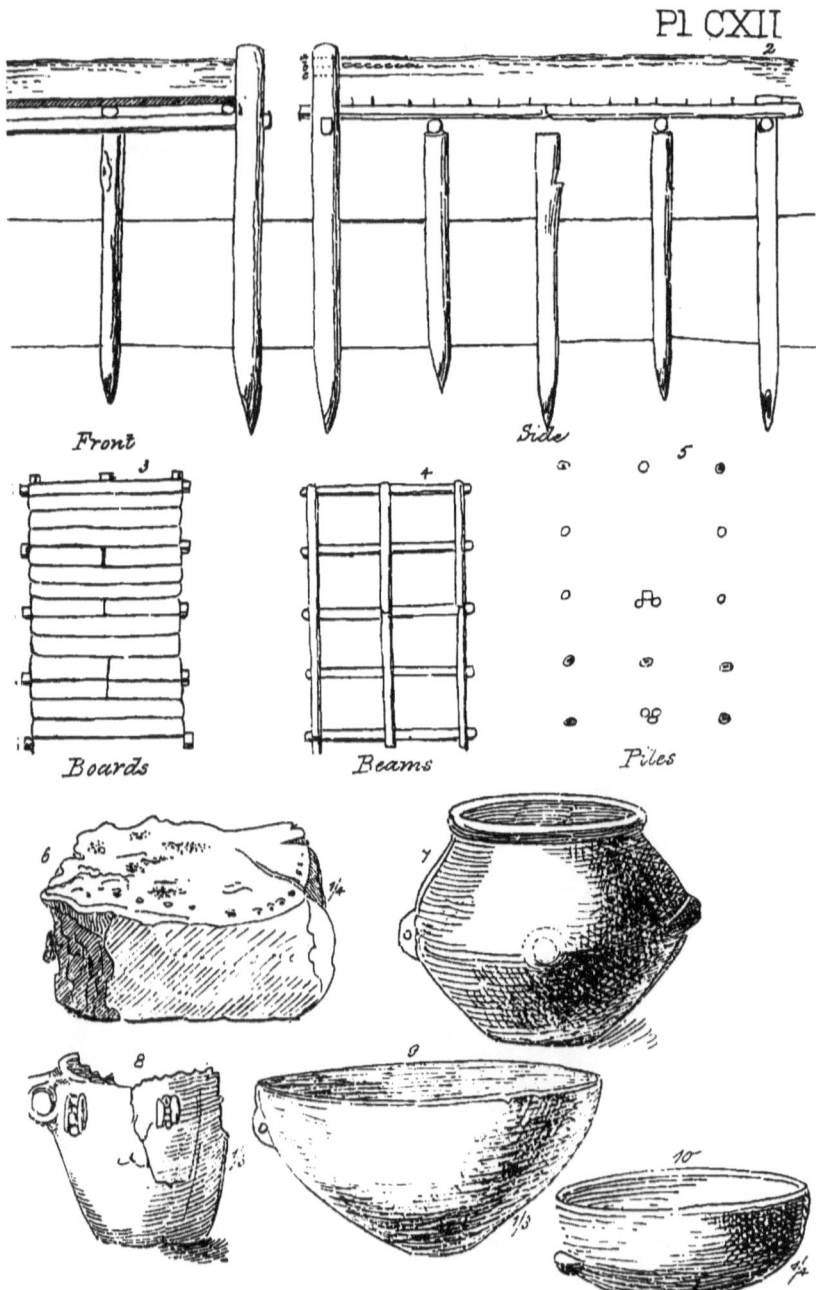

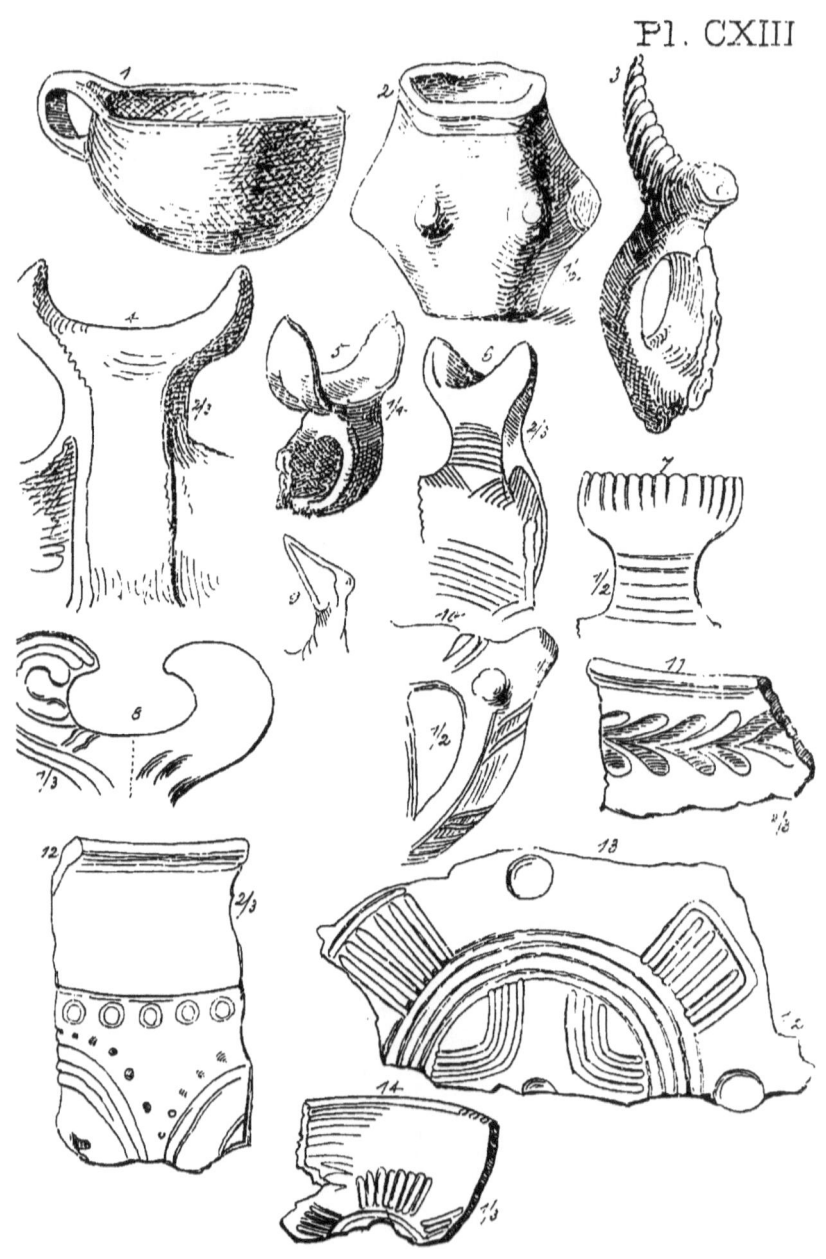

Pl. CXIII

TERRAMARA.

Pl. CXIV.

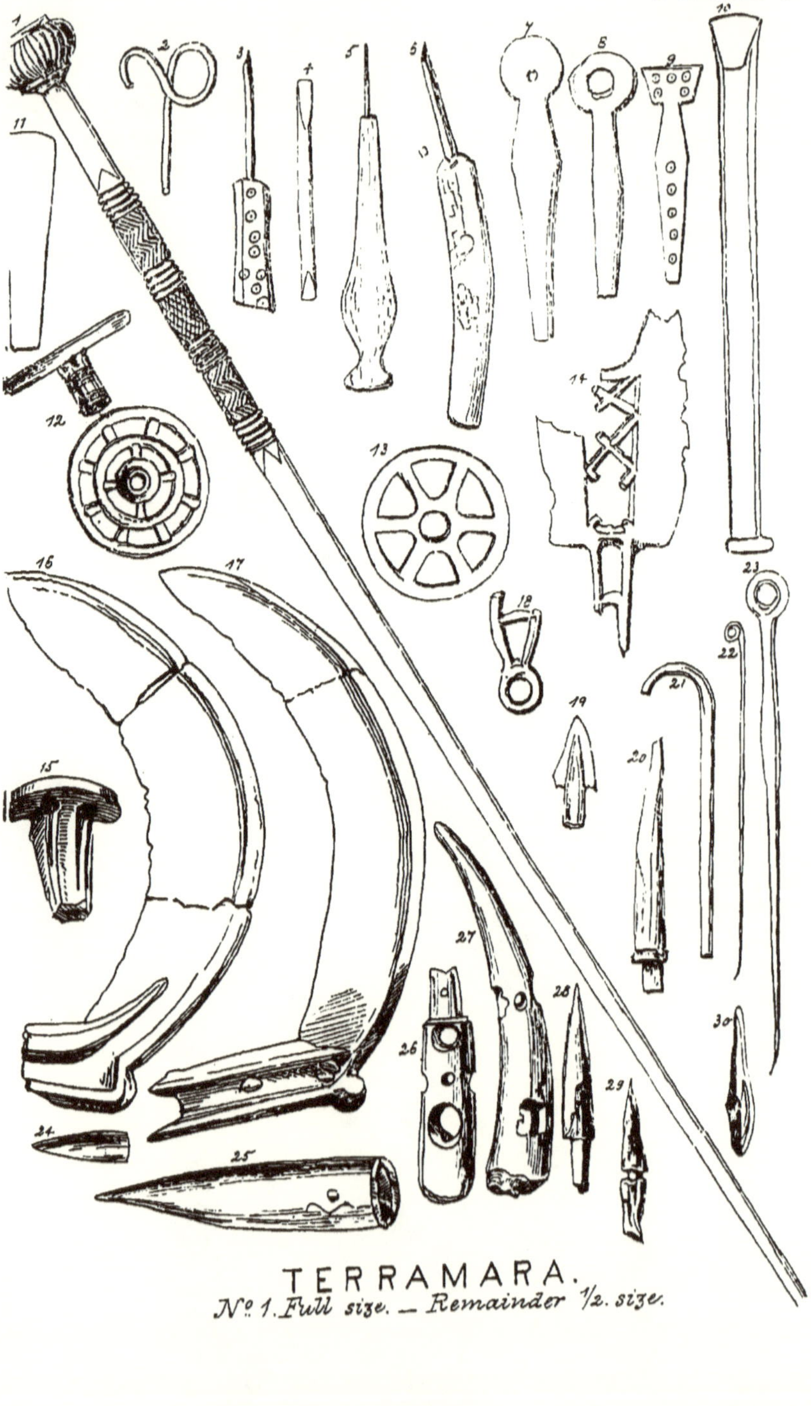

TERRAMARA.
N.º 1. Full size. — Remainder ½ size.

Pl. CXV.

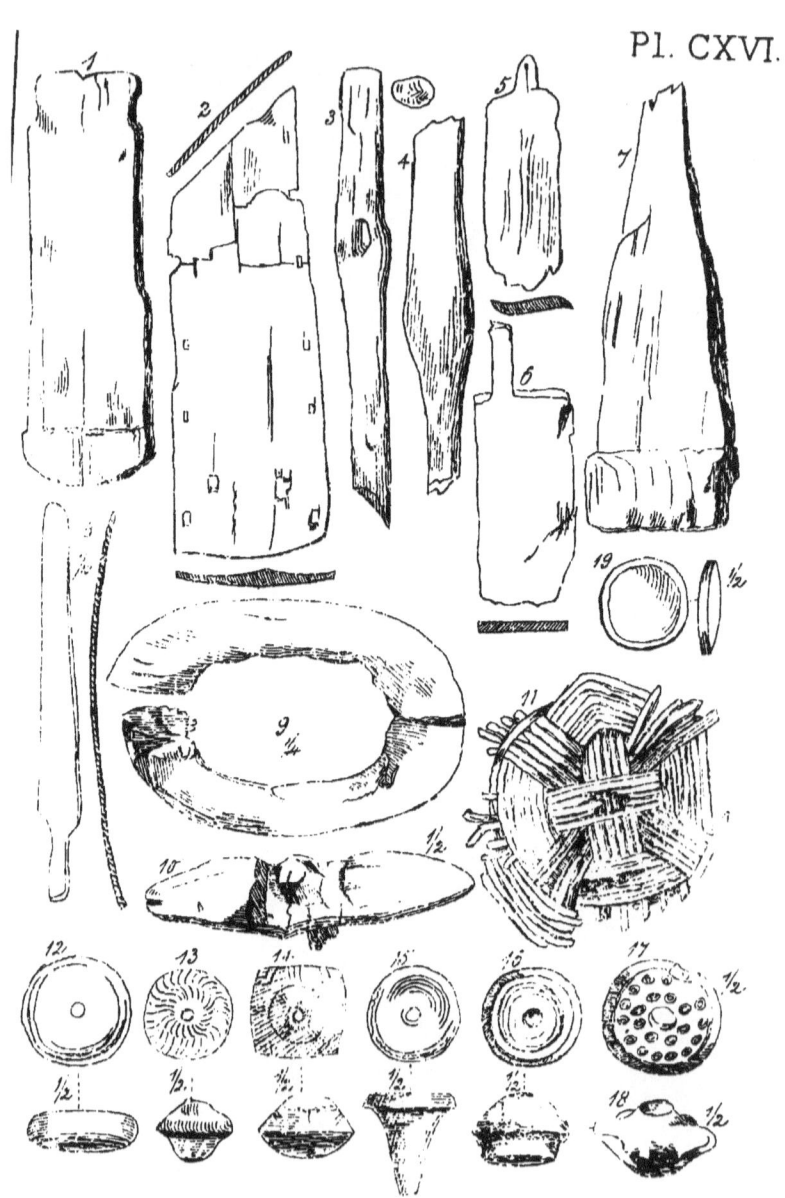

Pl. CXVI.

Pl. CXVII.

FOR COMPARISON

near the Lago di Viverone

IVREA

CUMAROLA near MODENA

SESTO CALENDE

IMOLA

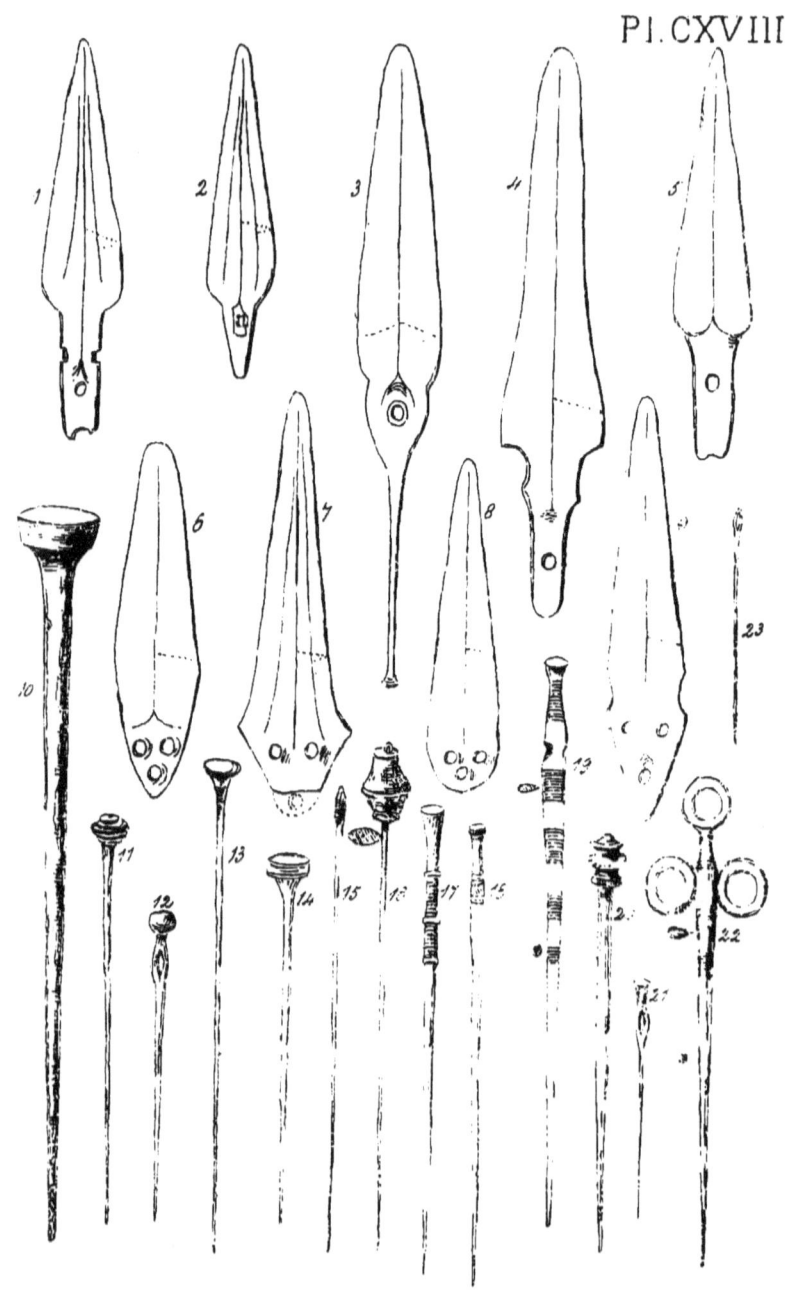

Pl. CXVIII

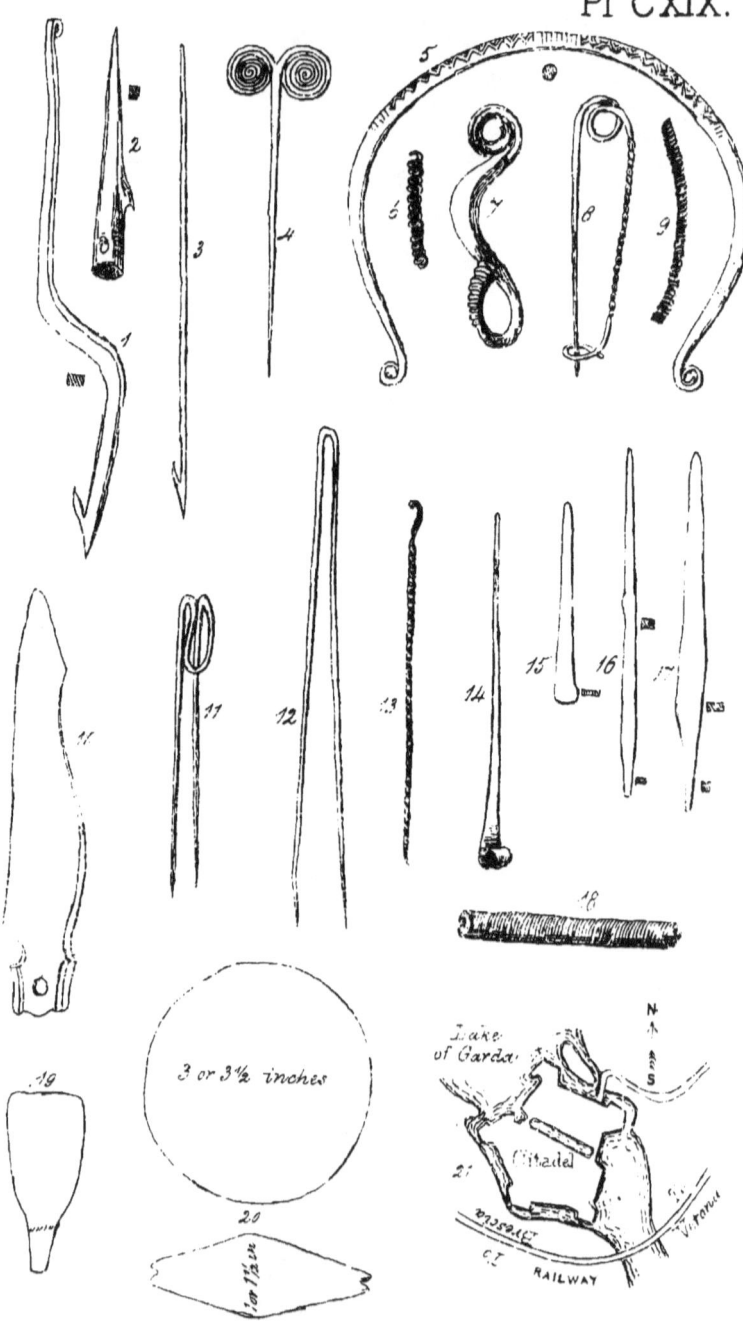

Pl CXIX.

PESCHIERA
Bronze. Copper. Stone: Fig: 1. to 20. half Size.

FOR COMPARISON. Pl. CXX.

(½ Full Size)

IMPLEMENTS OF COPPER FROM HUNGARY.
MAINLAND.

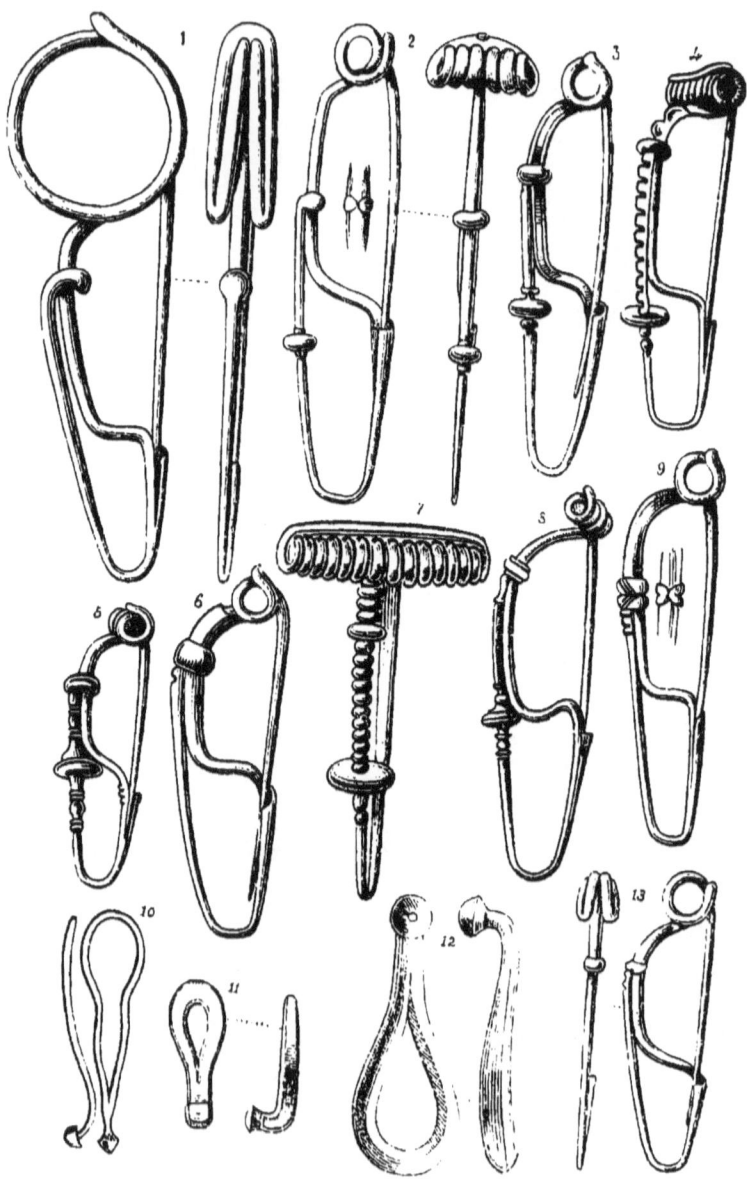

Pl. CXXII.

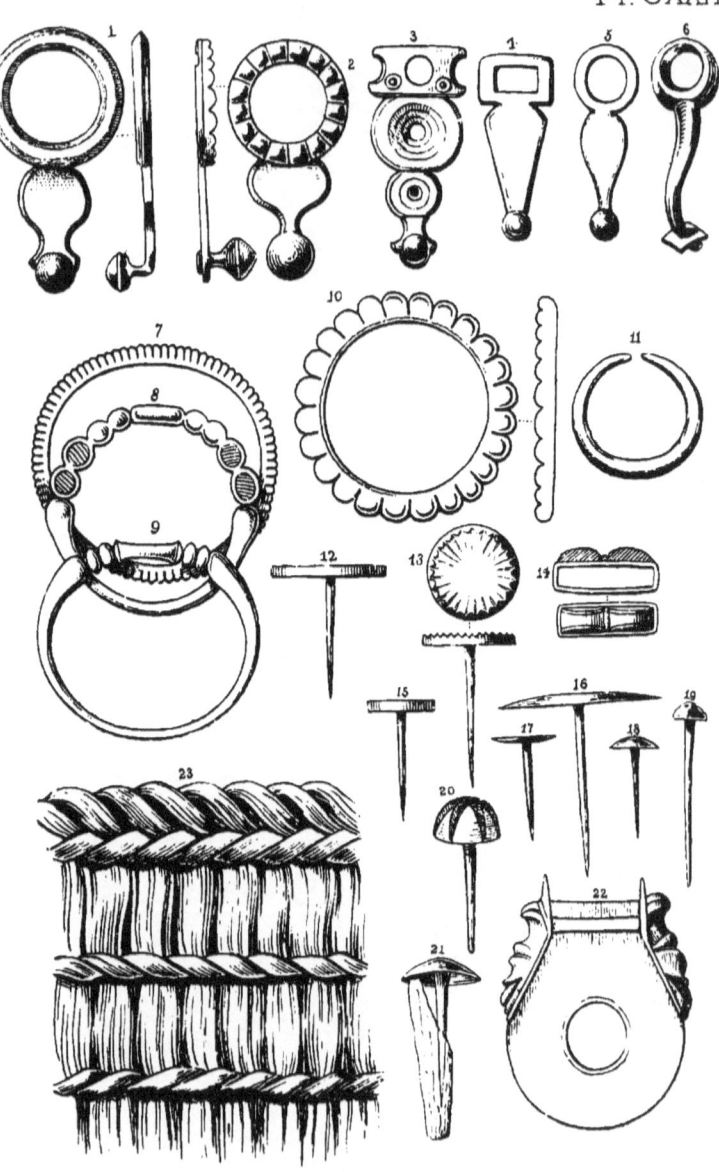

MARIN.
Fig 22 Full size – Rem ⅔ size.

Pl. CXXIII.

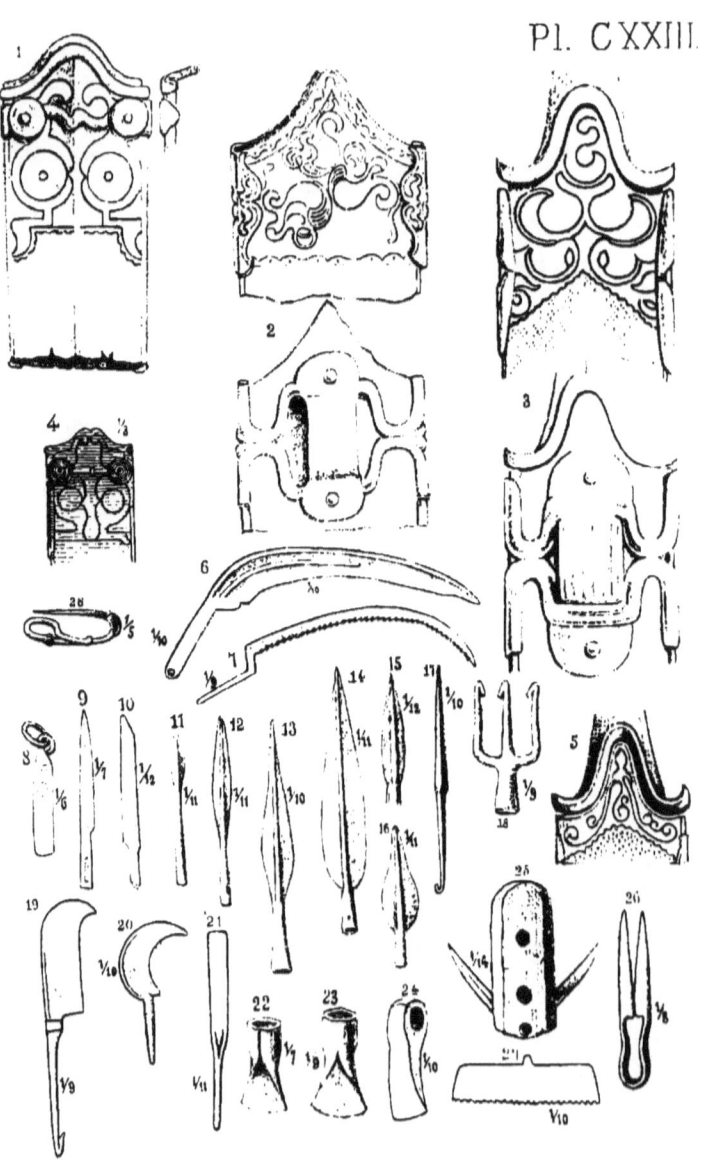

MARIN

Pl. CXXIV.

MARIN &c.

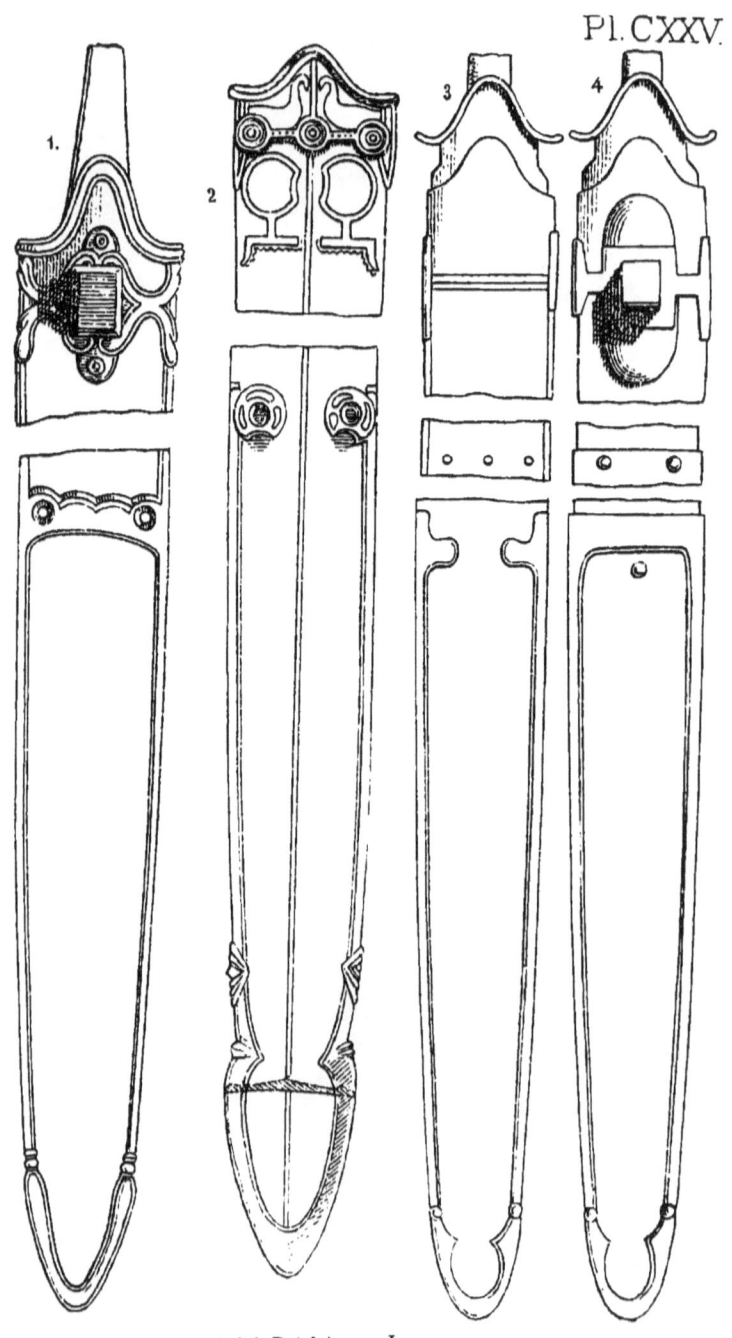

Pl. CXXV.

MARIN – *Iron.*

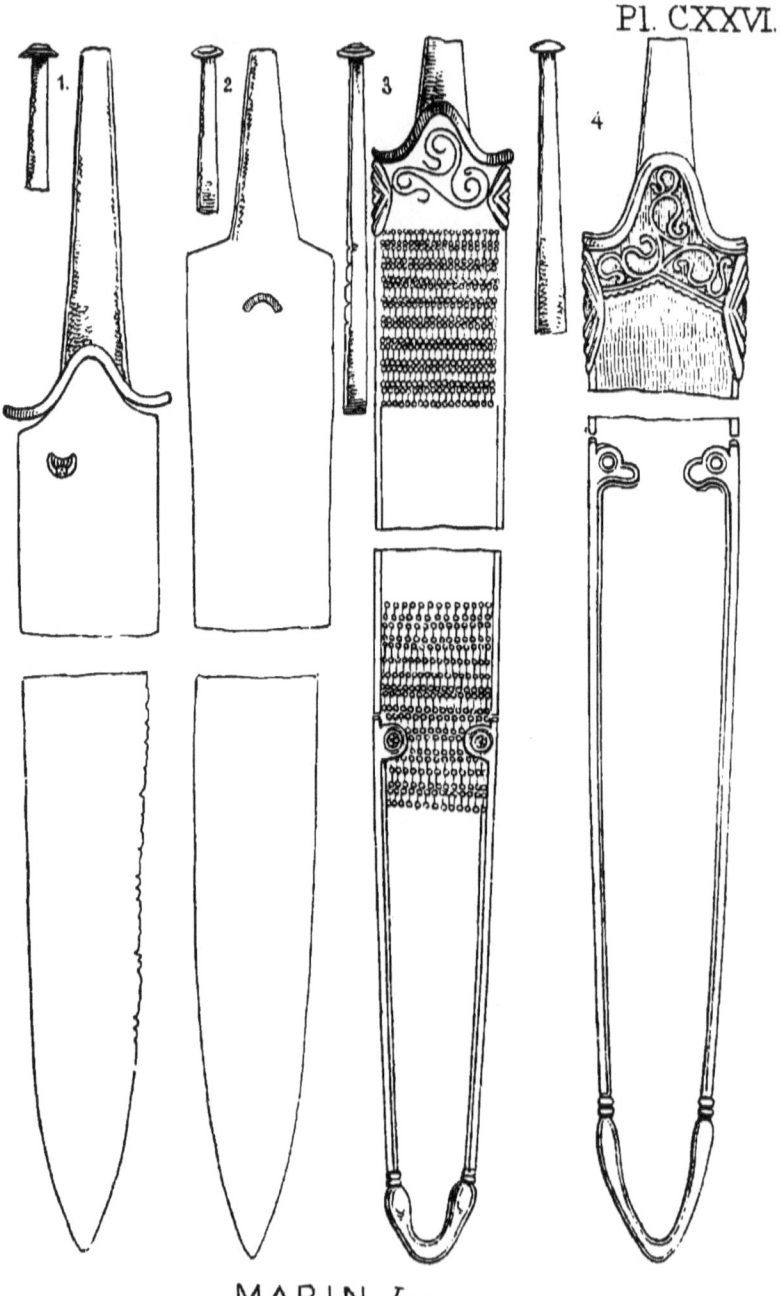

Pl. CXXVI.

MARIN-*Iron*.

Pl. CXXVII

MARIN *Iron*

Pl. CXXVIII.

MARIN *Iron.*

Pl. CXXIX.

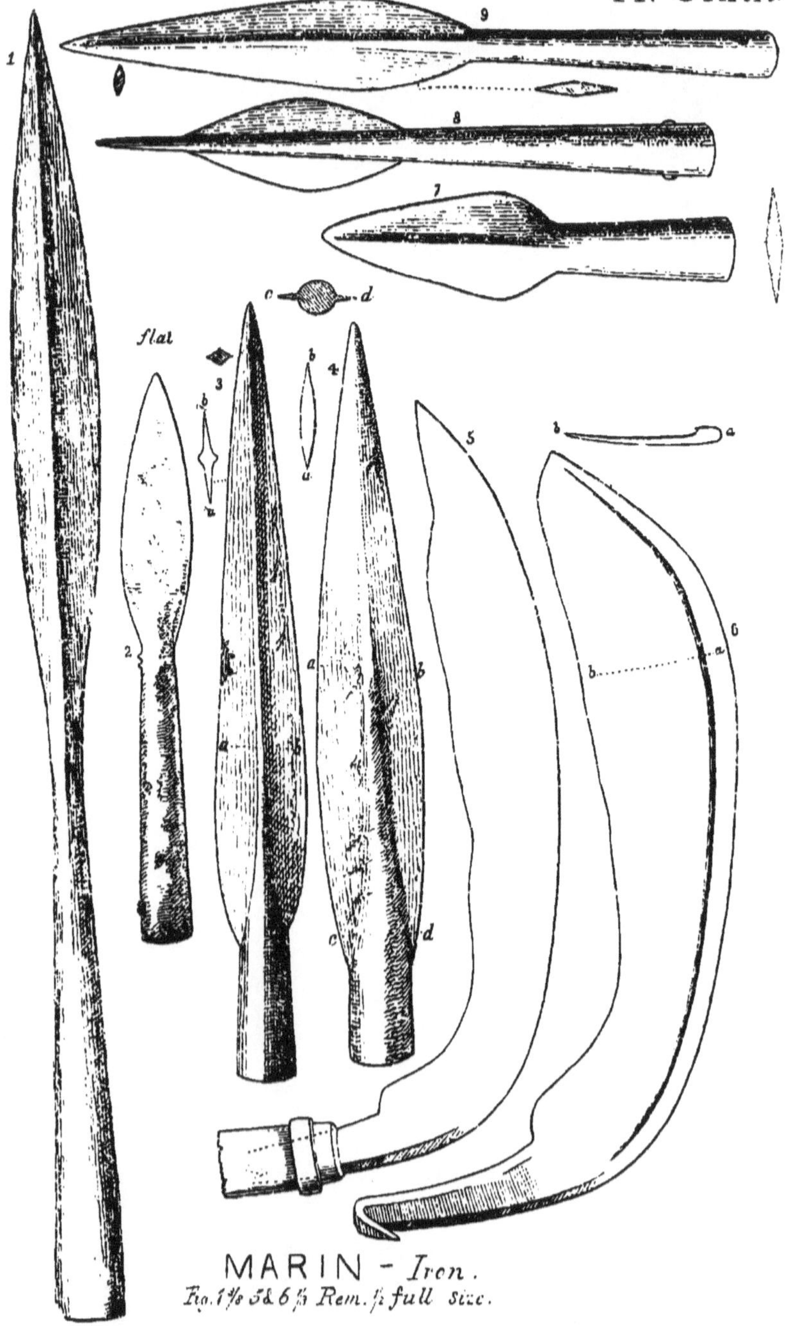

Pl. CXXX.

MARIN – Iron.
Fig. 1 ⅛. 5 & 6 ⅓. Rem. ½ full size.

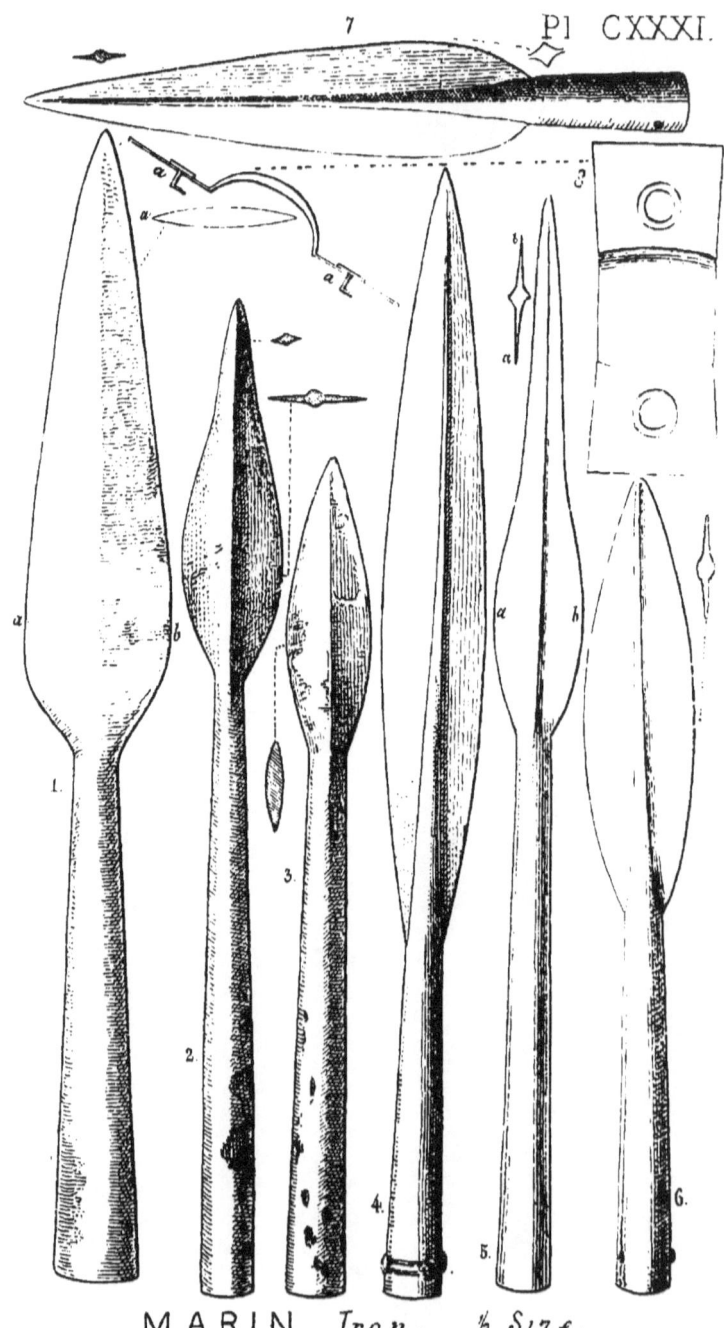

Pl CXXXI.

MARIN *Iron.* ½ Size.

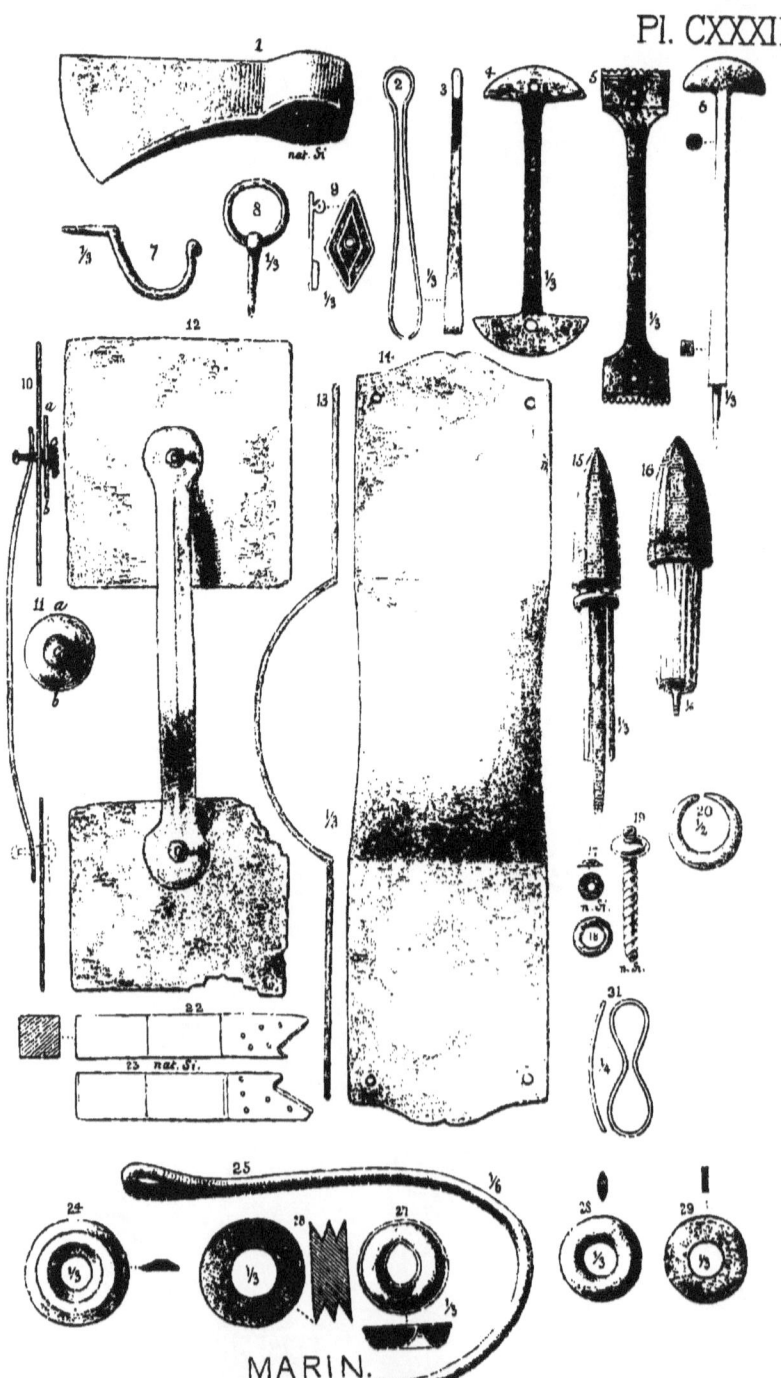

Pl. CXXXII.

MARIN.

Pl. CXXXIII.

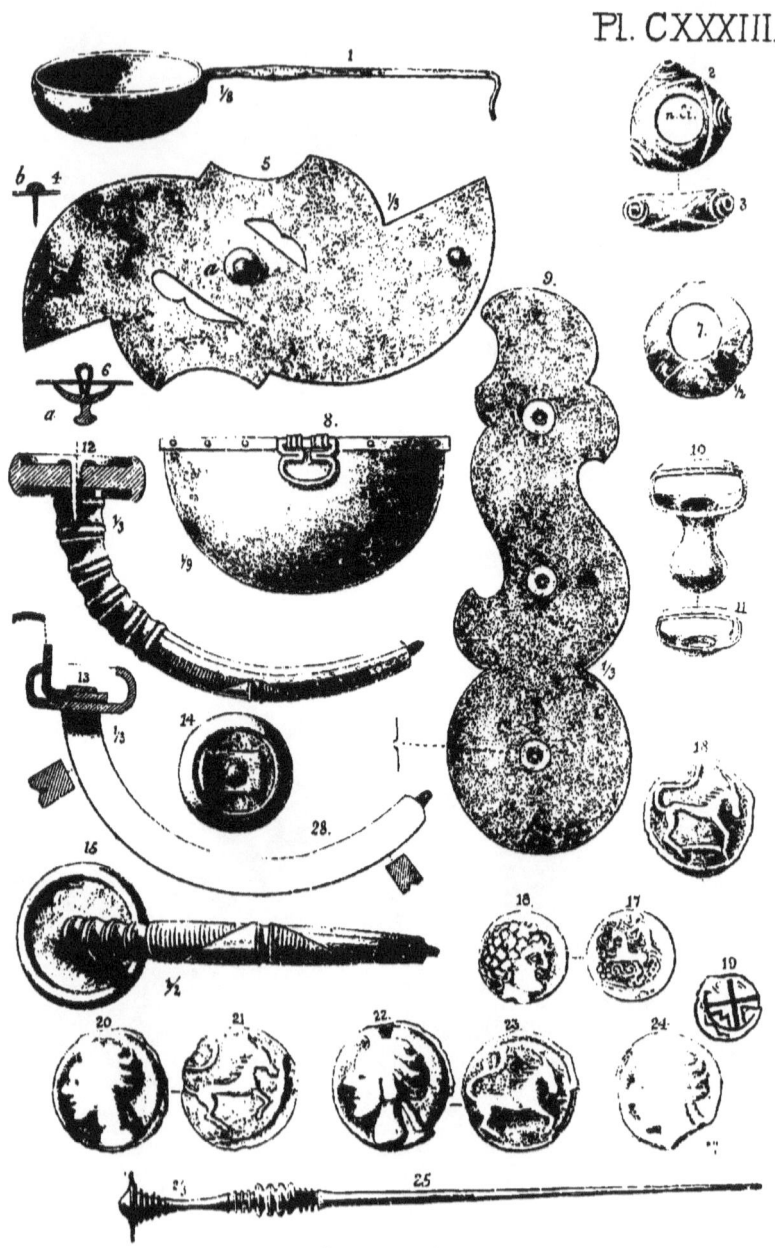

MARIN.

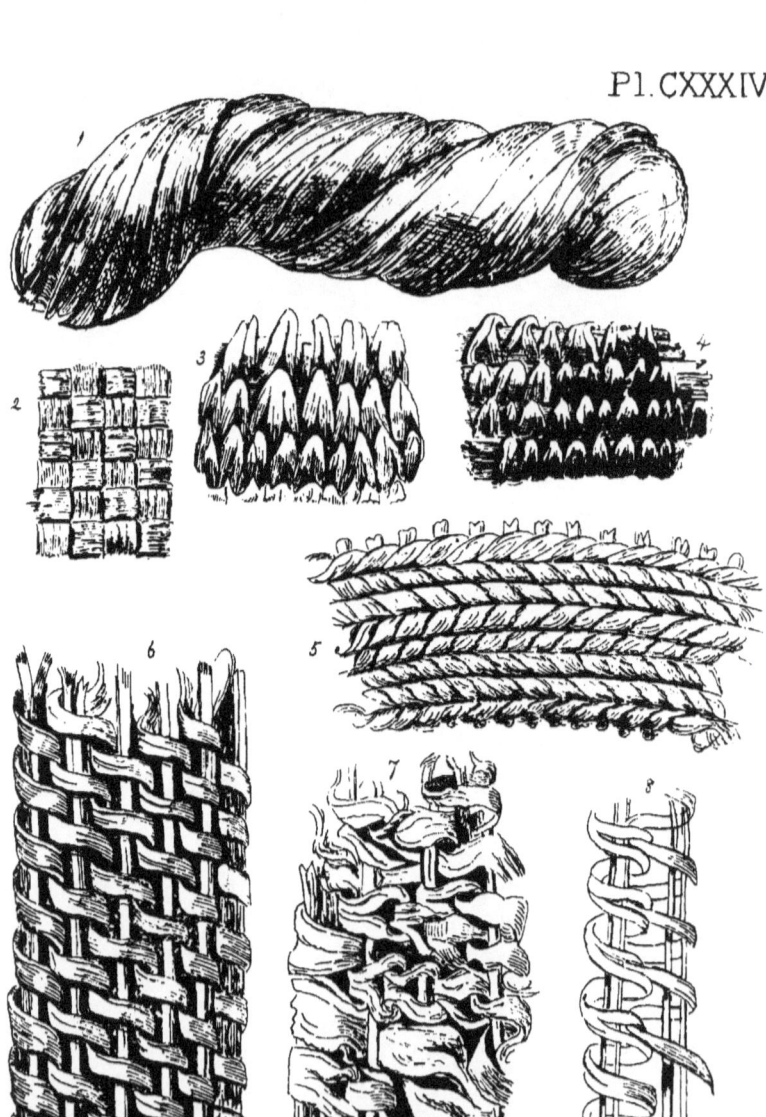

Pl. CXXXIV.

ROBENHAUSEN & WANGEN.
Bast. &c.

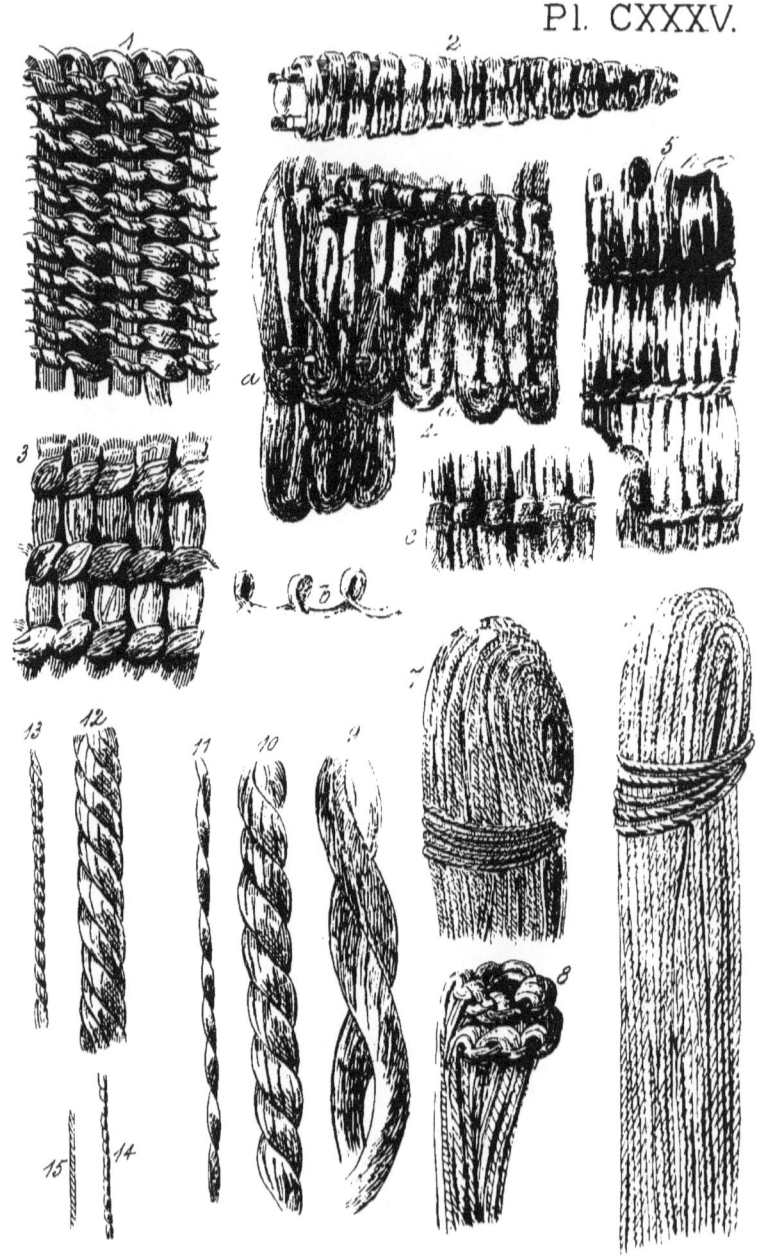

Pl. CXXXV.

ROBENHAUSEN & WANGEN.
Bast & Flax.

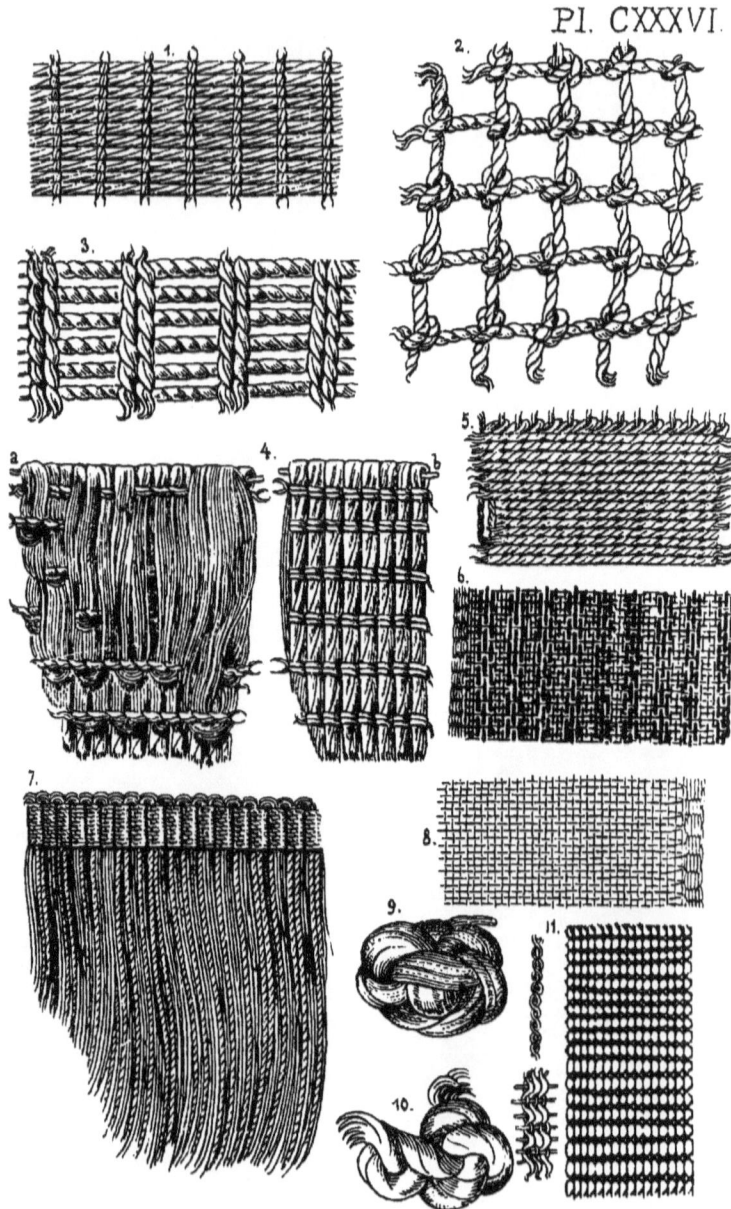

Pl. CXXXVI.

ROBENHAUSEN & WANGEN.
Flax.

Pl. CXXXVII.

ROBENHAUSEN &c   *Flax.*

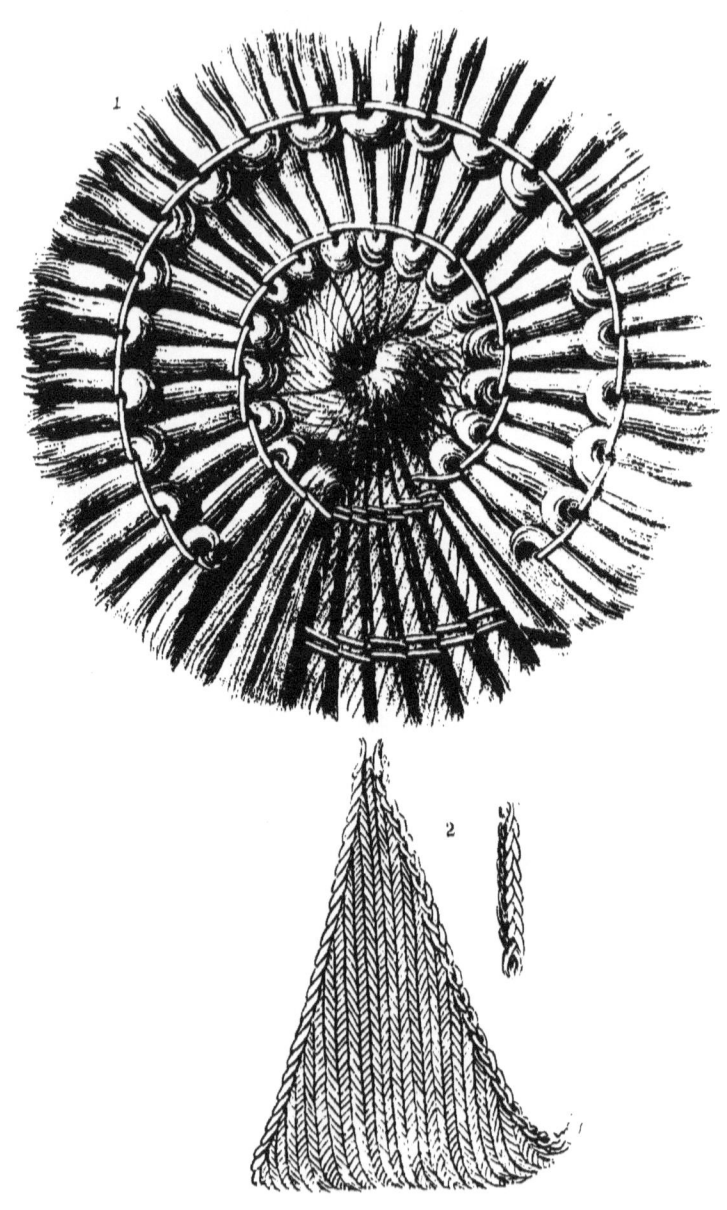

WANGEN & CORTAILLOD.

Pl. CXXXIX.

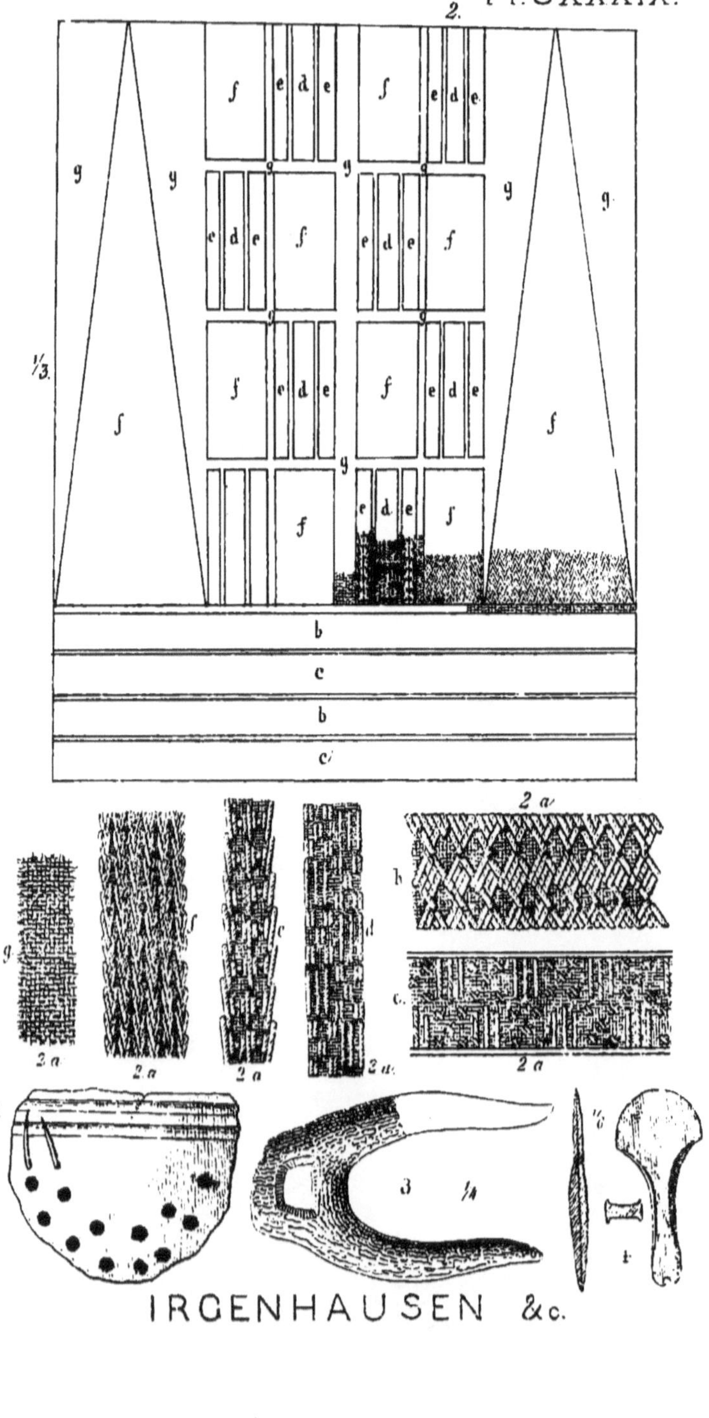

IRGENHAUSEN &c.

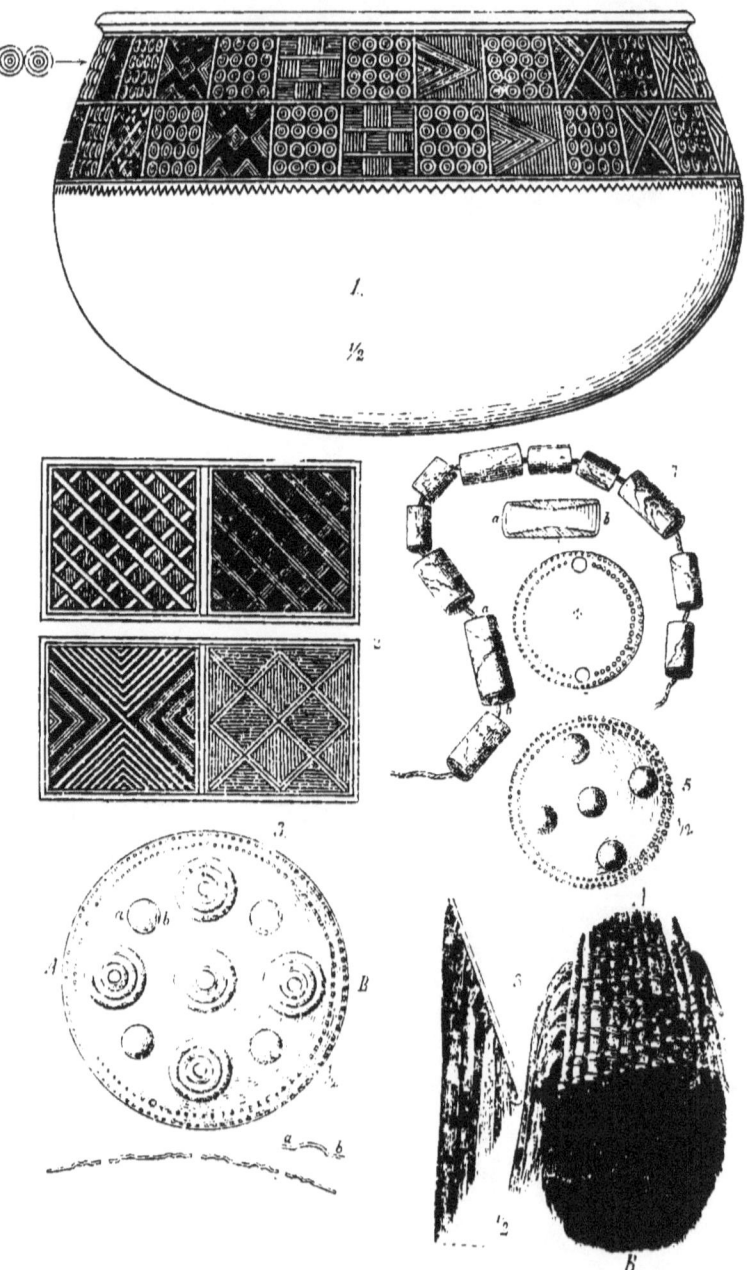

Pl. CXL.

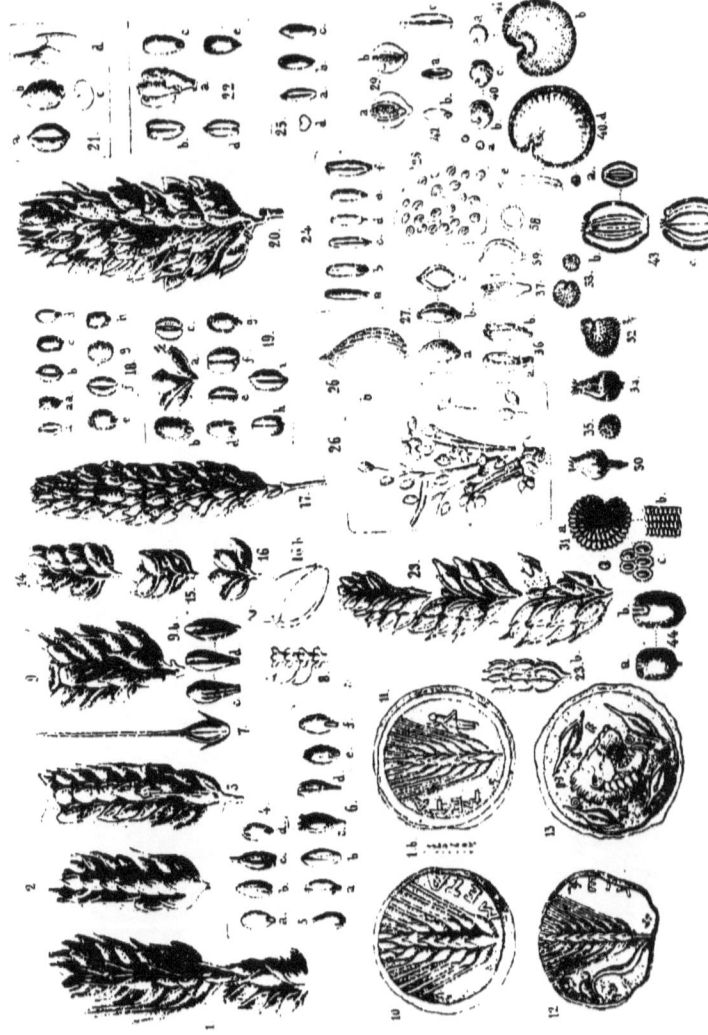

Pl. CXLI

PLANTS & SEEDS.

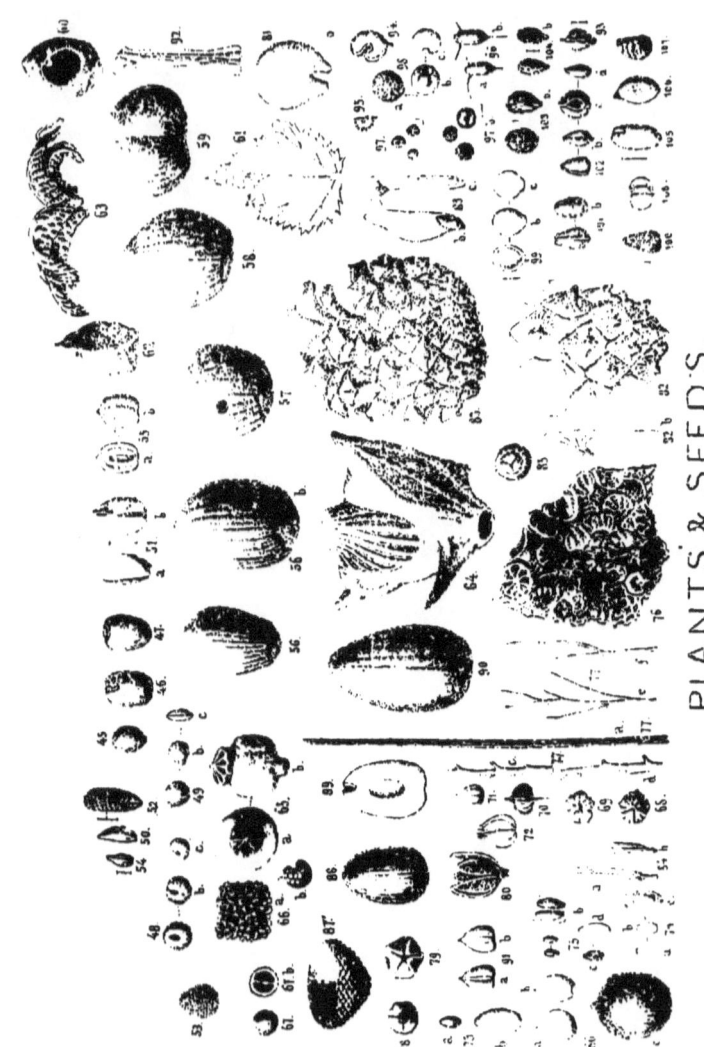

PLANTS & SEEDS.

Pl. CXLIII.

FOR COMPARISON MAIN LAND.

EBERSBERG.

Pl. CXLIV.

FOR COMPARISON   MAINLAND

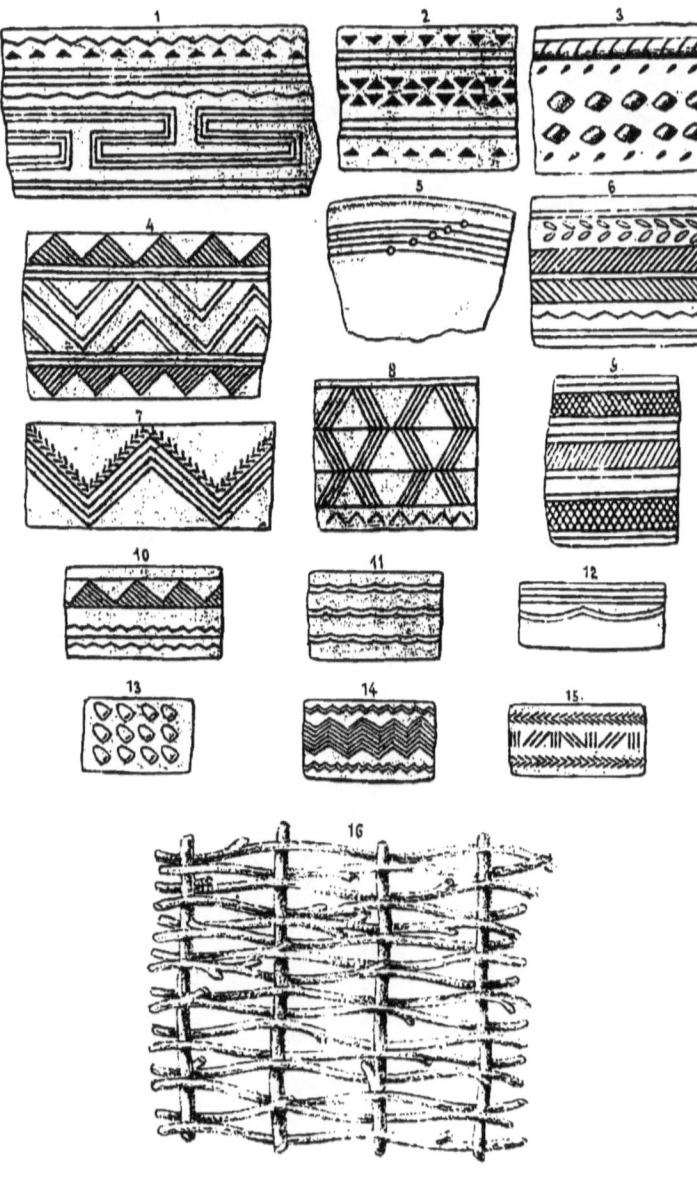

EBERSBERG

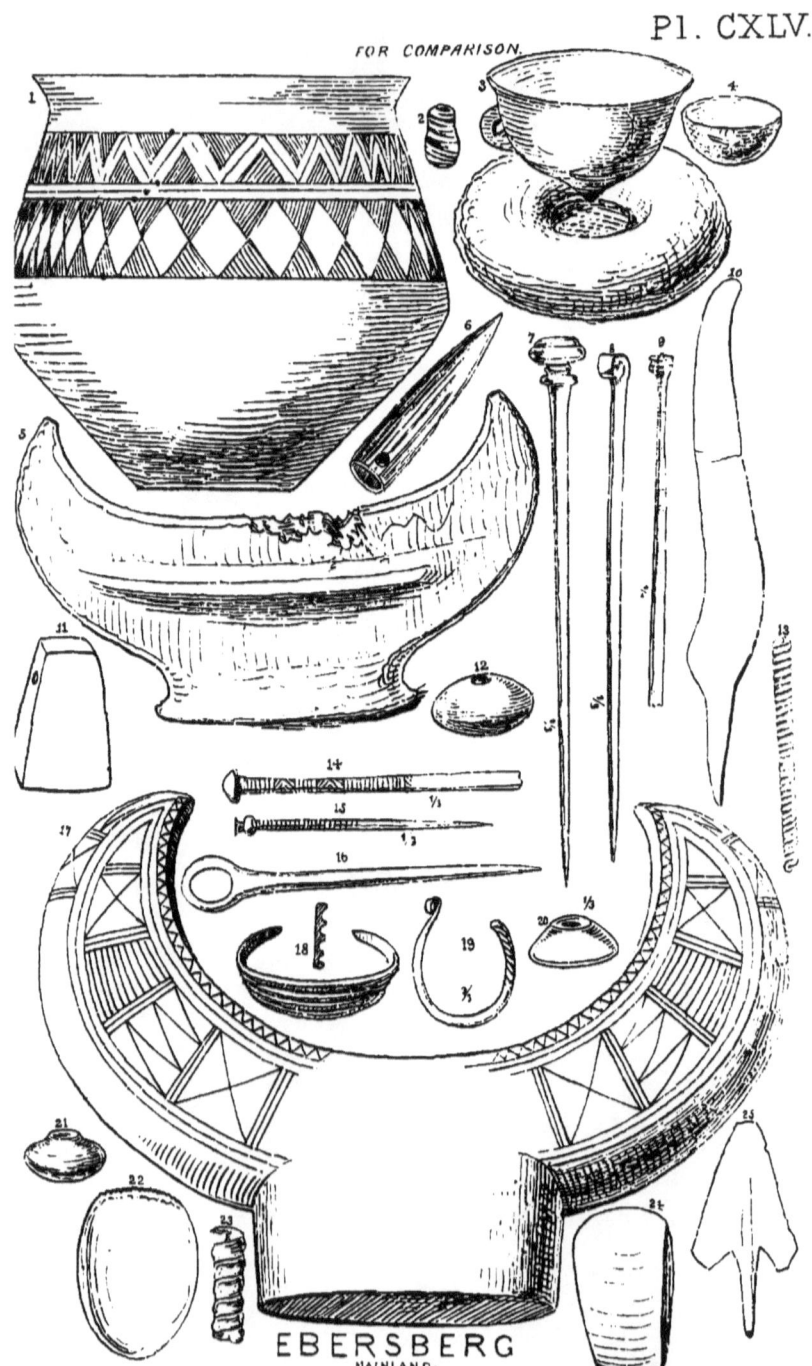

PL.CXLVI.

FOR COMPARISON. MAINLAND.

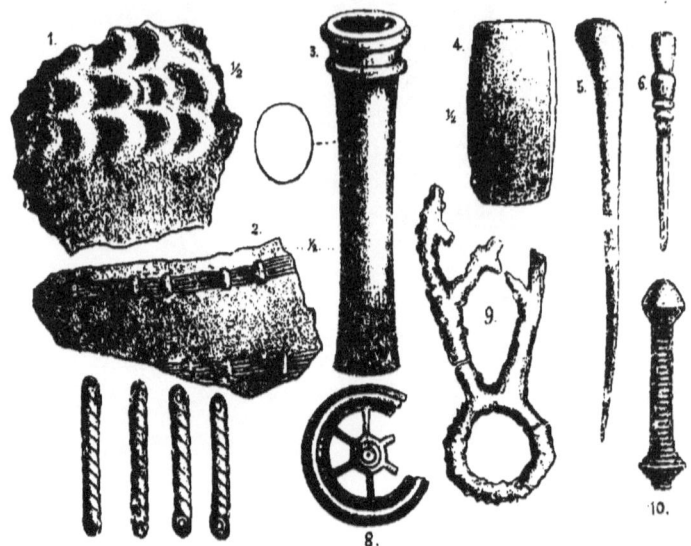

UETLIBERG.

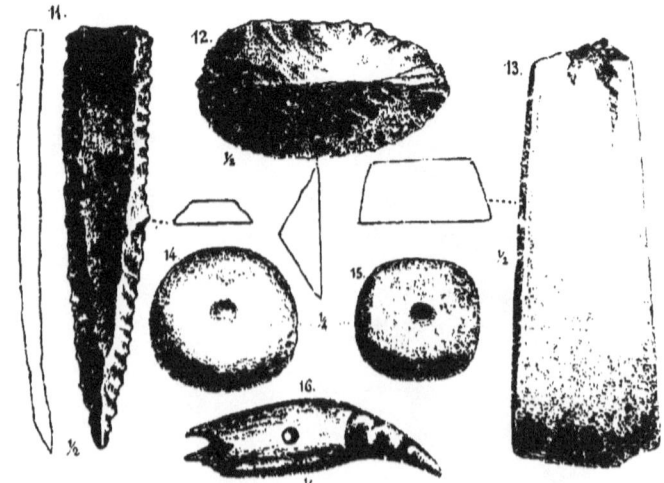

WINDISCH.

Pl. CXLVII.

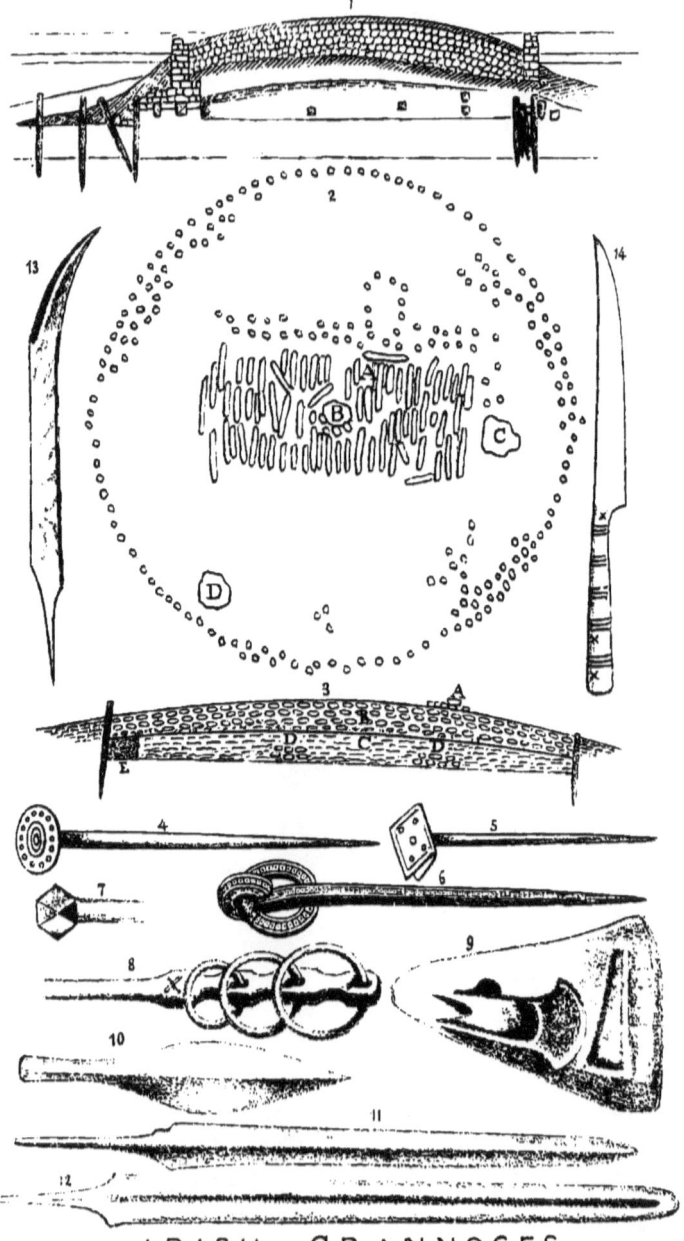

IRISH CRANNOGES
Copied from Sir W. R. Wilde's Catalogue & Arch. Journal Vol. VI

Pl. CXLVIII

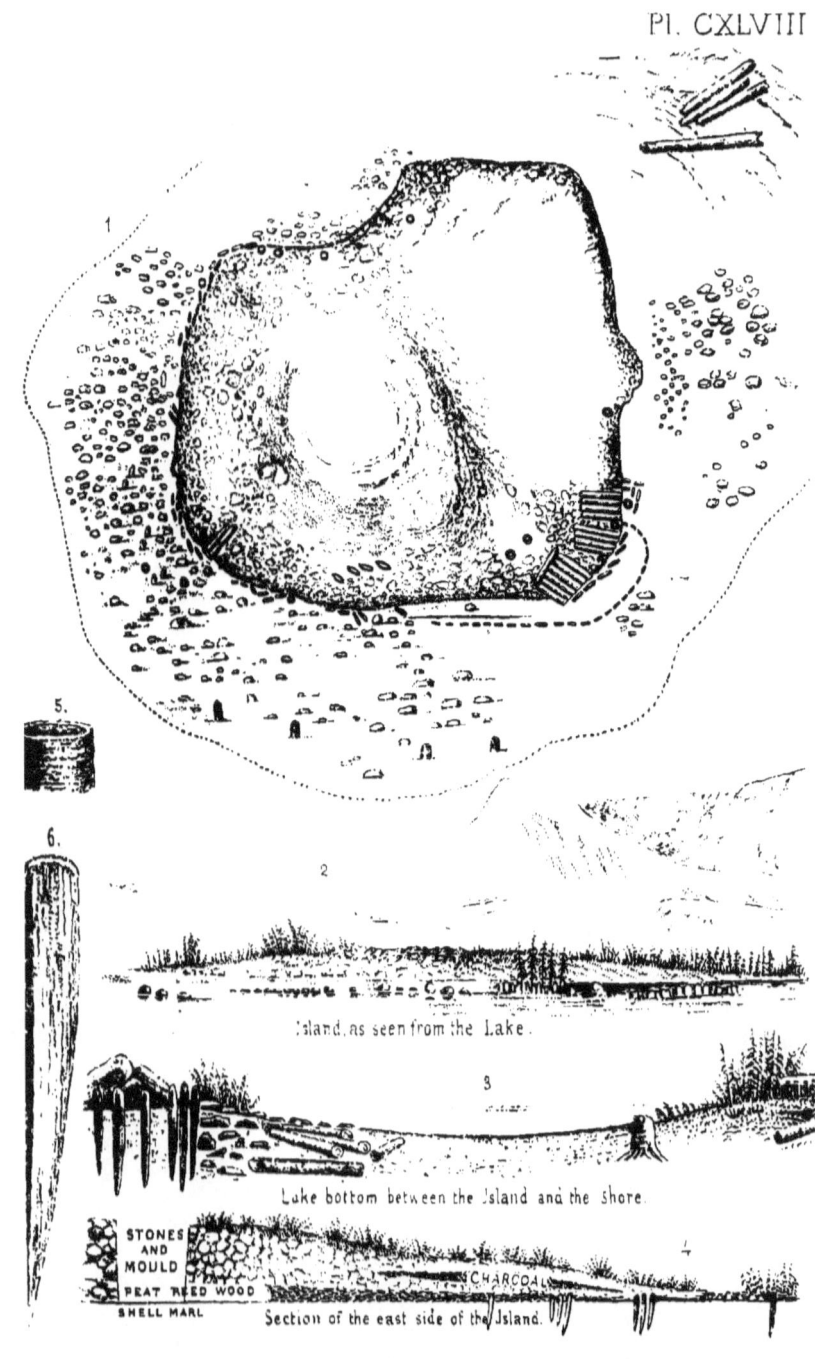

2. Island, as seen from the Lake.
3. Lake bottom between the Island and the Shore.
4. Section of the east side of the Island.

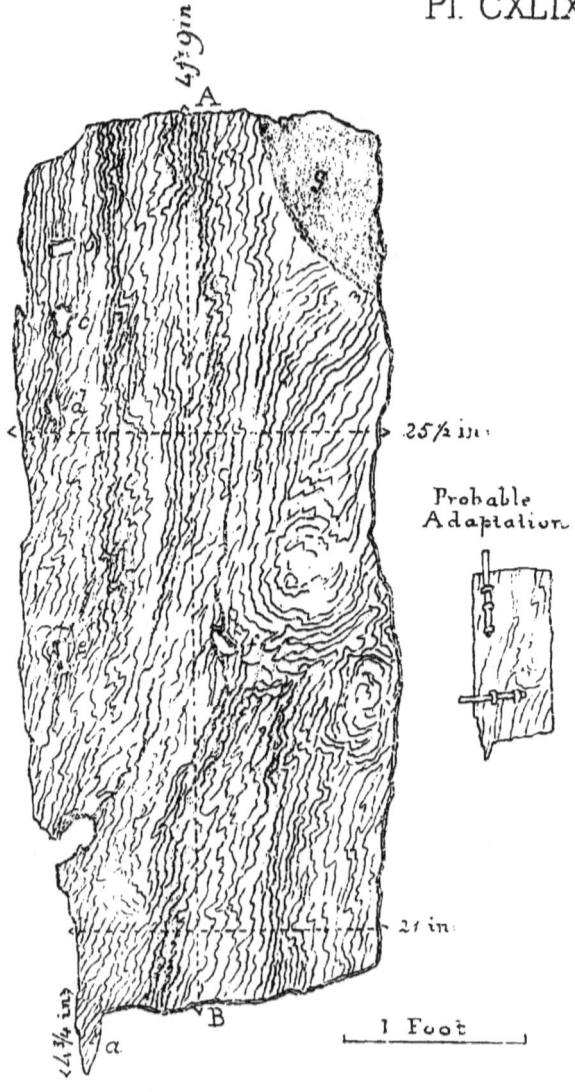

Pl. CXLIX.

Probable Adaptation

1 Foot

ROBENHAUSEN.
Wood.

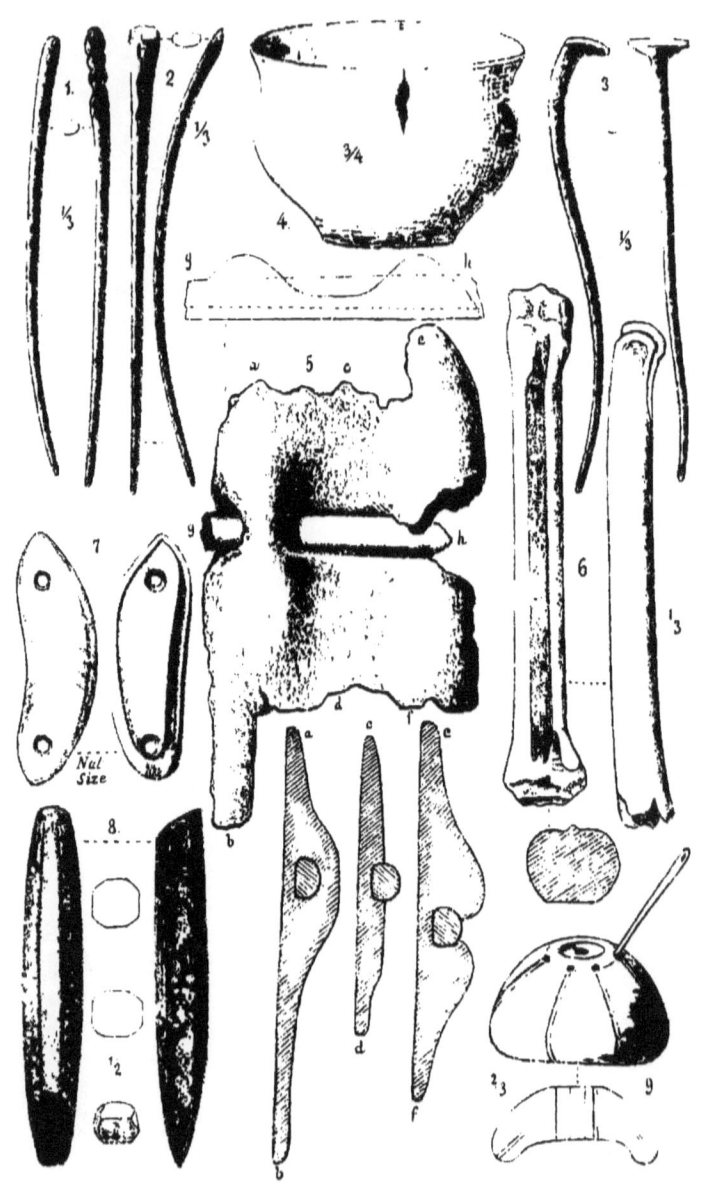

MÖRINGEN &c.

Pl. CLI.

LAKE OF BOURGET.

all ½ Size.

Pl. CLII.

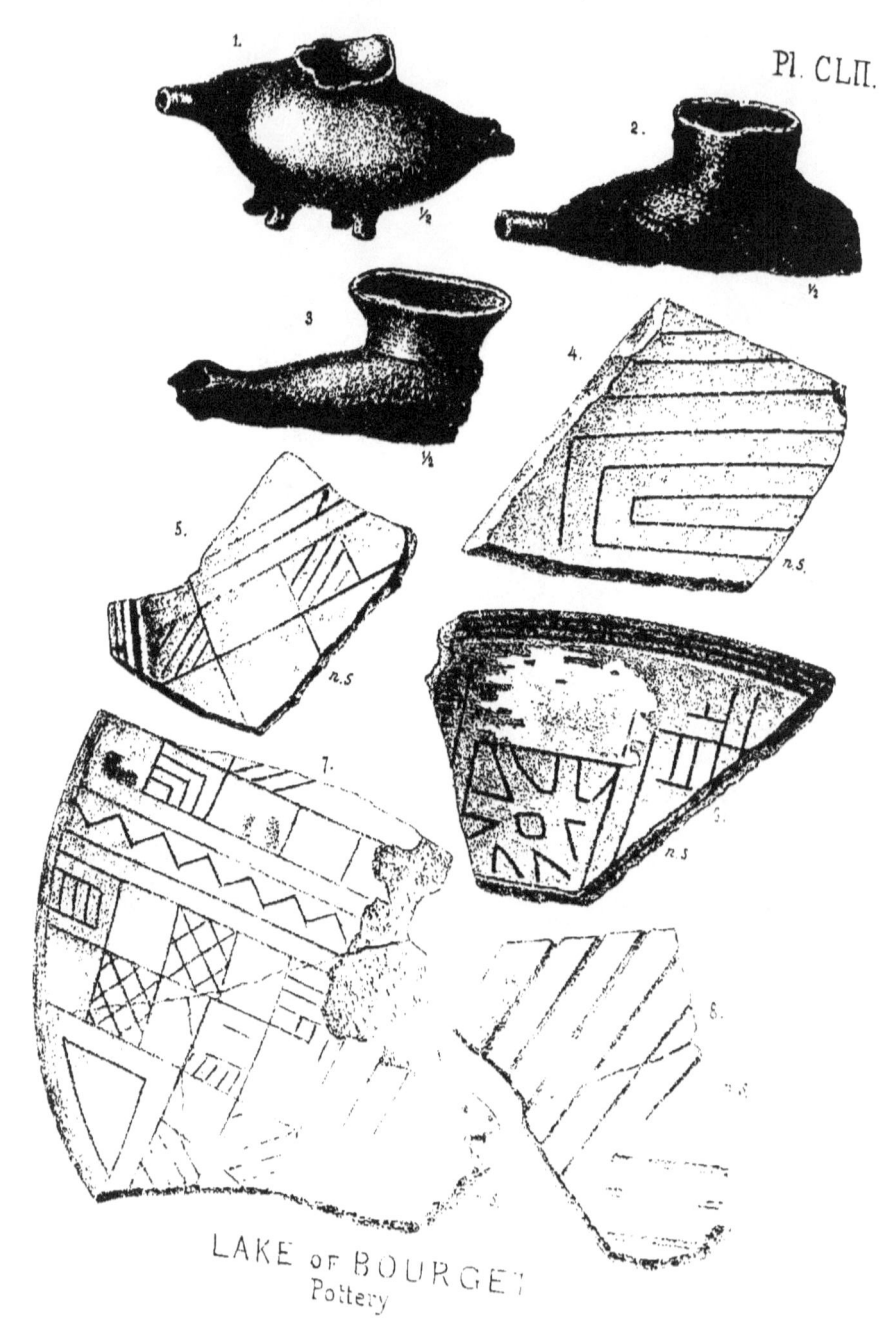

LAKE of BOURGET
Pottery

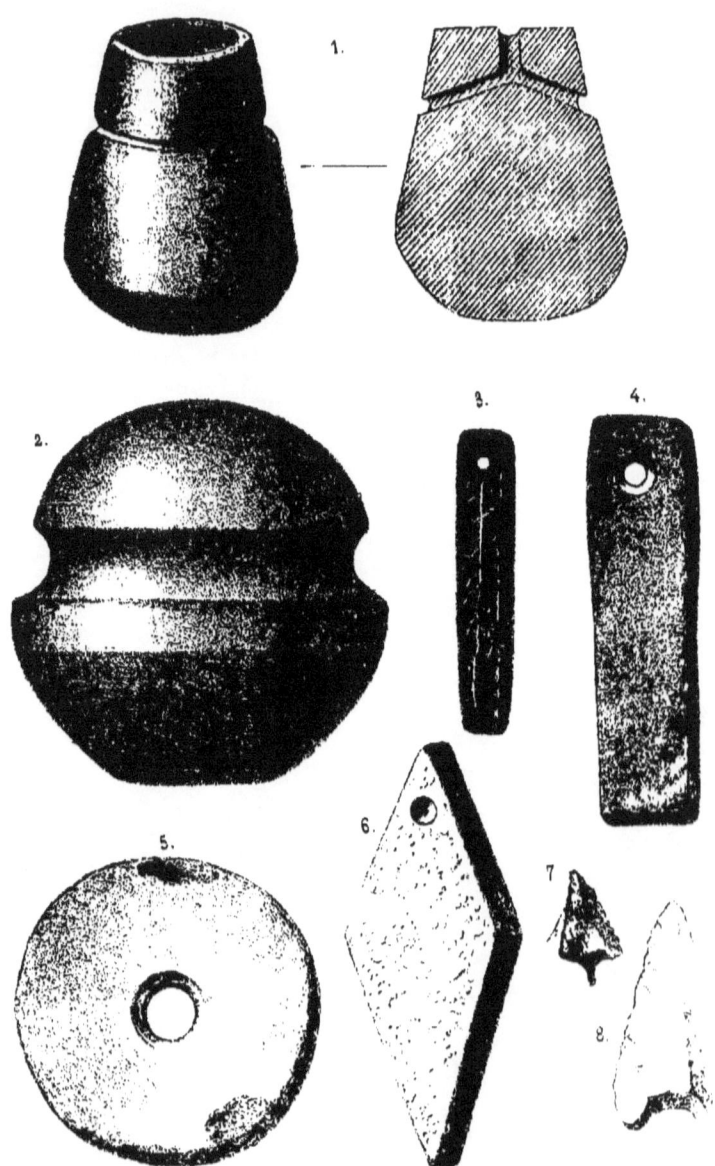

LAKE OF BOURGET.
Stone nat. Size.

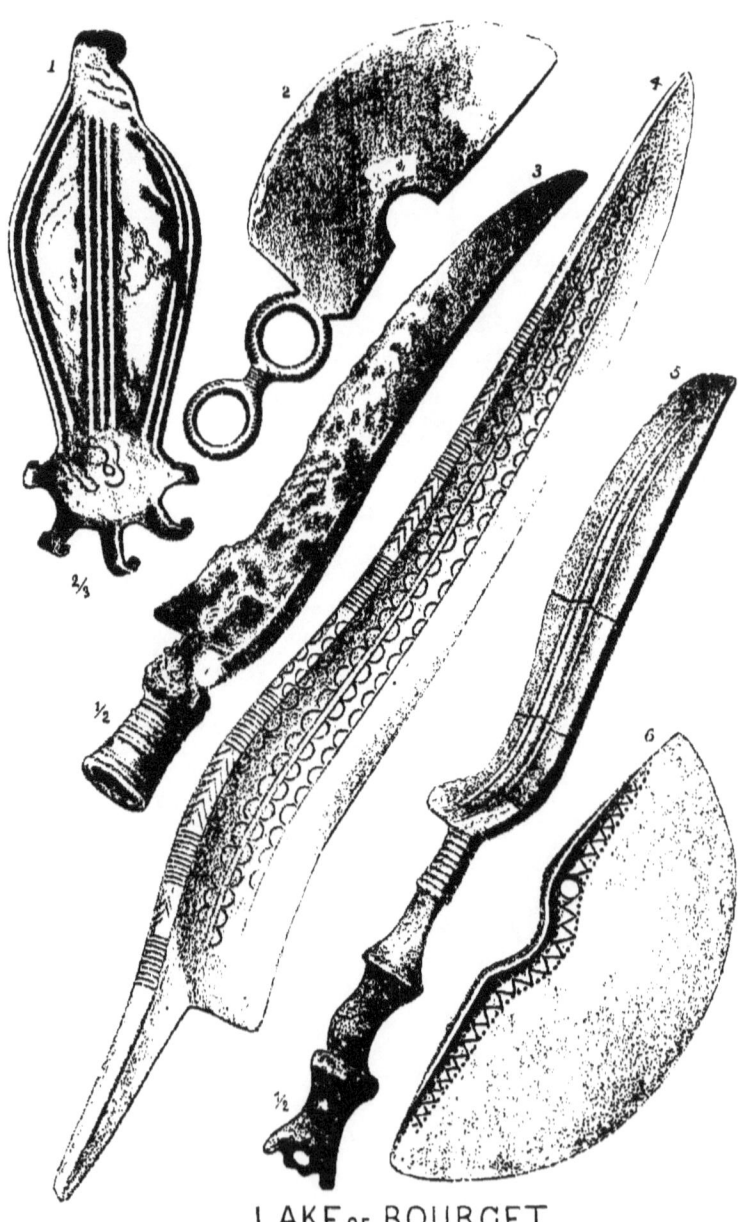

LAKE OF BOURGET.
Bronze.

Pl CLV.

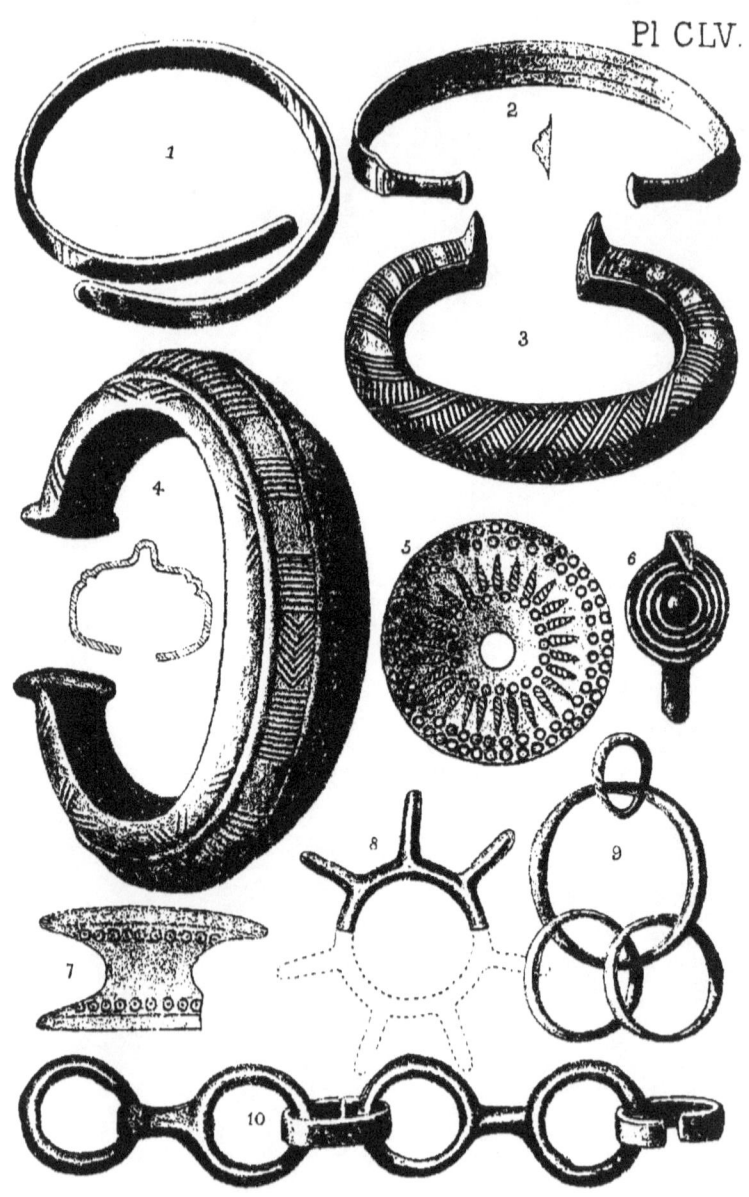

LAKE of BOURGET.
Bronze nat. size.

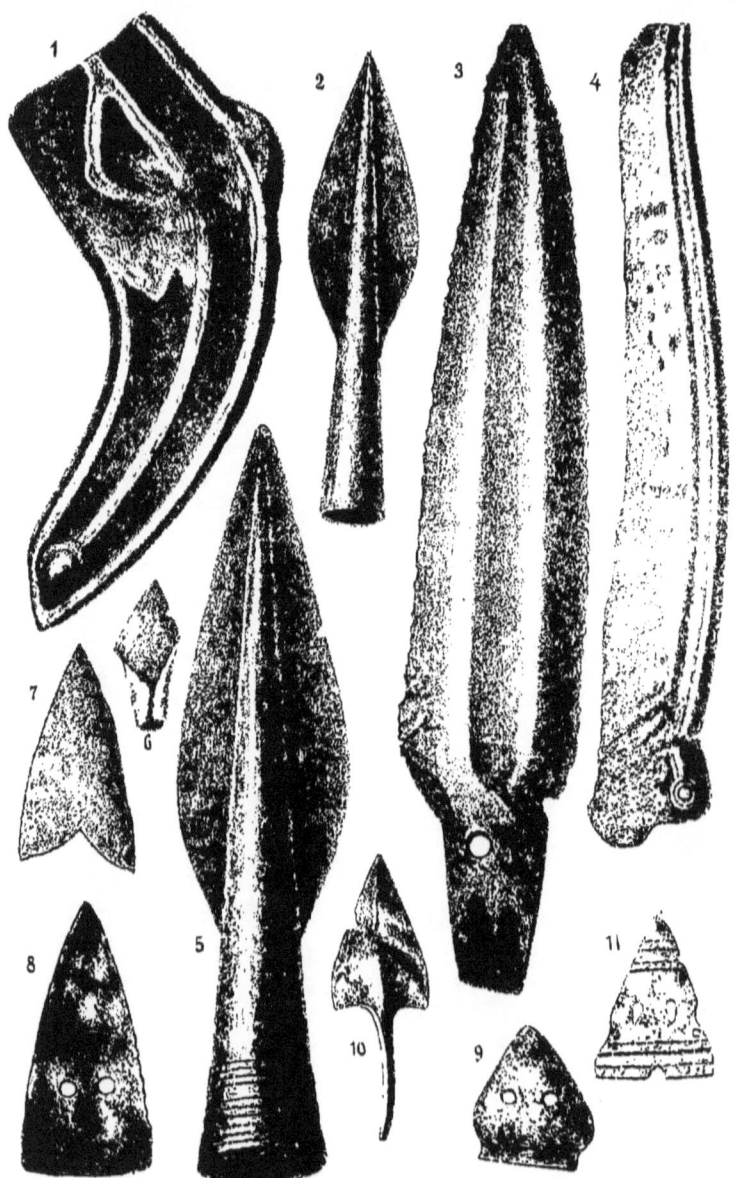

Pl. CLVI.

LAKE OF BOURGET
Bronze_nat.Size.

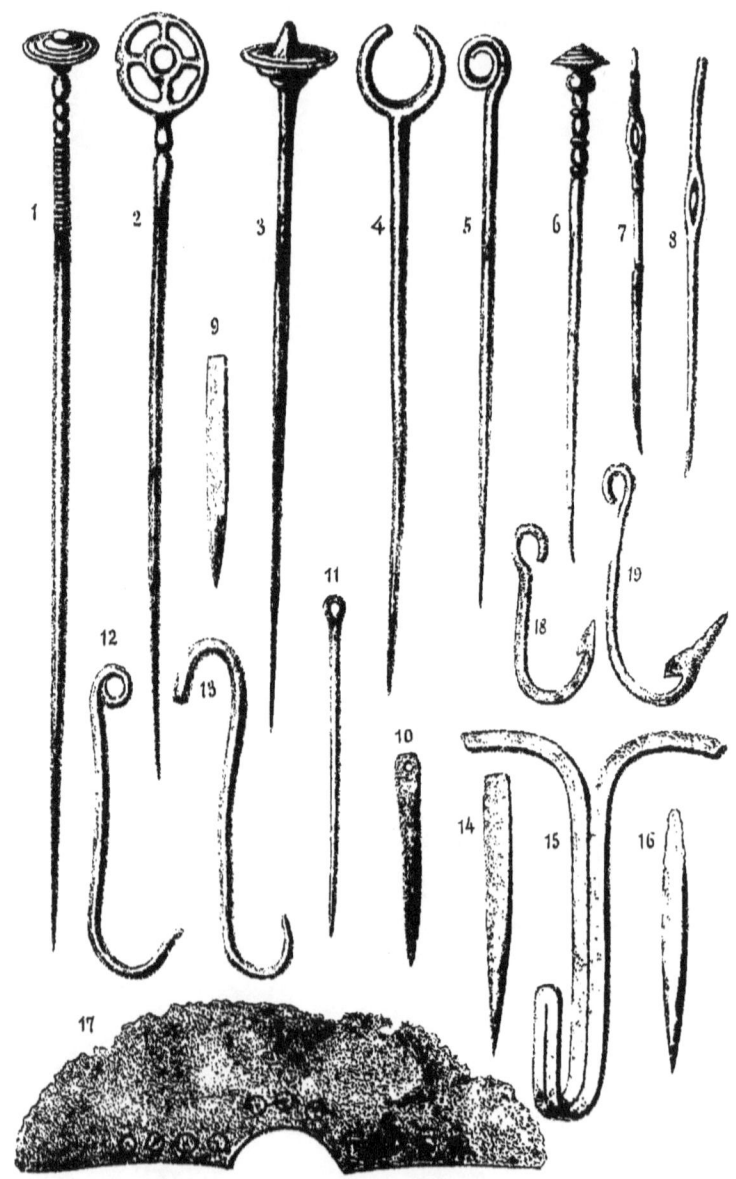

LAKE OF BOURGET
Bronze nat. size

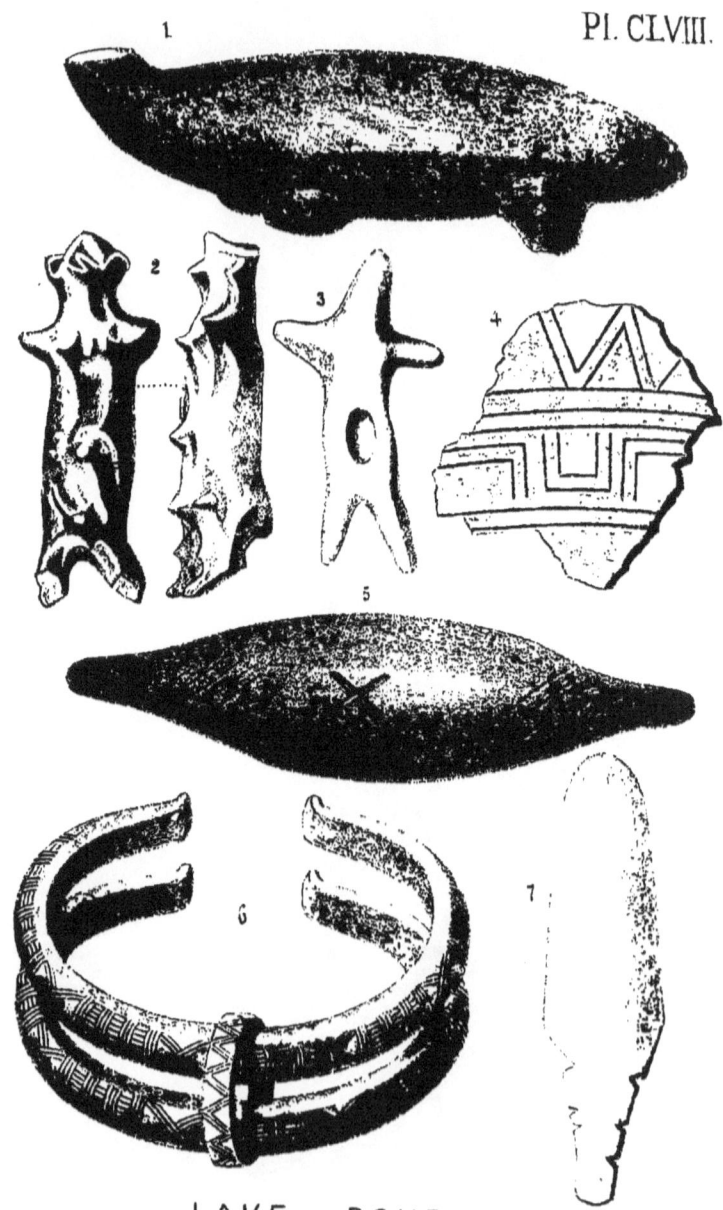

Pl. CLVIII.

LAKE of BOURGET.

Pl. CLIX.

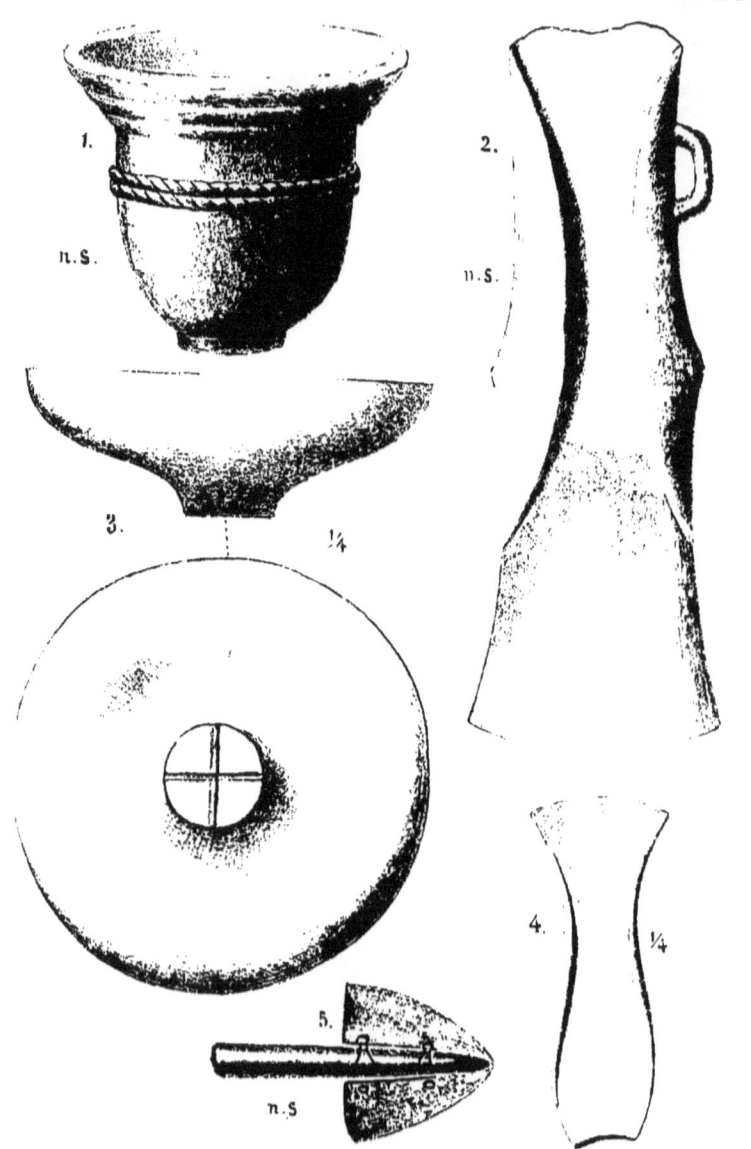

LAKE of BOURGET

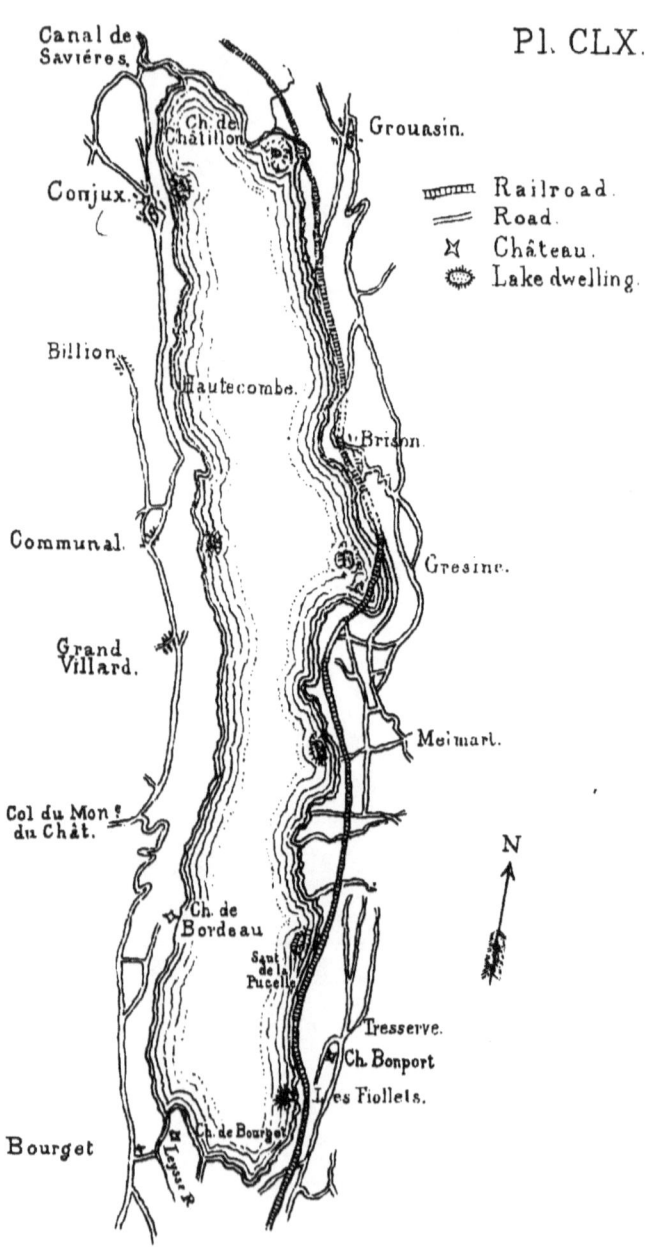

Pl. CLX.

LAKE OF BOURGET.
Scale.— 1/100 000.

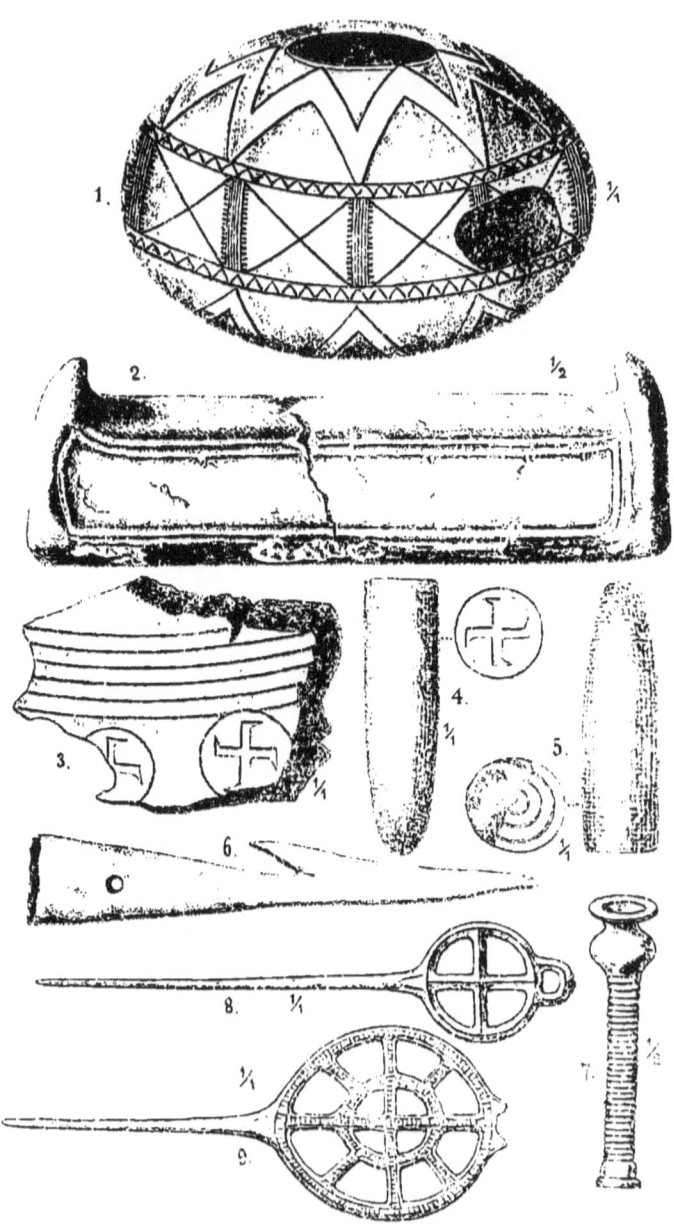

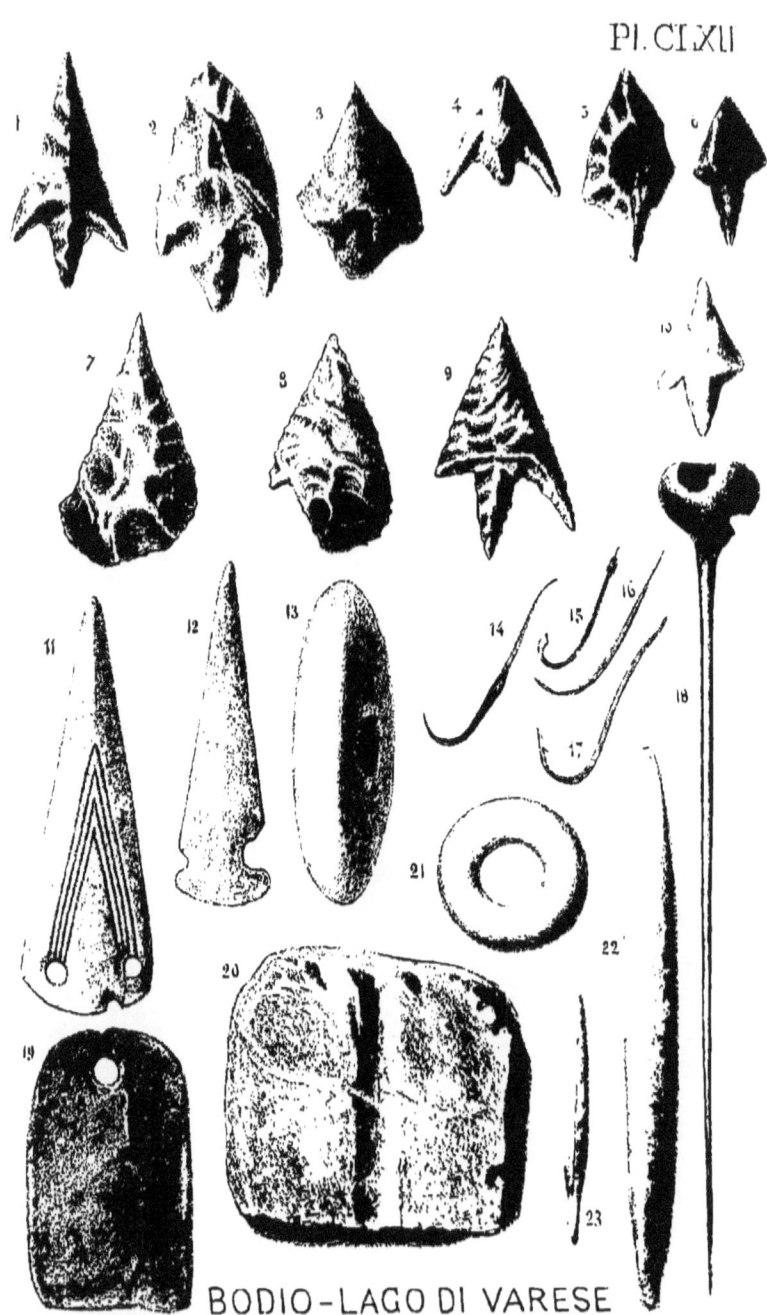

BODIO-LAGO DI VARESE

Pl. CLXIII.

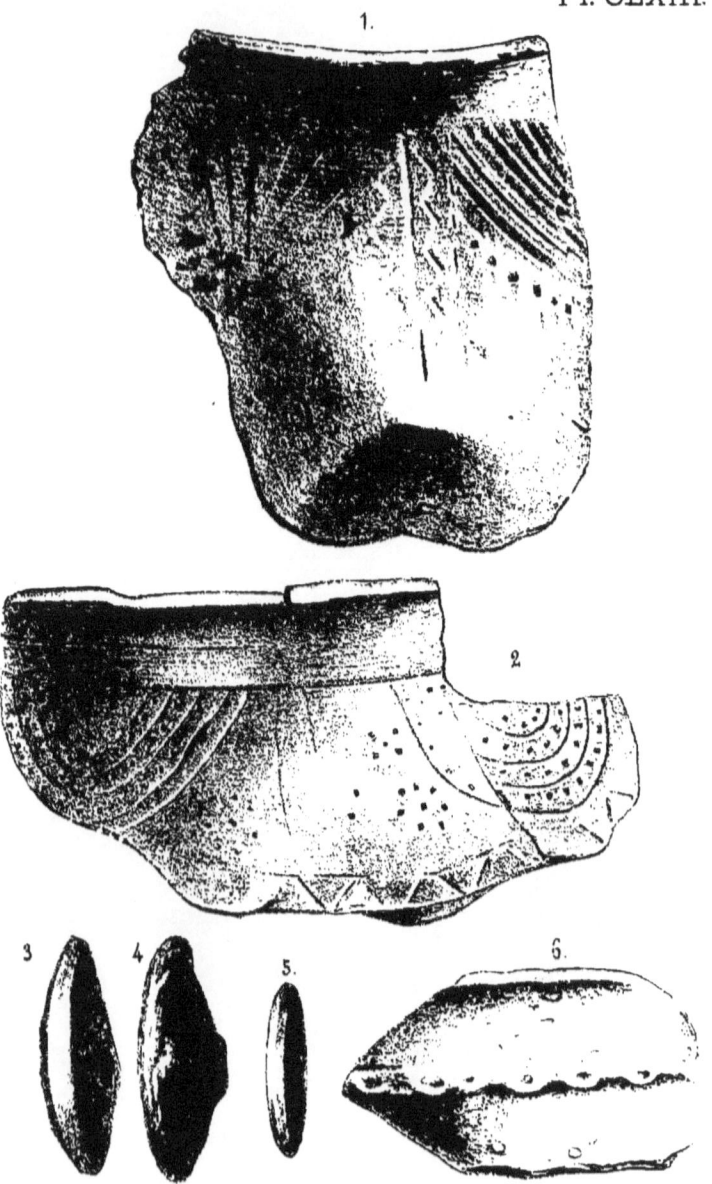

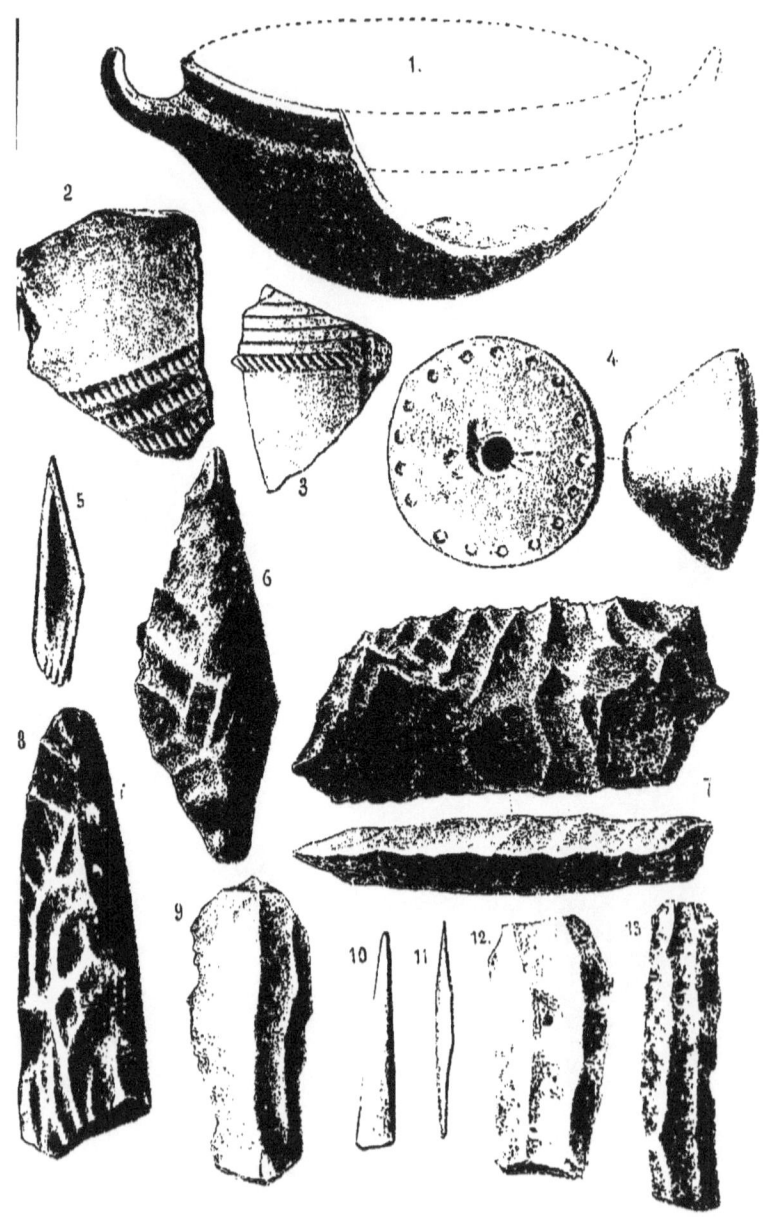

LAGO DI VARESE

Pl. CLXV.

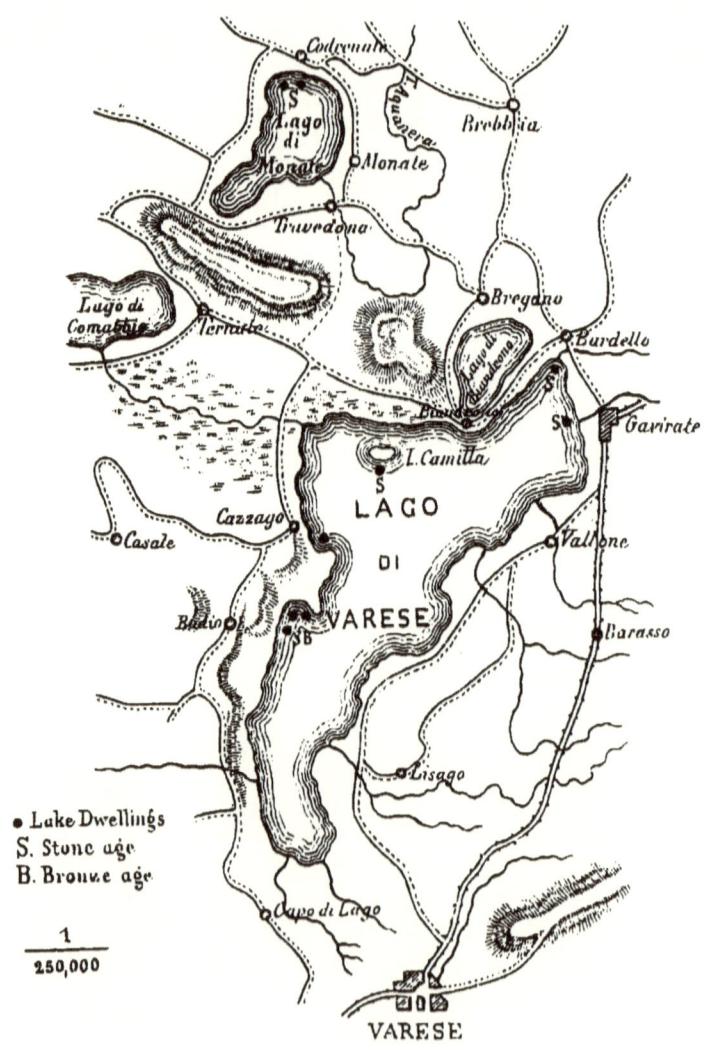

PLAN OF THE LAKES OF VARESE & MONATE

Pl. CLXVI.

LAKE OF PUSIANO.

LAKE OF GARDA.

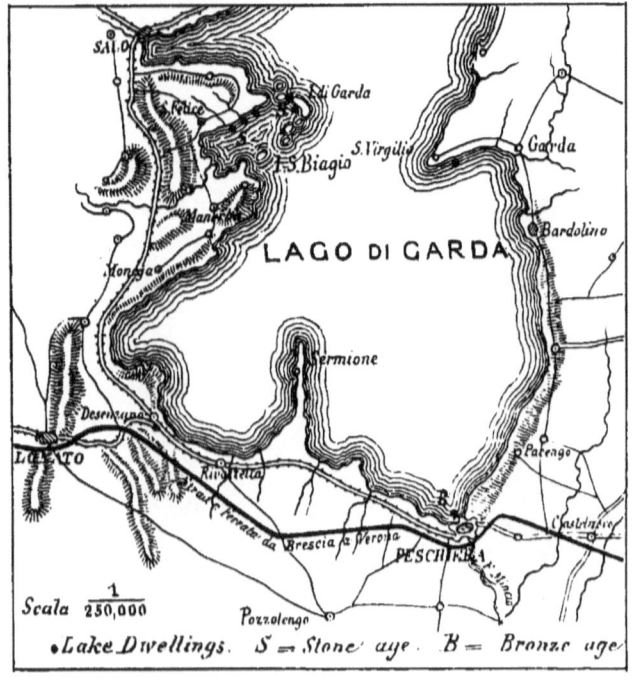

LAIBACH-MOOR

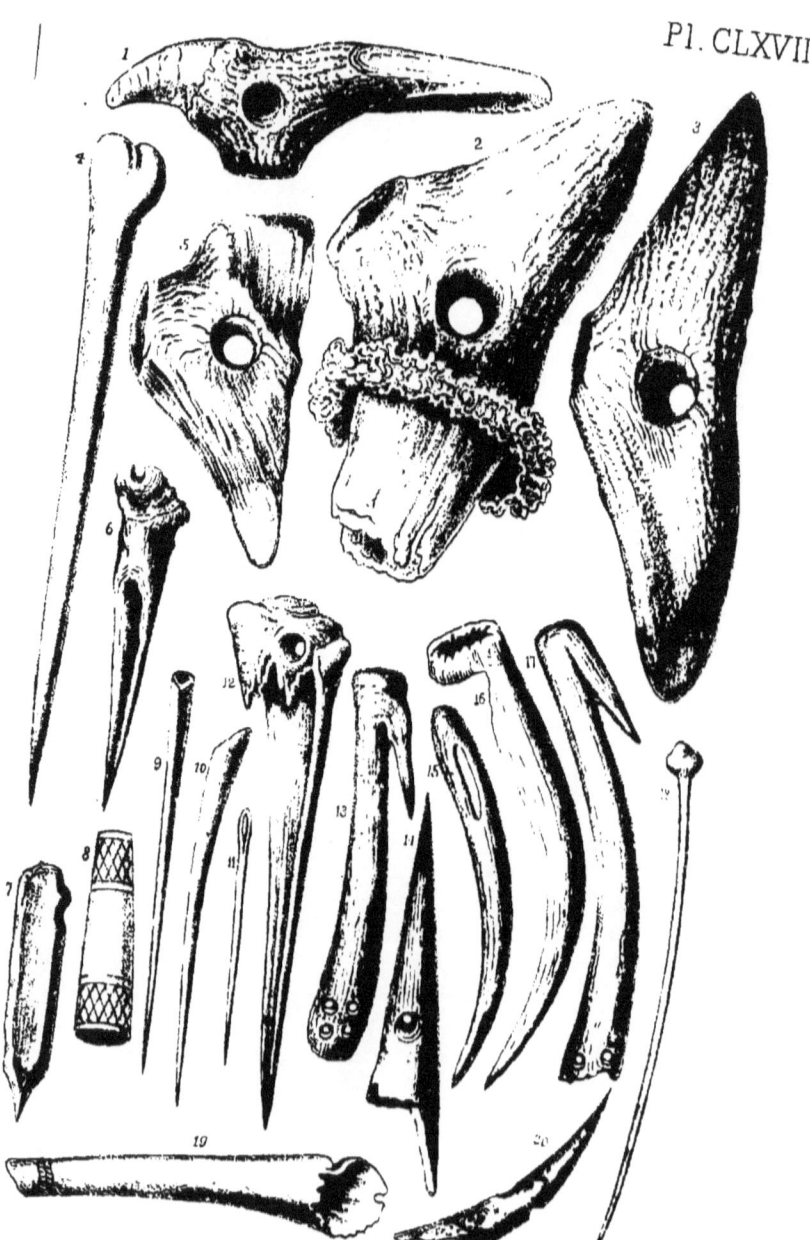

Pl. CLXVIII.

LAIBACH - MOOR.

Pl CLXIX.

1

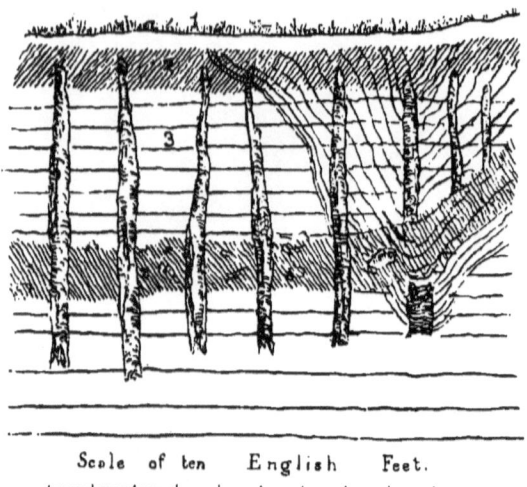

Scale of ten English Feet.

2

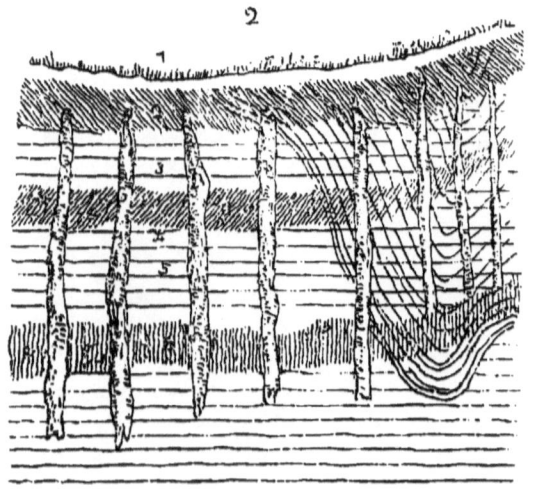

Scale of ten English Feet.

LAKE OF FIMON.

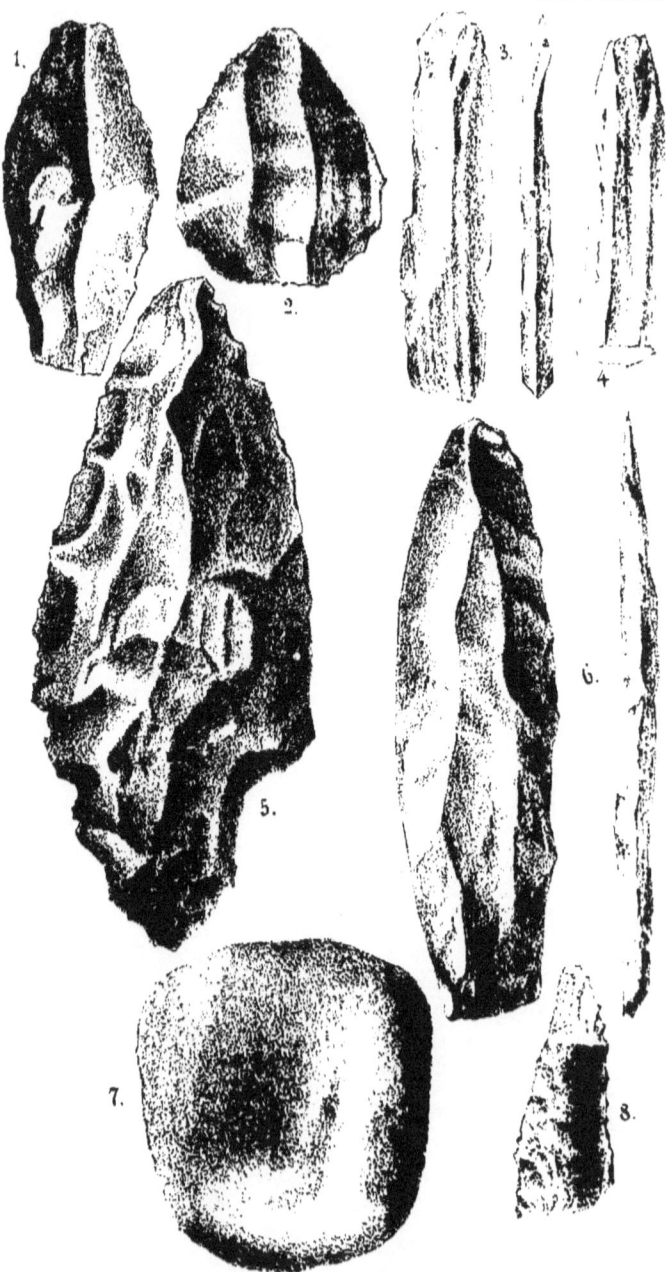

Pl. CLXX.

LAKE OF FIMON.
Lower Relic-bed-Stone Age.

LAKE OF FIMON.
Lower Relic-bed-Stone Age.

Pl. CLXXII.

LAKE of FIMON.
Lower Relic-bed Stone Age.

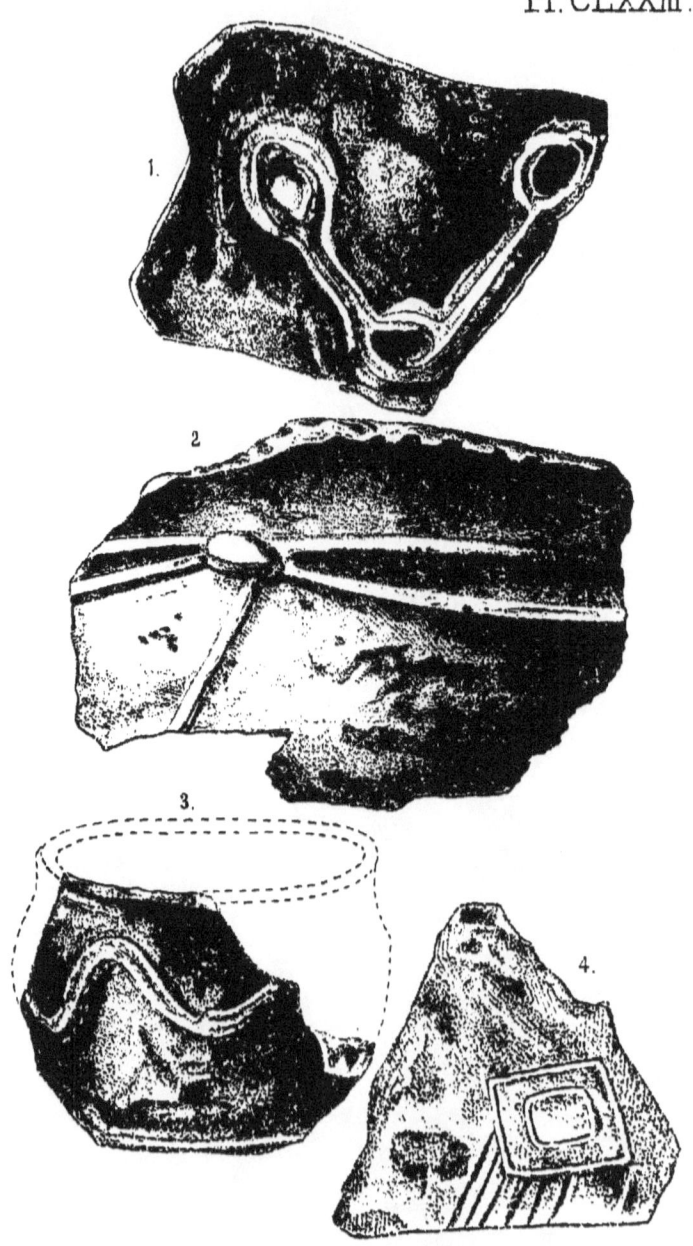

LAKE of FIMON
Lower Relic bed. Stone Age.

Pl. CLXXIV.

LAKE OF FIMON.
Lower Relic-bed. Stone Age.

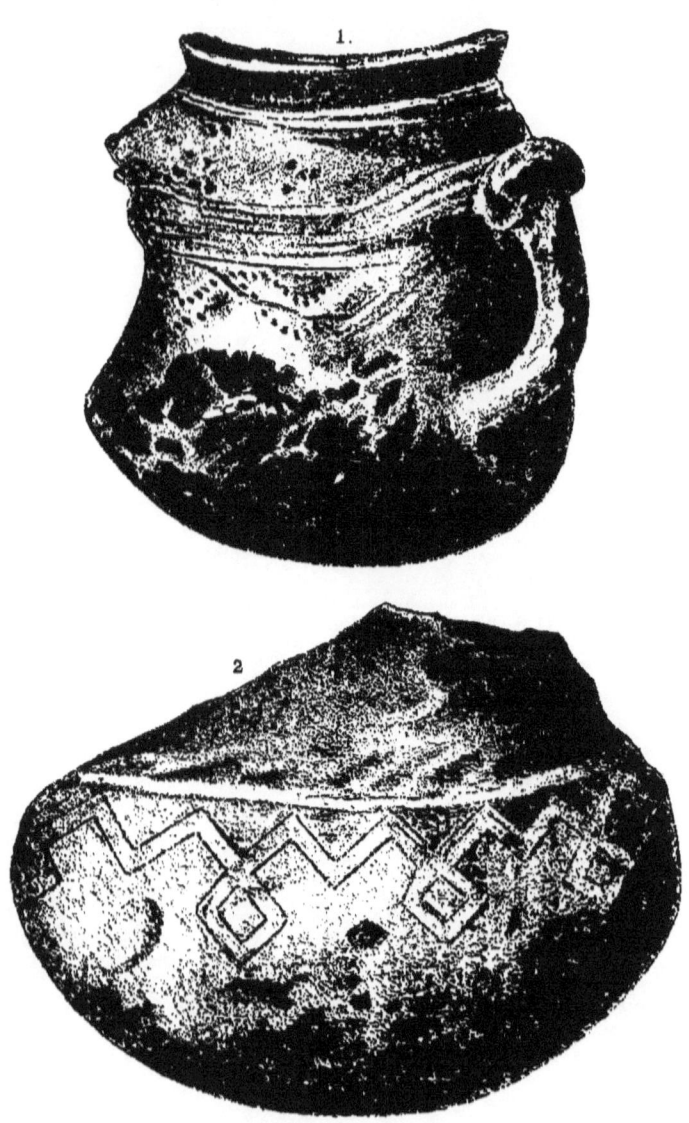

LAKE of FIMON.
Upper Relic-bed Bronze Age.

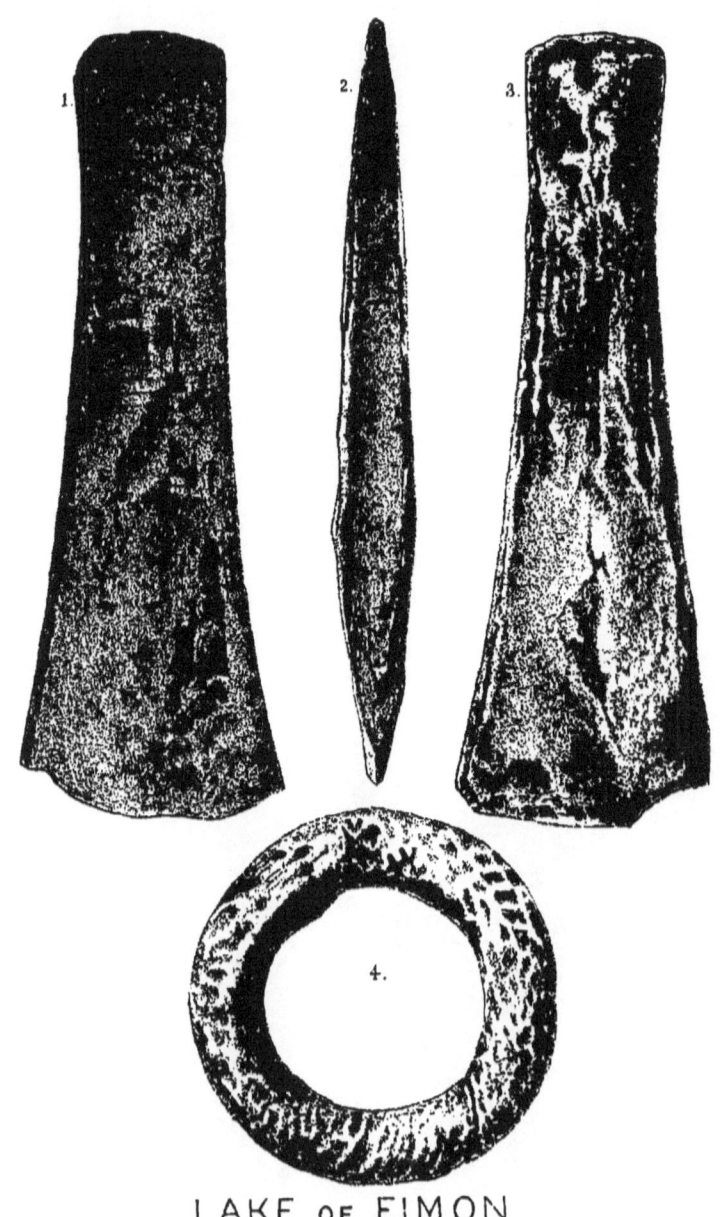

LAKE OF FIMON
Upper Relic-bed Bronze Age.

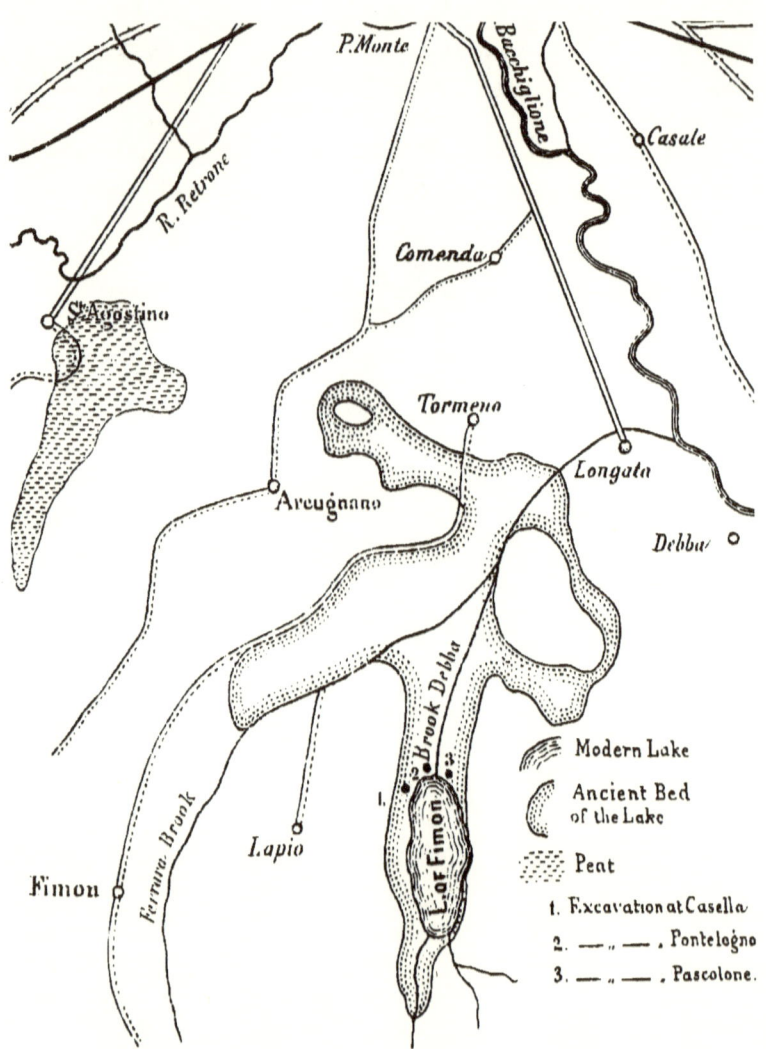

DISTRICT near the LAKE of FIMON.

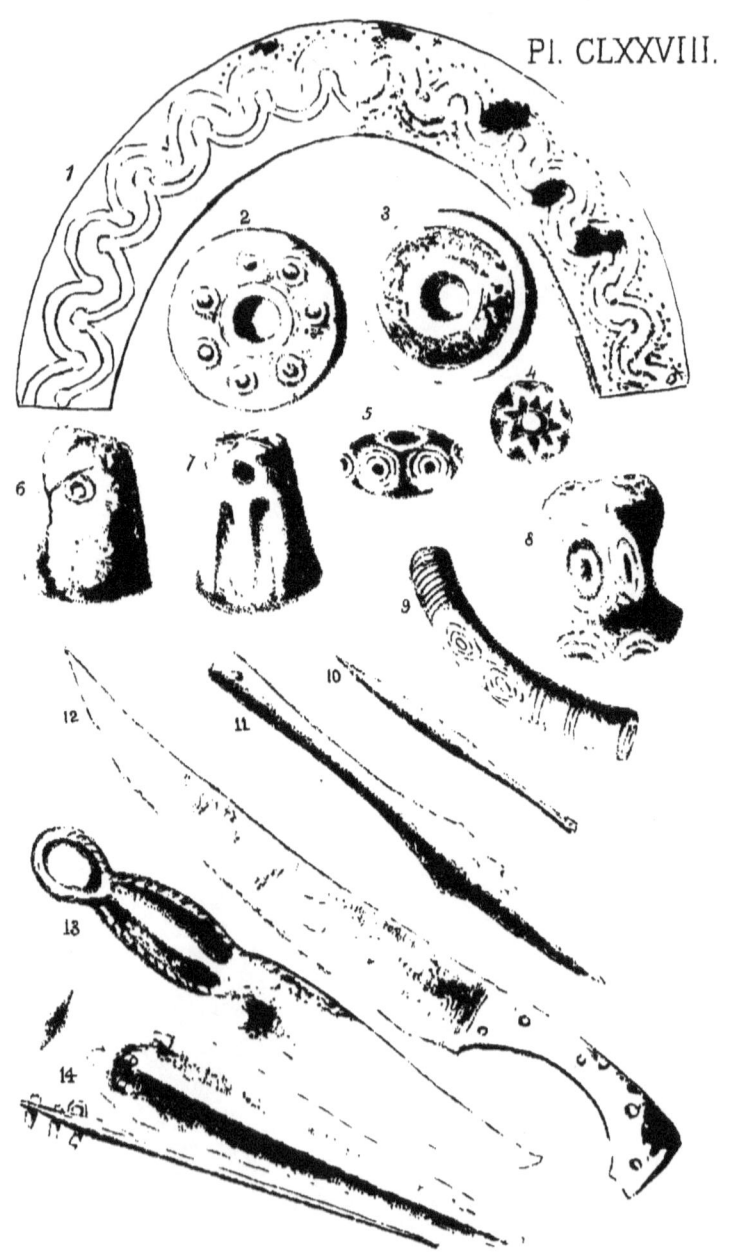

Pl. CLXXVIII.

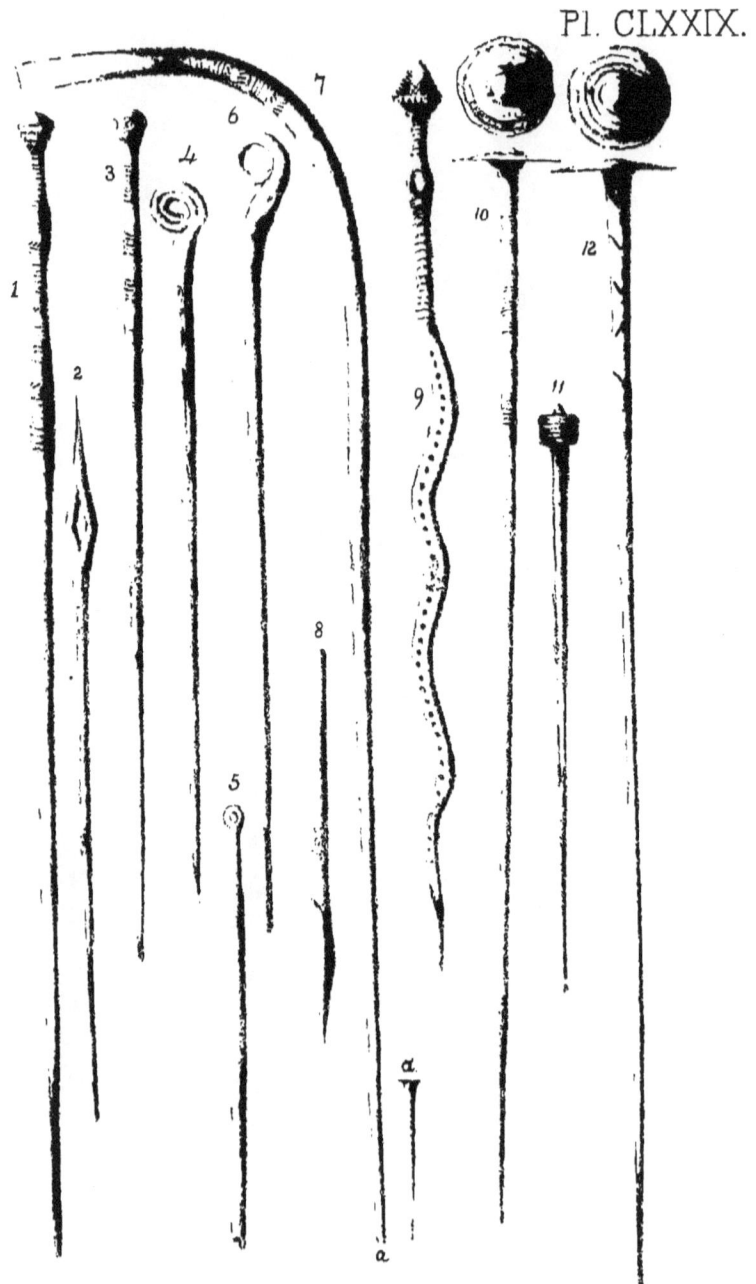

Pl. CLXXIX.

LAKE OF STARNBERG (*Rosen Insel.*)

Pl CLXXX.

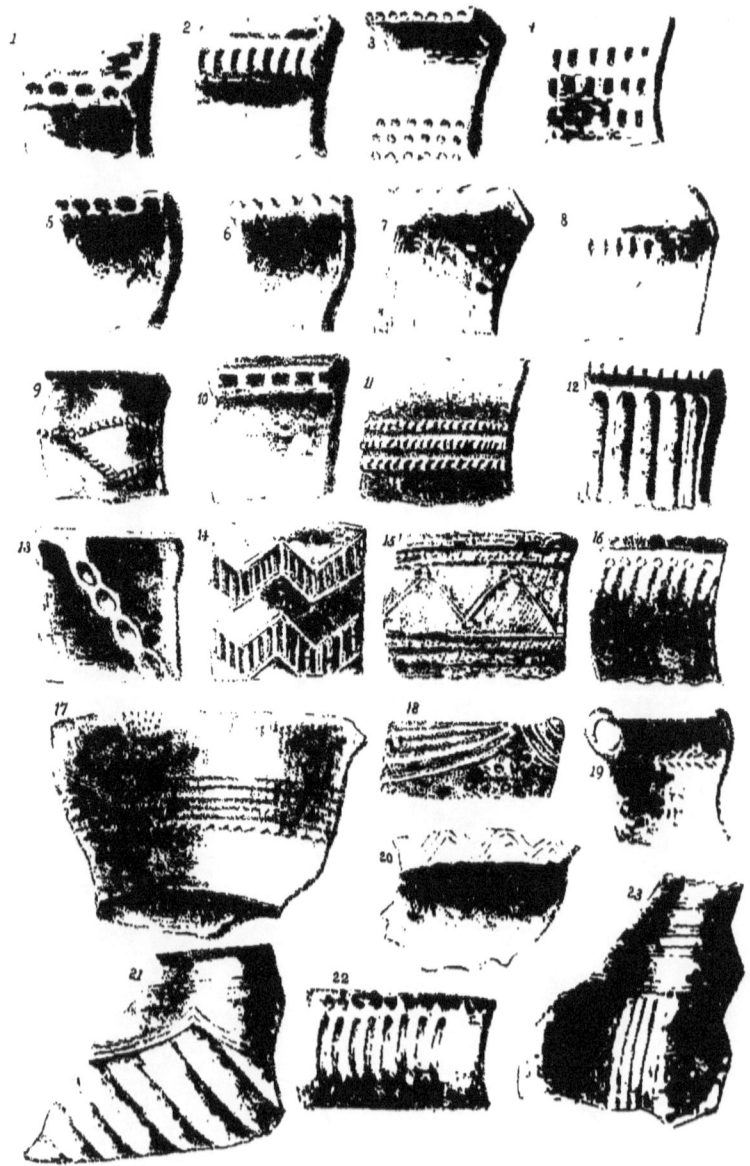

LAKE of STARNBERG. (Rosen Insel)

Pl. CLXXXI.

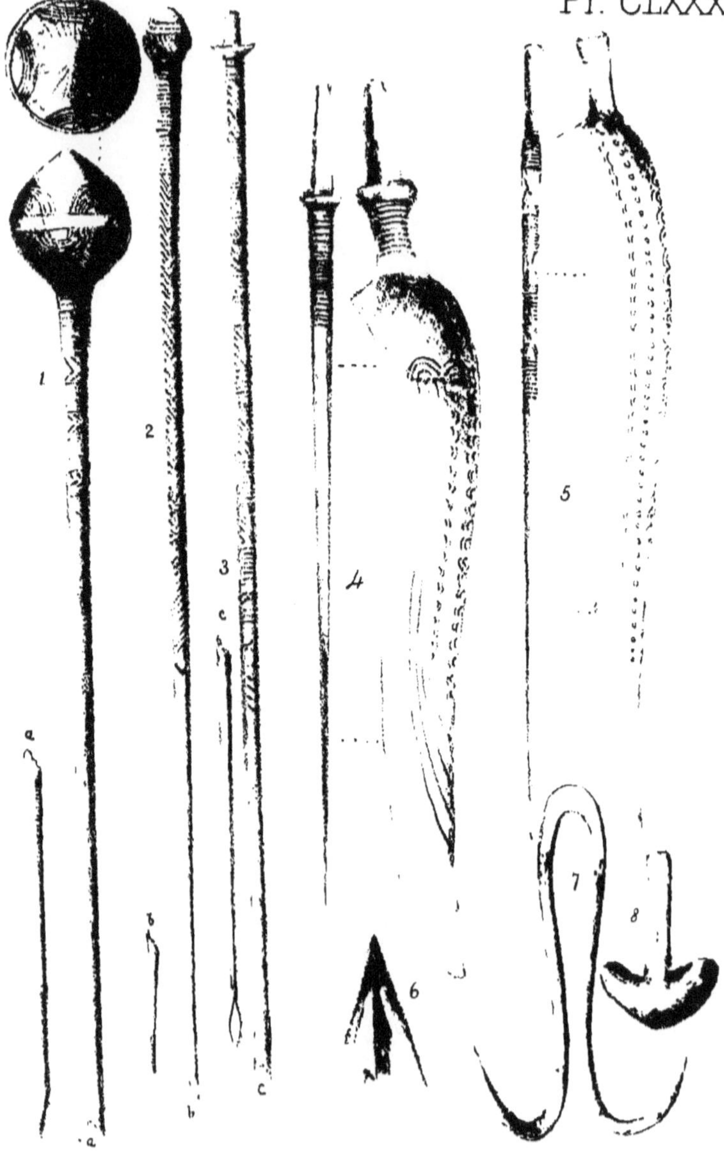

LAKE OF STARNBERG (Rosen Insel.

Pl. CLXXXII.

LAKE OF STARNBERG. (*Rosen Inscl.*)

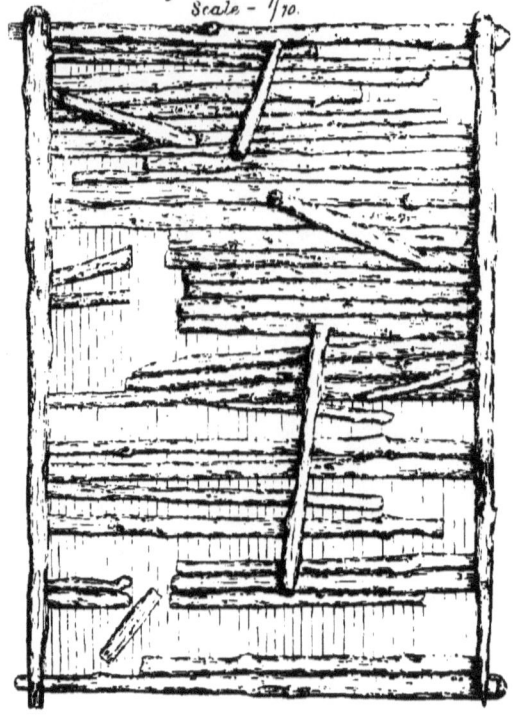

Birds eye view of the Platform
Scale – 1/10.

PLAN.

LAKE OF STARNBERG.
Rosen Insel.

Pl CLXXXIV

MOND SEE.
Forms of Earthenware Vessels without any ornamentation.

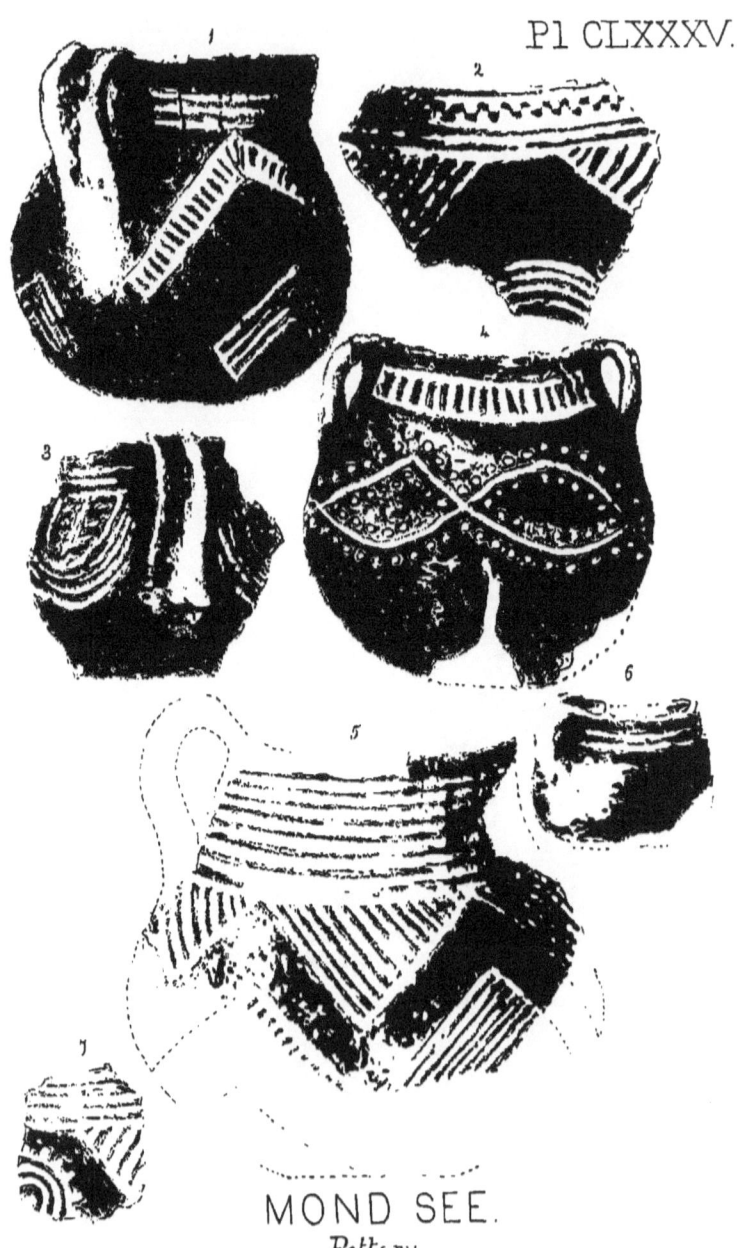

Pl CLXXXV.

MOND SEE.
Pottery.

Pl.CLXXXVII

MOND SEE.

Pl. CLXXXVIII.

MONDSEE.

PL. CLXXXIX.

MOND SEE.

ATTER SEE.

Pl. CXCI.

ATTER SEE.

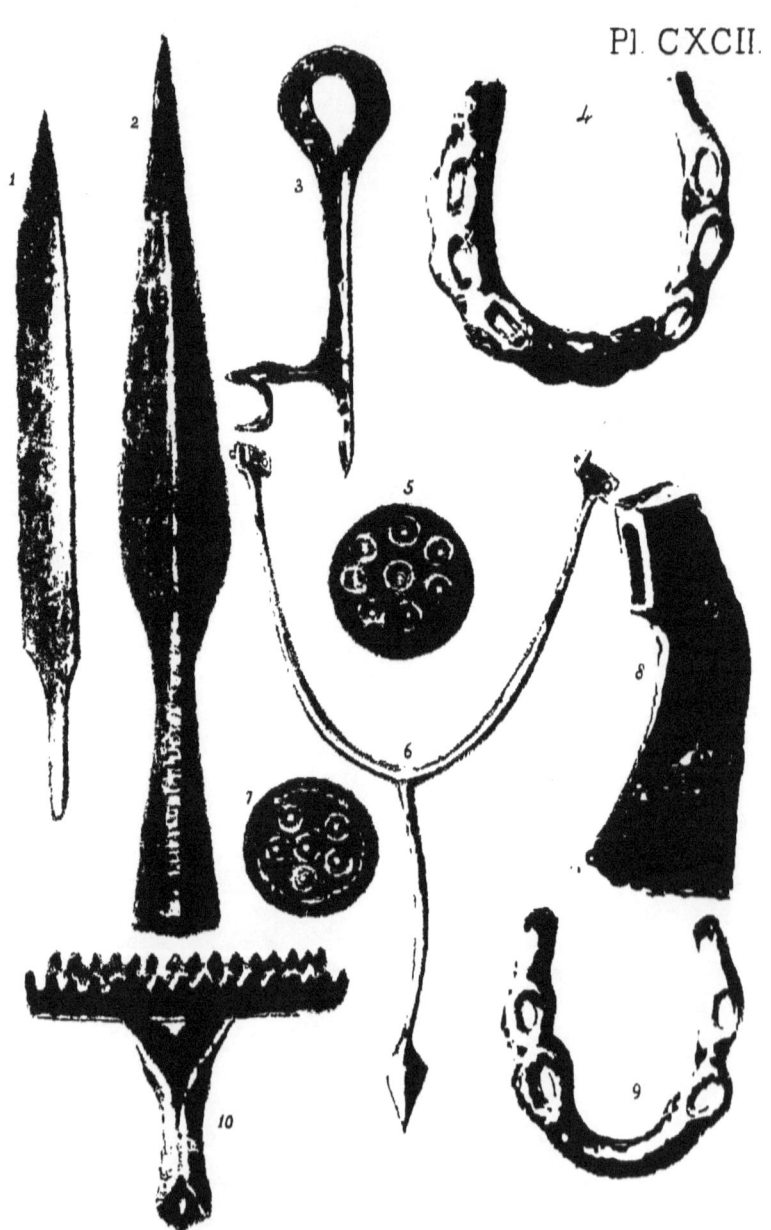

Pl. CXCII.

Pl. CXCIII.

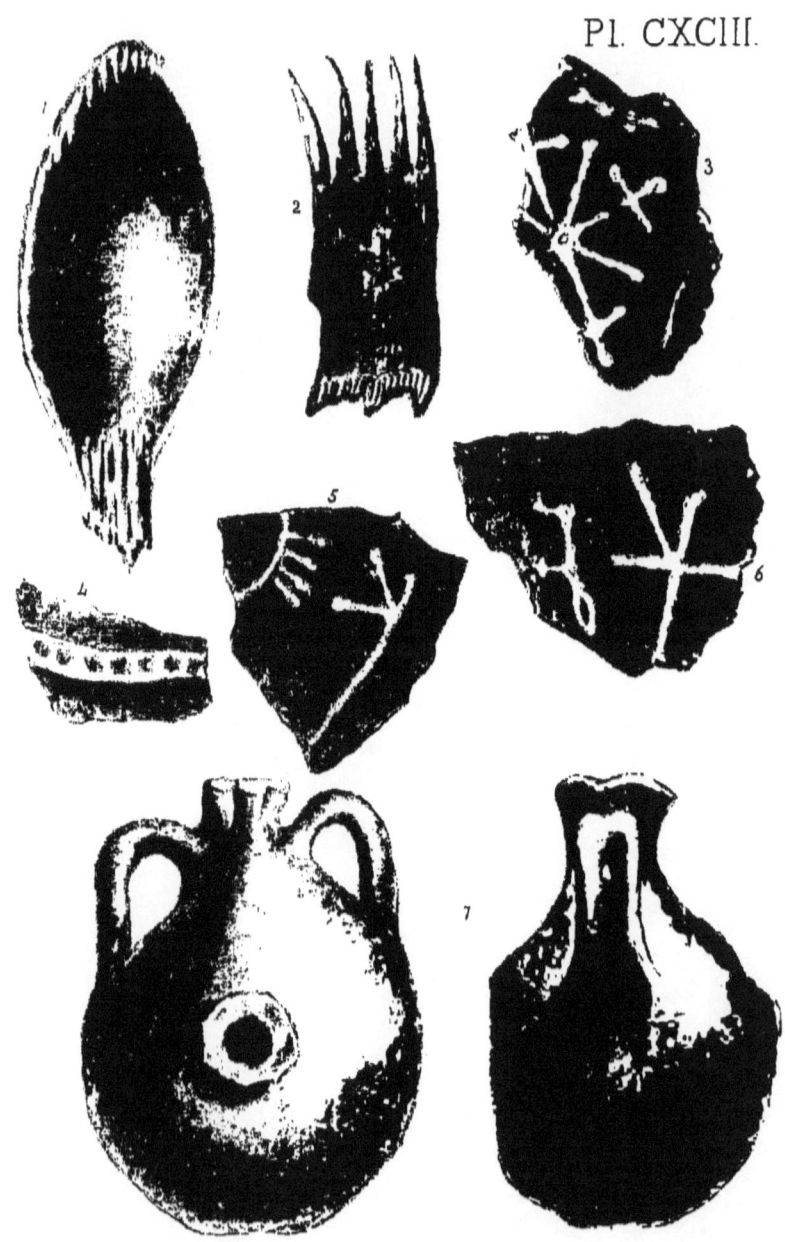

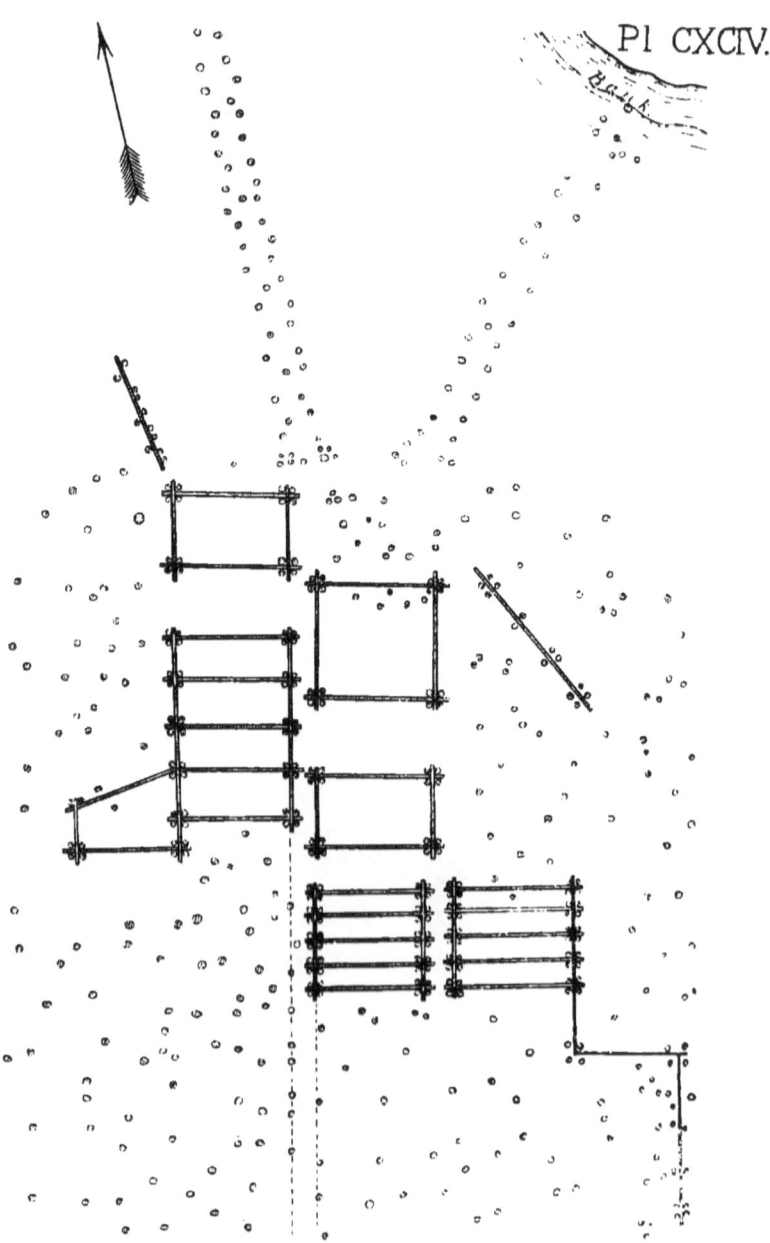

Pl CXCIV.

GRANDS ROSEAUX. (Lake of Paladru.)
SCALE.— ₃₅₀.

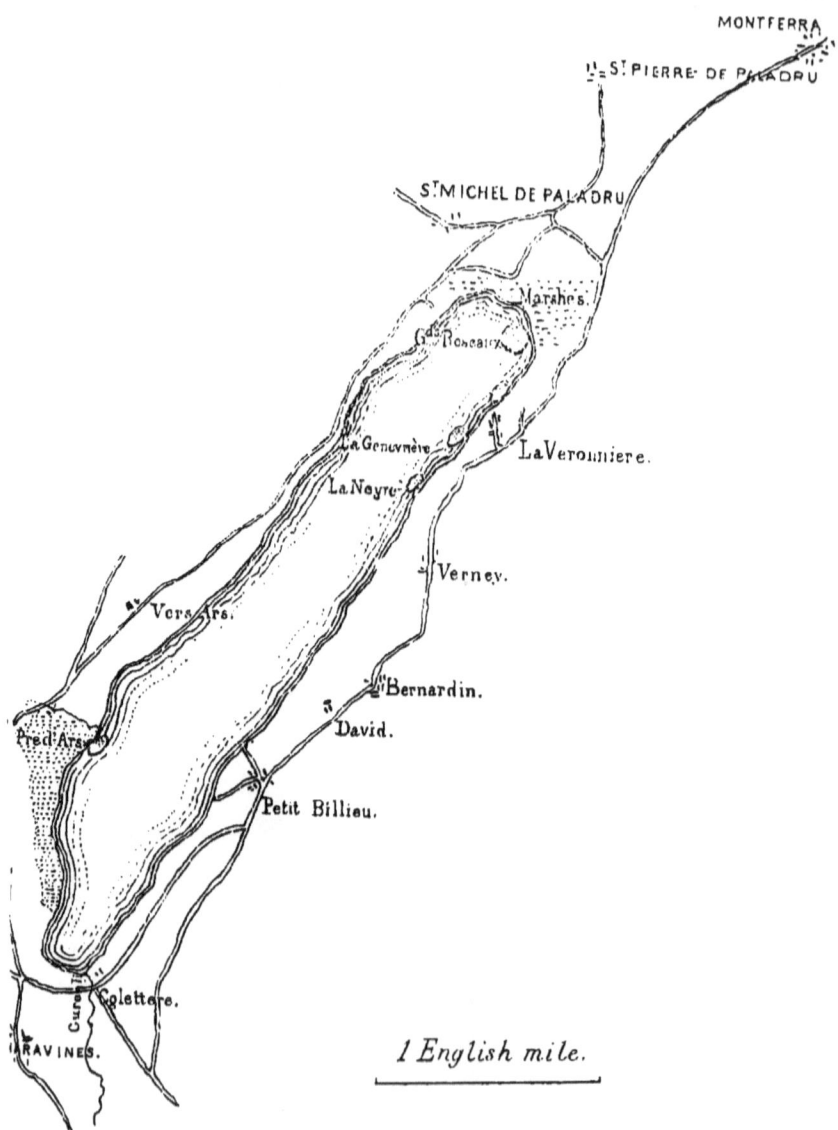

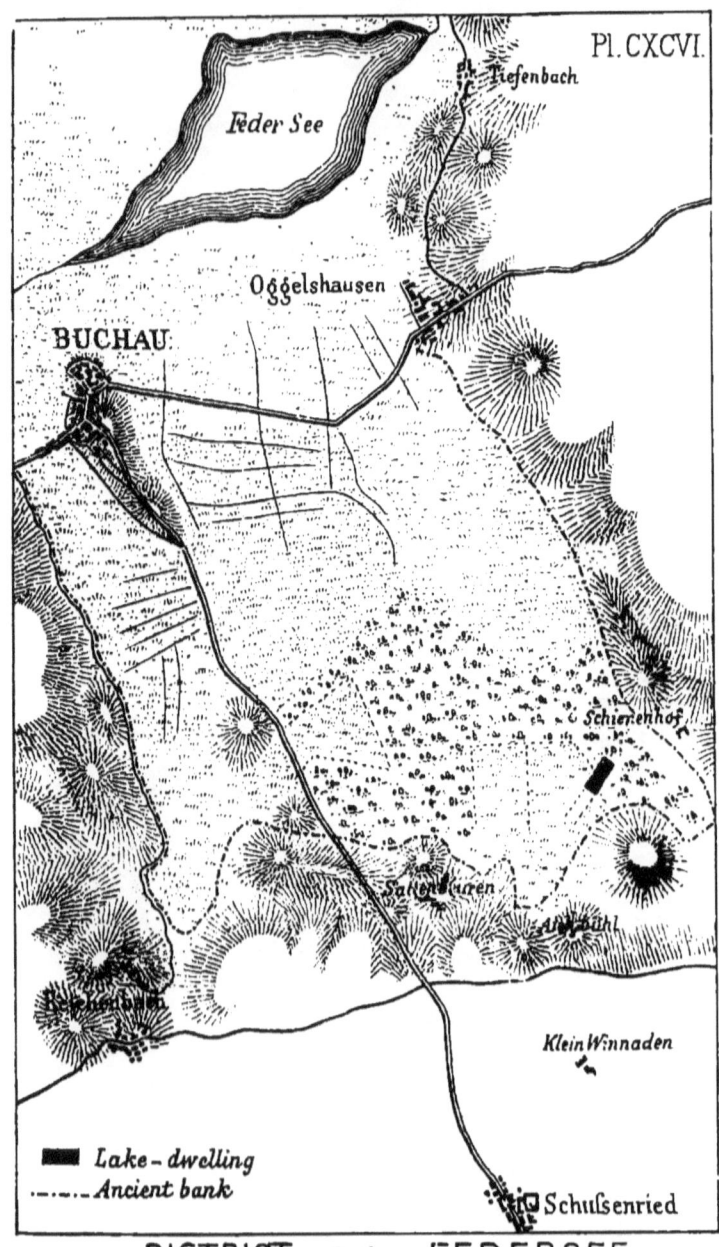

DISTRICT of the FEDERSEE

Pl. CXCVII

LAKE DWELLING of SCHUSSENRIED.

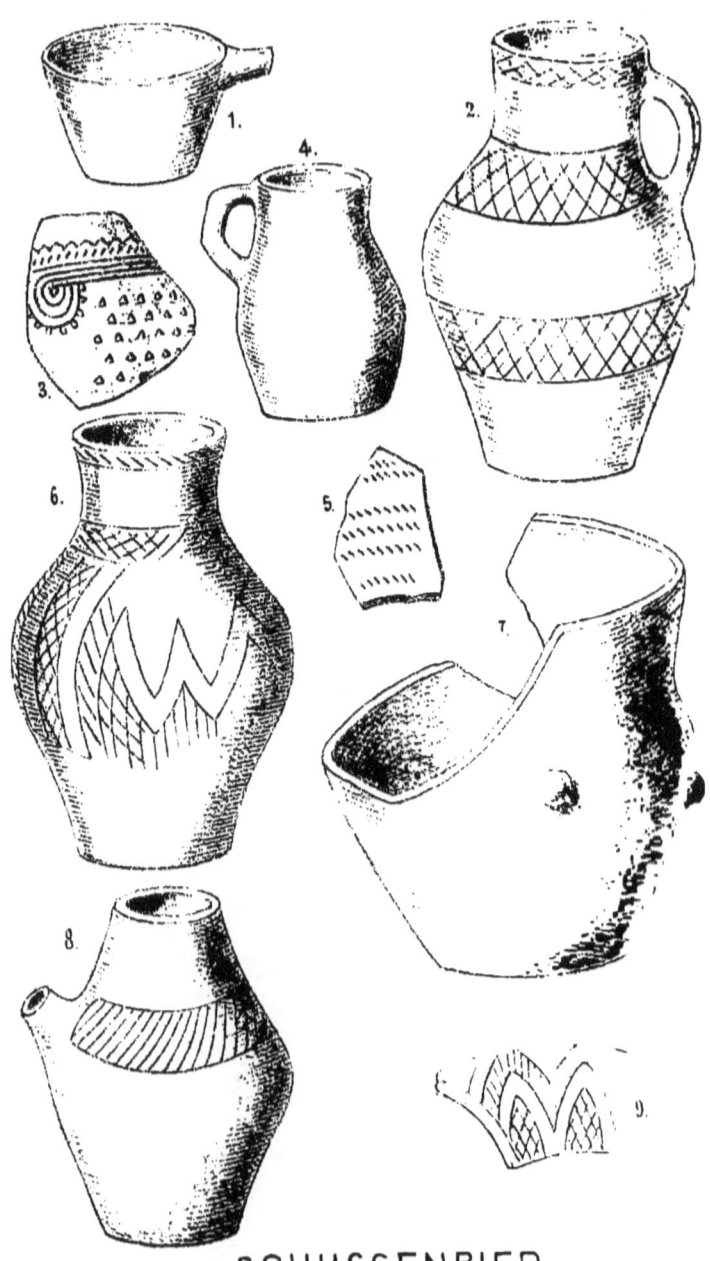

SCHUSSENRIED.
Pottery – all ½ Size.

Pl. CXCIX

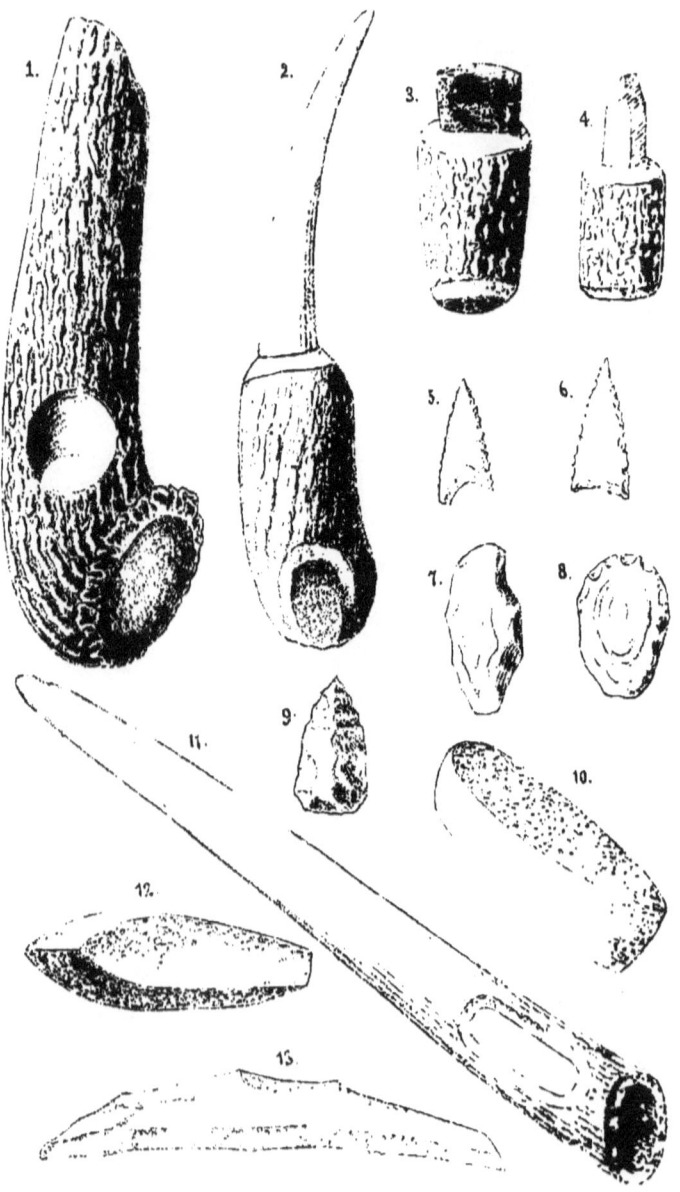

SCHUSSENRIED &c.

Pl. CCI.

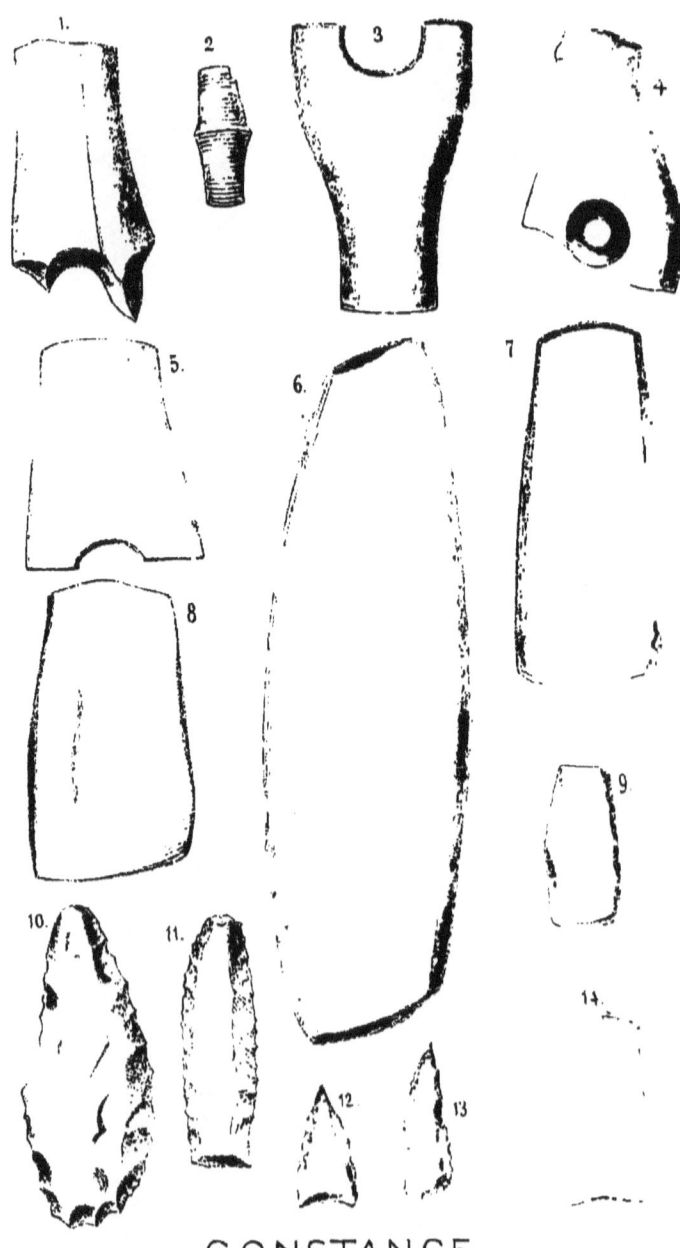

CONSTANCE.
Half size

Pl CCII.

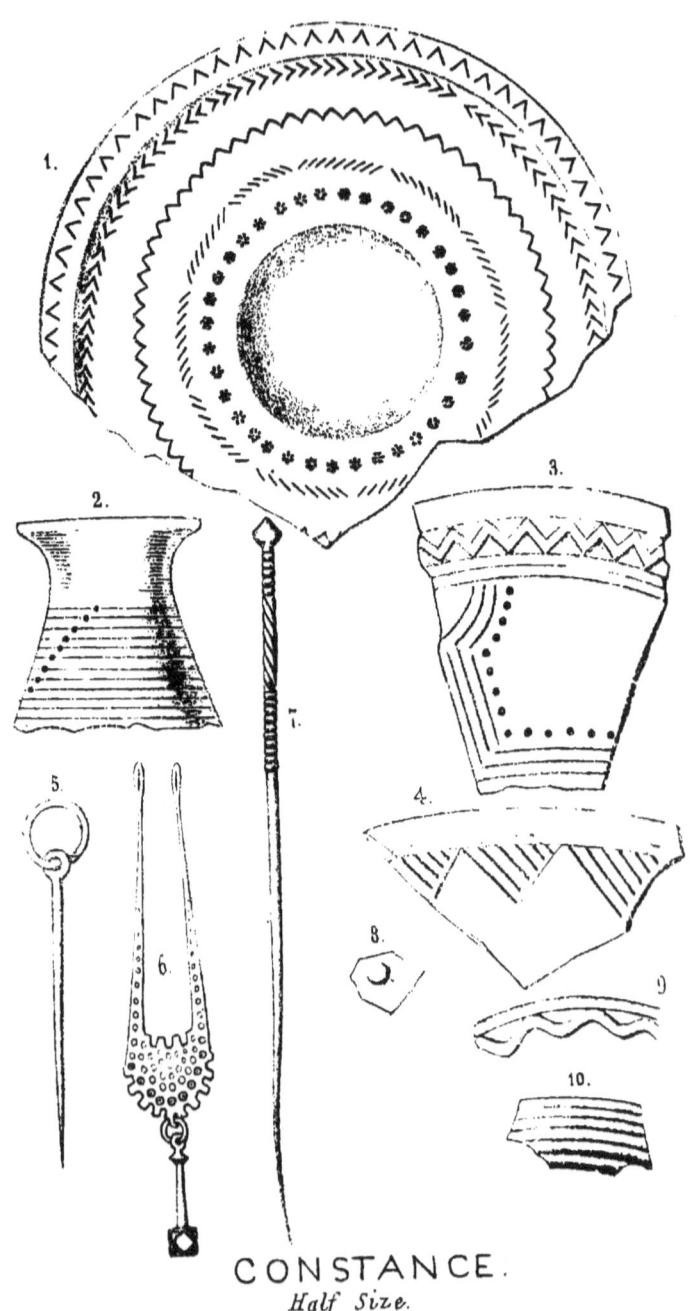

CONSTANCE.
Half Size.

Pl. CCIV.

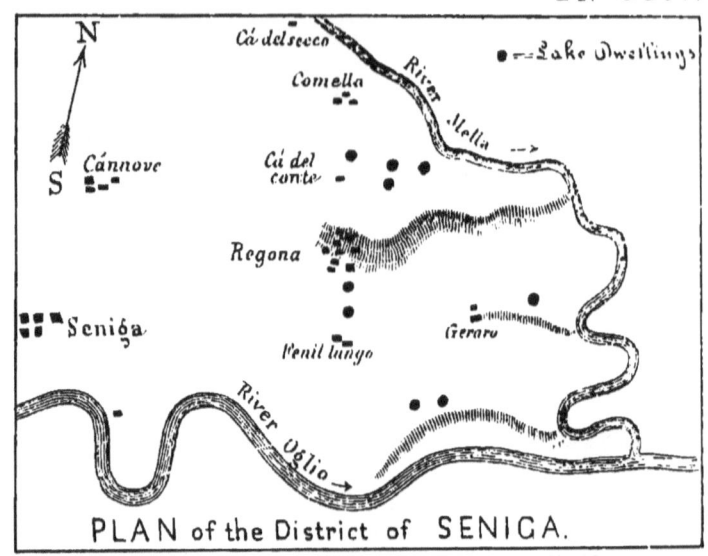

PLAN of the District of SENIGA.

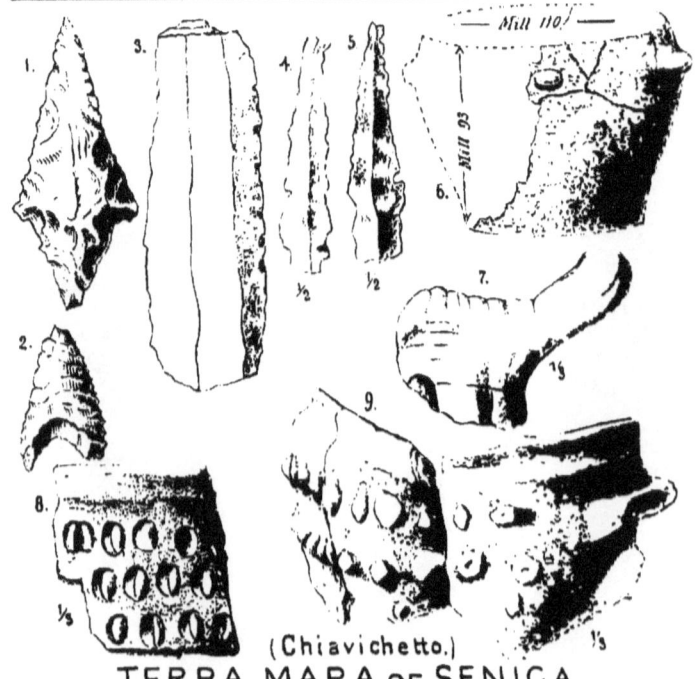

(Chiavichetto.)
TERRA MARA OF SENIGA

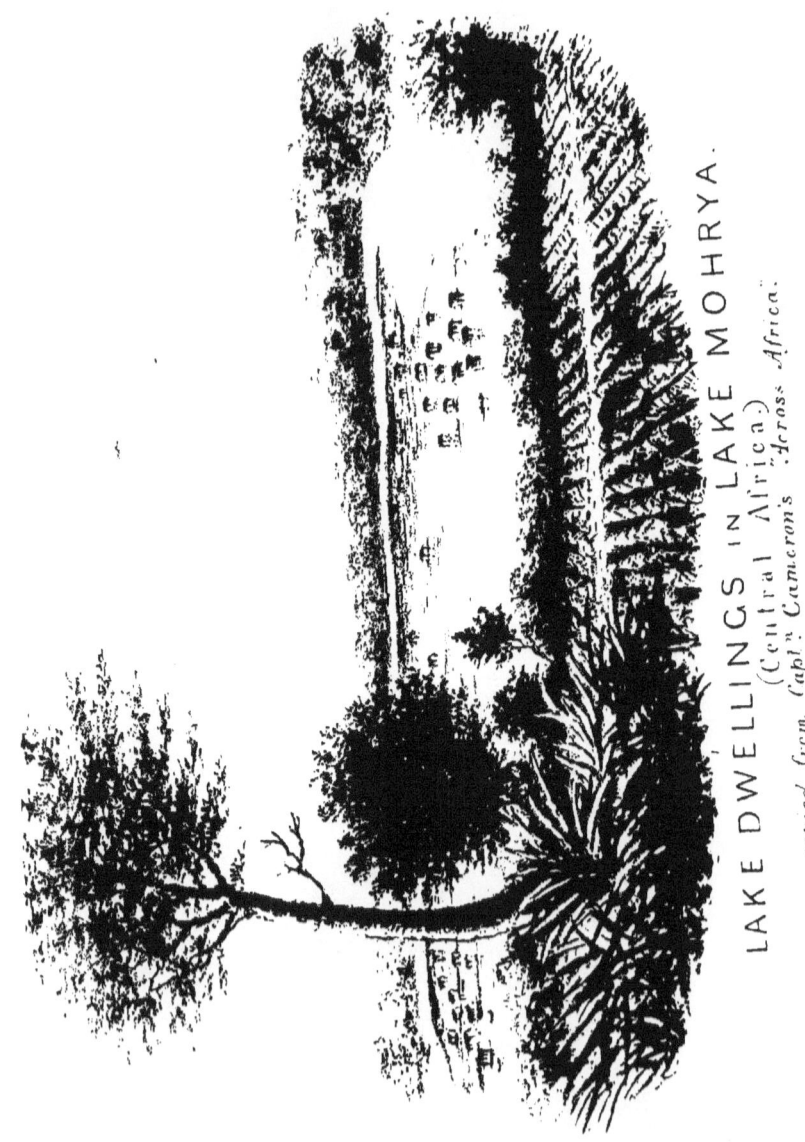

LAKE DWELLINGS IN LAKE MOHRYA.
(Central Africa)
copied from Captⁿ Cameron's "Across Africa".

GENERAL PLAN OF THE

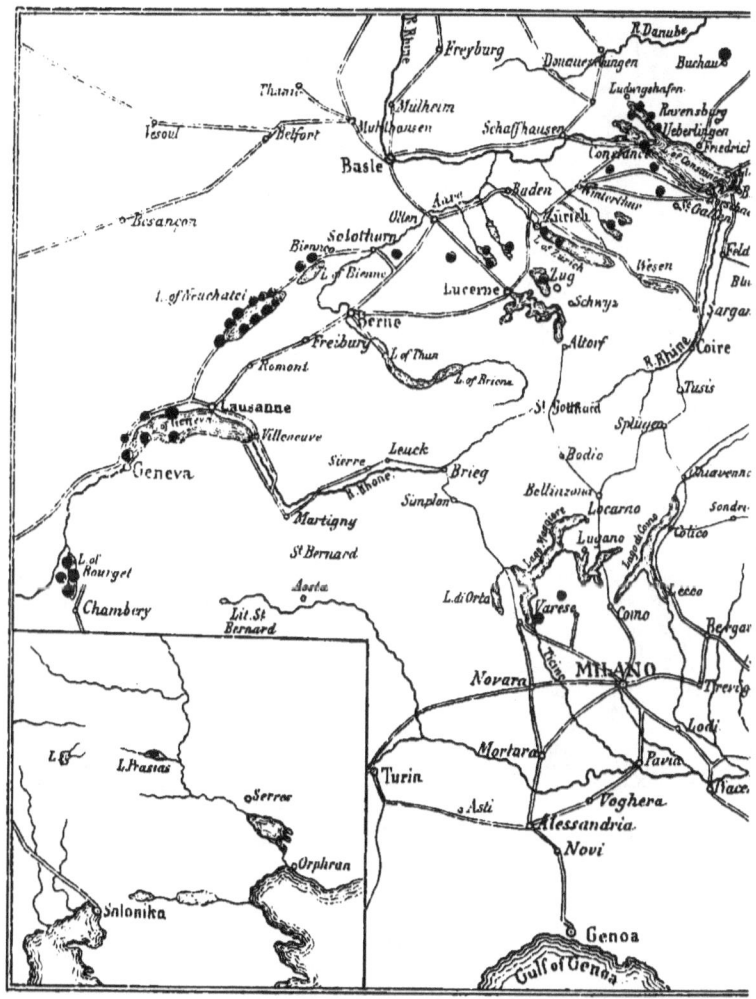

N³. The Terramara Settlements are not included. The Red marks

LAKE-DWELLING DISTRICT. Pl. CCVI.

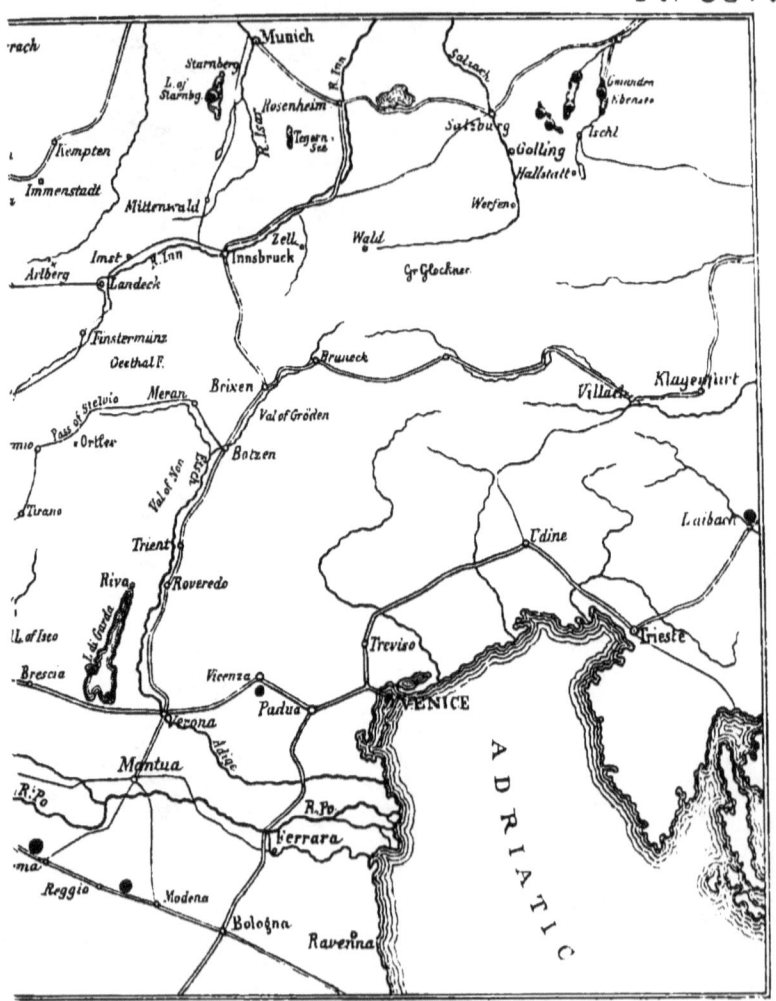

·dicate Pile Settlements both in the Lakes and in Peat Moors.
·ailways.

www.ingramcontent.com/pod-product-compliance
Lightning Source LLC
Chambersburg PA
CBHW032131010526
44111CB00034B/584